CONTENTS

Unwritten Rules	1
A Personal Note from the Author	3
Introduction: The Unspoken Code of Life	6
Chapter 1: The Power of Self-Awareness	12
Chapter 2: Learning to Fail	20
Chapter 3: The Art of Saying No	29
Chapter 4: Patience	38
Chapter 5: Courage Over Confidence	49
Chapter 6: The Power of Active Listening	58
Chapter 7: Building Trust	70
Chapter 8: The Unwritten Rules of Networking	83
Chapter 9: Embracing Vulnerability	96
Chapter 10: Reading Between the Lines	105
Chapter 11: Time Management	116
Chapter 12: Mastering the Art of Negotiation	127
Chapter 13: The Unspoken Etiquette of the Workplace	138
Chapter 14: Adaptability	149
Chapter 15: Imposter Syndrome	160

Chapter 15: Imposter Syndrome	171
Chapter 16: Money Myths You Learned Too Late	182
Chapter 17: Debt is Not Your Enemy, Ignorance Is	195
Chapter 18: The Unseen Cost of Lifestyle Inflation	207
Chapter 19: The Art of Investing in Yourself	218
Chapter 20: Financial Freedom Through Multiple Income Streams	230
Chapter 21: Handling Rejection with Grace	241
Chapter 22: The Power of Emotional Control	250
Chapter 23: Mindfulness for the Modern World	259
Chapter 24: Creating Mental Space	270
Chapter 25: Dealing with Life's Uncertainties	280
Chapter 26: Discovering Your Personal Values	290
Chapter 27: Passion vs. Persistence	300
Chapter 28: Aligning Your Life with Purpose	310
Chapter 29: The Power of Giving	320
Chapter 30: Legacy	330
Chapter 31: The Final Lesson	339
Epilogue: The Quiet Echo of Unwritten Truths	348
Glossary of Terms	353
References	359
Acknowledgements	366
Copyright Information	368
Disclaimer	369

UNWRITTEN RULES

Life Lessons We Never Learned In School

Dr Bhaskar Bora

A PERSONAL NOTE FROM THE AUTHOR

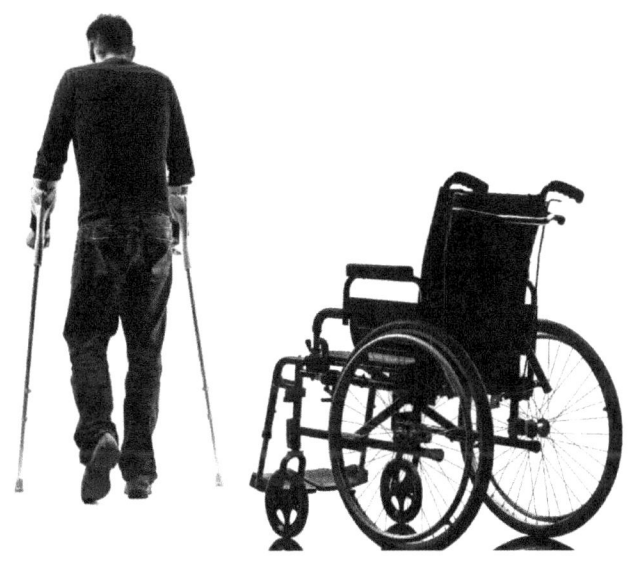

My journey, once marked by certainty and driven by purpose, has transformed in ways I could never have anticipated. It is no longer about grand achievements or the pursuit of external success, but about the quiet, tender moments that reveal the true essence of life—

moments of love, care, and presence. What you hold in your hands is not just a collection of words, but a testament to resilience, a story woven from the delicate threads of struggle, acceptance, and ultimately, renewal.

There was a time when my life flowed with the grace of a symphony, every note in perfect harmony. As a doctor, my days were filled with the pulse of life itself—offering hope, easing suffering, and healing with steady hands. The white coat I wore wasn't just a symbol of my profession; it embodied my very identity; an outward reflection of the healer I believed I was destined to be. The lives I touched, the people I helped—it all gave profound meaning to my existence.

But life, in its mysterious and unpredictable ways, had other plans. In one swift, unforeseen moment, the world I knew unraveled. First came the spinal cord injury, stripping away the physical strength I had relied upon. Then, the shadow of cancer darkened the horizon, a stark reminder of life's fragility. The world of medicine, where I once found so much joy and purpose, suddenly slipped away, leaving a vast emptiness in its wake—a silence where once there had been meaning.

Gone were the bustling corridors of the hospital, replaced by the quiet solitude of my home. No longer a "Doctor," I found myself standing at the edge of an uncertain future, my hands—once so steady with the knowledge of healing—trembling with questions I wasn't ready to face. Without the title, without the work that had defined me for so long, who was I? What was left of me when everything I had known was no longer within reach?

In that silence, in the stillness of a life interrupted, I began to uncover something unexpected. The role of a disabled husband and father, once a distant concept, became my new reality—one that held unexpected grace. What began as an effort to nurture my relationships, to find solace in this new world, slowly evolved into a profound inward journey.

I found healing in the spiritual—a rhythm of meditation, reading, and reflection that allowed me to rediscover the parts of myself I thought were lost. As I immersed myself in books, audiobooks, and hours of research, I began to understand that this new chapter of my life was not an ending, but a rebirth. The solitude of these years, the quiet hours of writing and reflection, gave birth to the very pages you hold in your hands now. It is with deep gratitude that I share these words with you, knowing that they carry with them not just knowledge but a piece of my soul. I hope that these reflections and insights offer you a fresh perspective on life and perhaps some nourishment for your own journey.

That we cannot control what the universe throws at us but how we react to those curveballs define who we are and what we make of our lives.

INTRODUCTION: THE UNSPOKEN CODE OF LIFE

In this vast theatre of existence, where each soul is cast into the roles of both actor and spectator, there lies a script unwritten, a code unspoken, whose lines are etched not on pages but within the subtle folds of life's ceaseless flow. These are the rules that govern the invisible threads binding each moment, each breath, and each decision. They are rules not bestowed by formal decree, nor are they whispered in the sanctified halls of education. Instead, they emerge, silently and indifferently, through the quiet orchestration of life's vicissitudes.

The traditional corridors of learning, with their structured syllabi and carefully curated lessons, paint only the broadest strokes of existence, leaving untouched the finer, more delicate lines that define the essence of what it means to truly live. We are taught how to compute the circumference of circles, to untangle historical events, and to dissect the intricacies of language. Yet, when faced with the labyrinthine complexities of human existence—when confronted with love unreciprocated, ambition unfulfilled, or dreams deferred—we find ourselves bereft of the wisdom to navigate such storms.

Thus, we wander, adrift, tethered not by certainty but by the fragile hope that experience itself might impart the teachings that education neglected to bestow. In this nebulous realm, the unwritten rules of life hold sway, unseen yet omnipresent, elusive yet inexorable. They guide us not with the clarity of textbooks or the precision of formulas, but through the intangible lessons learned in moments of quiet despair and fleeting triumph. These rules, whispered by the winds of time and circumstance, are the very foundation upon which this book is built.

It is not that we lack teachers in this realm, but that life itself becomes the sternest and most enigmatic instructor. Unlike the nurturing hand of a teacher in the classroom, life offers no clear directives, no gentle corrections. It does not pause to explain the meaning behind its riddles. Its lessons are often revealed through suffering, joy, and the full spectrum of human emotion, rather than through the sterile logic of facts and figures. Life's curriculum is nonlinear, its chapters disordered, its tests unannounced, and its wisdom hard-won.

Herein lies the crux of the journey we are about to undertake. This book does not seek to offer the certainties of formal education, nor does it pretend to possess the final answers to life's most persistent questions. Rather, it is a guide, a lantern held aloft in the deepening twilight, illuminating the shadowy paths of human existence. It seeks not to impose rules, but to reveal them—to uncover the hidden doctrines that shape our every interaction, our every choice, and our every thought. These are the unwritten rules that govern the very essence of what it means to be alive.

As we embark upon this odyssey together, it is essential to recognise that the lessons presented herein are not meant to be definitive. Life is too vast, too intricate, to be distilled into simple maxims or easy formulas. The unwritten rules we will explore are but fragments of a larger, unfathomable whole—glimpses into the mysterious workings of the universe, fleeting moments of clarity in an otherwise chaotic existence. They are neither right nor wrong, neither absolute nor immutable. Instead, they are the silent truths that have revealed themselves to those who have walked the path before us, truths that, once recognised, have the power to transform the way we move through the world.

We begin, as all journeys must, with a question: What is it that we truly seek? For it is only by understanding our deepest desires, our most profound needs, that we can hope to comprehend the rules that govern the fulfillment of those desires. The lessons of life are many, but they often converge upon a single truth: that to know oneself is the beginning of all wisdom. And so, our first step will be into the realm of self-awareness, the bedrock upon which all other knowledge rests.

Self-awareness, however, is no simple feat. It is not a matter of mere introspection or the cataloging of traits. It is a journey inward, a delving into the very depths of one's soul, where the shifting currents of desire, fear, and longing collide in an ever-changing dance. To be truly self-aware is to stand at the centre of this tempest and observe it without judgment, to recognise one's flaws and strengths without clinging to them, and to understand that the self is not a fixed entity but a fluid, evolving force.

From self-awareness, we will venture into the uncharted waters of failure, for it is here that many of life's most profound lessons are learned. Failure is a teacher like no other, and though its lessons are often harsh, they are also necessary. In a world obsessed with success, failure is often cast aside, hidden away, or treated as an aberration. Yet, it is through failure that we come to understand the limits of our abilities, the fragility of our aspirations, and the resilience of our spirit. We will learn that failure is not the end, but a crucial step on the path to mastery, a force that refines us and strengthens us in ways that success never could.

Following failure, we shall explore the intricate dance of human relationships, a realm where the unwritten rules are perhaps most deeply felt. Relationships are the crucible in which the self is both tested and transformed. They are the mirror through which we come to see ourselves more clearly, for it is only in the presence of others that we can fully understand who we are. Yet, relationships are fraught with complexity, with unspoken expectations, hidden desires, and the delicate balance of give and take. We will uncover the unwritten rules that govern how we connect with others, how we build trust, and how we navigate the inevitable conflicts that arise in any meaningful relationship.

As our journey continues, we will turn our attention to the world of work and career, a domain where success is often measured by external markers—titles, salaries, achievements—yet is governed by rules that go far beyond the superficial. We will learn that adaptability, more than intellect or ambition, is the key to thriving in this ever-shifting landscape. We will explore the unwritten etiquette of the workplace, the art of negotiation, and the value of time, that most precious and fleeting of resources. In doing so, we will come to understand that true success is not about climbing the proverbial ladder, but about finding fulfillment in the work we do and the lives we lead.

From the professional realm, we shall delve into the intricacies of financial wisdom, another area where the formal education system so often fails us. We are taught the mechanics of economics, the principles of accounting, yet we are never shown how to wield money as a tool for freedom, rather than as a shackle. We will explore the myths that surround wealth, the dangers of debt, and the subtle lure of materialism. We will come to see that financial freedom is not about accumulation, but about alignment—about ensuring that our financial choices reflect our deepest values and aspirations.

Yet, no exploration of life's unwritten rules would be complete without a foray into the realm of emotional resilience and mental well-being. Life is not a gentle tutor; it does not shield us from suffering or hardship. But within that suffering lies the potential for profound growth, for it is through adversity that we come to know our true strength. We will learn the art of mindfulness, of being present in a world that constantly seeks to distract us, and we will discover the power of letting go—of releasing the burdens that weigh us down, whether they be fears, regrets, or attachments.

Finally, we shall ascend to the highest peaks of existence, where the search for meaning takes precedence. We will explore the nature of purpose, the importance of values, and the deep yearning that lies at the heart of the human experience. We will come to understand that meaning is not something to be found, but something to be created—an act of will, a declaration of intent, a choice made each day. And in doing so, we will glimpse the final, most profound unwritten rule of life: that to live fully is not merely to exist, but to participate in the creation of one's reality, to be both the artist and the canvas, the dreamer and the dream.

This is the journey we shall undertake together—a journey into the unspoken, the unwritten, the unknown. And though the path may be winding, though the terrain may be treacherous, it is a path worth walking, for it leads to the heart of what it means to truly live. Let us begin.

CHAPTER 1: THE POWER OF SELF-AWARENESS

There is a vast and uncharted realm within each human, a kingdom not bound by the ordinary laws of the physical world. It is a domain not governed by seasons or time, but by the rhythm of thought, emotion, and perception. This kingdom is a place of quietude, where the silent whispers of the soul reign, where the echoes of the past meet the aspirations of the future in a ceaseless dance. Yet, for many, it remains a shadowed territory, a land only dimly perceived and rarely explored with intent.

This inner world, rich with meaning and complexity, is the very seat of self-awareness, the unshaken pillar upon which the edifice of personal growth rests. To understand oneself is not merely to reflect upon the habits or thoughts that flicker across the surface of consciousness. It is to delve into the very essence of being, to observe with an eye unclouded by illusion, and to listen to the subtle undertones that guide our actions and reactions.

In the traditional sense, education seeks to illuminate the mind with external knowledge—facts, equations, historical narratives, and societal structures. Yet, no amount of intellectual mastery can grant us the key to our internal world, for that journey is not one of memorization or intellect, but of introspection. Formal education neglects this deeper voyage, leaving us to navigate the vast wilderness of self-awareness alone, often without map or compass. The lessons of self-awareness are not written in books but are etched in the contours of lived experience, whispered through moments of quiet reflection and illuminated in the crucible of emotional turmoil.

To embark on the path of self-awareness is to step into this wilderness, to brave its uncertainties, and to explore the terrain of the soul with courage and curiosity. What, then, is this awareness that we seek? It is a multi-faceted jewel, a prism through which the light of our existence is refracted into myriad hues. It is the ability to stand apart from oneself, to observe without judgment, and to comprehend the forces that shape our inner lives. It is both a state of being and a practice—a continual unfolding, a deepening of understanding that evolves as we do.

To be truly self-aware is to recognise the kaleidoscope of emotions, thoughts, and desires that rise and fall within us like the tides of a vast ocean. We are not static beings; we are in constant motion, our inner world a swirl of impressions, fears, hopes, and aspirations. And yet, we so often move through life unaware of the forces that propel us. We react without understanding, act without intention, and speak without reflection. To be self-aware is to break this cycle of unconscious existence. It is to become the quiet observer of one's internal landscape, to witness without being swept away by the currents of emotion or impulse.

But self-awareness does not come easily. It is a practice that must be cultivated, like a garden tended with care and patience. The first step on this path is the willingness to turn inward, to pause in the ceaseless rush of daily life and listen to the quiet voice within. This voice, often drowned out by the noise of external obligations and distractions, speaks not in words but in the subtle language of feeling, intuition, and reflection. It tells us who we are, not in the roles we play or the achievements we amass, but in the deeper currents of our being.

To become self-aware is to cultivate this inner listening, to attune oneself to the fluctuations of thought and feeling, and to begin to discern the patterns that shape our inner lives. These patterns, like the currents of a river, are often invisible to the casual observer but have a profound impact on the direction of our lives. They are the habits of thought, the unconscious beliefs, the emotional reactions that guide us, often without our knowledge. To become aware of these patterns is the first step toward mastery.

Emotions, those elusive and ephemeral forces, are often the most difficult to understand. They rise suddenly, like storm clouds gathering on the horizon, and can engulf us before we are even aware of their presence. We are often swept away by their power, acting in ways that we later regret, or suppressing them in an effort to maintain control. Yet, emotions are not to be feared or denied; they are messengers, bearing vital information about our inner state. They tell us where we stand in relation to the world, signaling our desires, our fears, our needs, and our values.

To be self-aware is to cultivate the ability to observe these emotions without becoming entangled in them. It is to stand at the centre of the storm, watching the clouds gather and disperse, without being swept away by the wind. This requires a deep mindfulness, a steady attention to the flow of feeling and thought. It is not about controlling or repressing emotion, but about understanding its source, its meaning, and its purpose. For emotions, when observed with clarity, can guide us toward deeper self-understanding.

This brings us to the delicate balance between our strengths and weaknesses. In the realm of self-awareness, these are not fixed traits, but dynamic forces that shape our behaviour and our interactions with the world. Our strengths are those qualities that we naturally cultivate, the aspects of ourselves that bring us success, fulfillment, or joy. But even strengths, when left unchecked, can become distorted, turning into their shadow counterparts. Confidence can turn to arrogance, ambition to greed, and compassion to self-sacrifice. To be self-aware is to recognise this balance, to know when our strengths serve us and when they begin to hinder us.

Equally important is the recognition of our weaknesses, those aspects of ourselves that we often seek to hide or deny. These are the places where we struggle, where we feel vulnerable, where we fall short. Yet, it is often through the very acknowledgment of these weaknesses that we find the potential for growth. To deny them is to remain stagnant, but to face them with honesty and humility is to open the door to transformation. In this recognition of our limitations, we plant the seeds of our expansion.

Self-awareness, then, is not merely an act of understanding, but an act of creation. For once we see ourselves clearly, we are no longer bound by the unconscious patterns that have shaped our lives. We become the artists of our existence, capable of shaping our responses to the world, rather than reacting blindly to the circumstances around us. This is the essence of personal mastery: the ability to govern oneself, not through sheer force of will, but through a deep and abiding understanding of the forces at play within us.

It is important to recognise that self-awareness is not a solitary pursuit. Though it requires introspection, it is deeply intertwined with our relationships with others. For it is often through our interactions with the world that we come to know ourselves. The people we encounter act as mirrors, reflecting back to us aspects of ourselves that we might otherwise overlook. In the presence of another's joy, we may recognise our capacity for empathy. In the face of another's anger, we may see our tendencies toward defensiveness.

These reflections are invaluable, for they offer us the opportunity to see ourselves from a perspective outside our limited view. Yet, we must also be cautious, for these reflections can be distorted by the biases, projections, and expectations of others. To be self-aware is not to accept every reflection as truth, but to sift through the myriad perceptions that come our way, seeking the clarity that lies beneath. It is to engage in a dialogue with the world, not as passive recipients of feedback, but as active participants in the ongoing process of self-discovery.

In this process of discovery, we must also turn our attention to the larger forces that shape our lives—our culture, our environment, our past experiences. For we are not isolated beings, existing in a vacuum, but are deeply embedded in the fabric of life. Our sense of self is shaped by the stories we are told, the roles we are expected to play, the values we are encouraged to uphold. And yet, to be truly self-aware is to recognise these influences without being confined by them. It is to understand that while we are shaped by our circumstances, we are not defined by them.

This is a critical distinction, for self-awareness is not about accepting a fixed identity. It is about understanding the fluid, evolving nature of the self. We are not static beings, confined to the roles or identities we were assigned in childhood or adolescence. We are constantly evolving, constantly shifting, and to be self-aware is to embrace this process of evolution with curiosity and openness. It is to recognise that who we are today is not who we were yesterday, nor who we will be tomorrow.

As we continue on this path of self-awareness, we must do so with a sense of reverence for the process. There will be moments of revelation, when the clouds part and we see ourselves with startling clarity. And there will be moments of confusion, when the path ahead seems obscured and we are left to grapple with the uncertainty of not knowing. But through it all, we must remain committed to the journey, trusting that each step we take brings us closer to the truth of who we are.

In this first chapter of life's unwritten rules, we have only begun to scratch the surface of self-awareness. Yet, even this brief exploration reveals the immense power that comes from understanding ourselves—not as static beings, but as ever-evolving creatures, shaped by the forces of emotion, thought, and circumstance. The path ahead is long, winding through the many facets of personal growth and self-mastery, but with each step, we come closer to realizing the fullness of our potential.

To be self-aware is to be awake to the richness of life, to see the world not through the narrow lens of ego or habit, but through the expansive vision of one who understands that the greatest journey we will ever undertake is the one within ourselves. It is to know, in the deepest sense, that the self is not a fixed point but a horizon—always receding, always inviting us to explore further, to dive deeper, to seek that which lies beyond.

And so, the journey continues.

CHAPTER 2: LEARNING TO FAIL

Why Setbacks Are Stepping Stones

The human heart, with all its aspirations, desires triumph. It seeks the glittering peaks of success, often at the expense of understanding the landscape of failure, that vast and fertile terrain that must be crossed if any summit is to be reached. Yet, there is a perilous misconception that permeates our collective consciousness: that failure and success are polar opposites, that one stands as the negation of the other, when in truth, they are but two sides of the same coin. This fundamental misunderstanding of failure has led countless souls to fear it, to avoid it at all costs, and to internalize it as a personal deficiency when it inevitably occurs.

But the path to mastery in any field, whether personal or professional, is paved not only with victories but with missteps, disappointments, and moments of profound failure. What we often fail to recognise is that failure is not merely a detour on the road to success—it is the road itself. It is the very soil from which the seeds of resilience, wisdom, and innovation spring forth. Failure is the anvil upon which the soul is tempered, the crucible through which we are refined. In this light, failure becomes not a point of shame or regret, but a necessary stage in the process of becoming.

Consider the many layers of failure. It is not a singular, monolithic event but rather a series of experiences—some minor, some catastrophic—each offering its own lesson, each with its own unique texture. To fail at something is to engage in a dialogue with life, to receive feedback from the universe about what works and what does not, about where our strengths lie and where our growth is needed. It is an opportunity for reflection, for adjustment, for recalibration.

Failure is not something to be avoided but to be embraced, for it offers us insights that success often conceals. Success can be a seductive mask, hiding from us the weaknesses and blind spots that we might otherwise overlook. In success, we are often lulled into complacency, content with our achievements and unaware of the flaws that lurk beneath the surface. But failure strips away these illusions. It confronts us with the stark reality of our limitations, and in doing so, it gives us the chance to confront those limitations, to learn from them, and ultimately, to transcend them.

The Psychological Barriers to Embracing Failure

Why, then, do we fear failure so deeply? The answer lies not only in the external pressures of society but in the intricate workings of the mind itself. From an early age, many of us are conditioned to equate failure with inadequacy, with a lack of inherent ability or worth.

This mindset, often referred to as a fixed mindset, leads us to believe that our skills, talents, and intelligence are static and unchangeable. In this view, failure becomes a confirmation of our limitations, a sign that we are simply not capable of succeeding in a given endeavor.

This fixed mindset is insidious in its effects. It stifles growth, discourages risk-taking, and fosters a deep fear of failure. Those who operate from a fixed mindset often shy away from challenges, preferring the safety of tasks they know they can accomplish with ease. They avoid situations where their abilities might be tested or questioned, and in doing so, they limit their potential for growth and discovery.

In contrast, those with a growth mindset—a concept popularized by psychologist Carol Dweck—view failure not as a verdict on their abilities but as a necessary part of the learning process. For them, abilities and intelligence are not fixed traits but malleable qualities that can be developed through effort, practice, and experience. In this view, failure is not a reflection of one's intrinsic worth but a stepping stone on the path to mastery. Those with a growth mindset embrace challenges, take risks, and persist in the face of setbacks, knowing that each failure brings them closer to success.

Cultivating a growth mindset requires a shift in perspective, a reimagining of failure as an ally rather than an enemy. It involves recognizing that failure is not something to be feared but something to be learned from, that each setback is an opportunity for growth, and that the road to success is rarely linear or smooth. This mindset shift is critical for personal development, for it frees us from the paralyzing fear of failure and opens the door to new possibilities.

Historical Examples: Failure as a Prelude to Success

History is replete with stories of individuals who, by learning to embrace failure, ultimately achieved greatness. These stories serve as reminders that failure is not a barrier to success but an essential ingredient in its recipe.

Take, for example, Abraham Lincoln, one of the most revered figures in American history. Before his ascent to the presidency, Lincoln endured a long string of personal and political failures. He lost his job, failed in business, suffered the death of his fiancée, and was defeated in several elections. Yet, each failure strengthened his resolve, deepened his understanding of leadership, and refined his sense of purpose. It was through these failures that Lincoln developed the resilience and fortitude necessary to lead the nation through one of its darkest periods.

Or consider the story of Thomas Edison, the inventor who revolutionized the world with his creation of the electric light bulb. Edison's journey to success was marked by thousands of failed experiments. When asked about these failures, Edison famously replied, "I have not failed. I've just found 10,000 ways that won't work." This perspective is emblematic of the growth mindset—Edison did not view his failed attempts as defeats but as valuable lessons that brought him closer to his goal. His persistence, his willingness to learn from failure, ultimately led to one of the most significant technological advancements in history.

Another powerful example is that of J.K. Rowling, the author of the Harry Potter series. Before she became one of the best-selling authors in history, Rowling faced a series of devastating setbacks. She was a single mother, living on welfare, and struggling with depression. Her manuscript for Harry Potter and the Philosopher's Stone was rejected by twelve different publishers before it was finally accepted. But Rowling did not allow these rejections to define her. She persisted, fueled by her belief in the story she had created, and in time, her perseverance paid off in ways she could never have imagined.

These stories—and countless others like them—illustrate a crucial truth: failure is not a dead end but a detour, a necessary part of the journey toward success. It is through failure that we gain the experience, the resilience, and the insight required to achieve our goals. It is through failure that we learn to adapt, to innovate, and to persevere.

The Transformative Power of Failure

If we are to truly learn from failure, we must approach it not with fear or shame, but with curiosity and openness. Failure has the power to transform us, to deepen our understanding of ourselves and the world around us, if we are willing to engage with it fully.

One of the most profound lessons that failure teaches us is the importance of humility. Success can breed arrogance, a false sense of invincibility that blinds us to our flaws and limitations. Failure, on the other hand, strips away these illusions, forcing us to confront our imperfections and vulnerabilities. It reminds us that we are not infallible, that we are not all-knowing, and that there is always more to learn. This humility is essential for growth, for it keeps us grounded and open to new ideas, new perspectives, and new possibilities.

Failure also teaches us resilience—the ability to persevere in the face of adversity. To fail and rise again, to continue forward despite setbacks, is to cultivate a strength of spirit that cannot be easily broken. Resilience is not merely the ability to endure hardship, but the capacity to learn from it, to adapt, and to emerge stronger on the other side. Those who learn to fail are those who learn to rise, again and again, until success is achieved.

Moreover, failure can be a powerful catalyst for innovation. When we fail, we are forced to rethink our approach, to question our assumptions, and to seek out new solutions. Many of the world's greatest inventions and discoveries were born out of failure. Edison's light bulb, for example, was the result of countless failed experiments, each of which brought him closer to a working solution. The same can be said of countless scientific breakthroughs, technological advancements, and artistic achievements—failure is often the precursor to innovation.

Yet, for failure to be transformative, we must approach it with the right mindset. We must be willing to reflect on our failures, to analyze them with a critical but compassionate eye, and to extract the lessons they offer. This requires self-awareness, a willingness to look inward and examine our motivations, decisions, and actions. It requires us to take responsibility for our failures, rather than blaming external factors or other people. It is only through this process of reflection that we can learn from our failures and use them as stepping stones to success.

Failure and the Fear of Judgment

One of the greatest barriers to embracing failure is the fear of judgment—the fear of what others will think or say if we fall short of our goals. This fear can be paralyzing, preventing us from taking risks, from pursuing our dreams, or from putting ourselves in situations where failure is a possibility. We worry that failure will lead to embarrassment, ridicule, or rejection, and so we stay within the confines of what is safe and familiar.

But the truth is that the judgment of others is often far less severe than we imagine. People are far more likely to admire resilience and persistence than to mock failure. In fact, many of the world's most successful individuals have failed publicly, sometimes spectacularly, only to rise again with renewed strength and determination. Their failures did not define them; their response to those failures did.

To learn to fail is to learn to release the fear of judgment. It is to recognise that the opinions of others are fleeting, and that true success is not measured by external validation but by internal growth. It is to understand that failure is not something to be hidden or ashamed of, but something to be celebrated as part of the journey.

The Role of Compassion in Failure

As we learn to fail, it is essential that we also

learn to cultivate self-compassion. Failure can be a painful experience, one that evokes feelings of shame, frustration, or disappointment. In these moments, it is easy to be harsh with ourselves, to engage in self-criticism or to internalize our failures as reflections of our worth. But this kind of self-punishment only serves to deepen the wounds of failure and to prevent us from learning the lessons it offers.

Self-compassion, on the other hand, allows us to approach failure with kindness and understanding. It reminds us that failure is a universal experience, that everyone falters at some point in their lives, and that our worth is not determined by our successes or failures. When we are compassionate with ourselves, we create a space in which we can reflect on our failures without judgment, and in doing so, we open the door to growth and healing.

Embracing Failure as Part of the Journey

Failure is not the enemy of success; it is its most faithful companion. It is the crucible in which our character is tested, the forge in which our resilience is shaped, and the path that leads us to greater wisdom, innovation, and achievement. To learn to fail is to learn to grow, to evolve, and to reach heights that would otherwise remain unattainable.

The journey to success is not a straight line, but a winding road, full of detours, obstacles, and setbacks. Failure is not a stop sign on this road; it is a guidepost, pointing us toward the lessons we need to learn and the adjustments we need to make. It is through failure that we discover our true potential, that we develop the strength to persevere, and that we find the courage to continue forward, even when the way is uncertain.

Success is not about avoiding failure, but about embracing it, learning from it, and using it as a stepping stone to greater things. To fail is not to fall short; it is to take another step on the journey toward success. And in that journey, failure is not something to be feared—it is something to be welcomed, for it is the key to unlocking our true potential.

CHAPTER 3: THE ART OF SAYING NO

In the corridors of existence, where life unfurls its manifold choices, there is a word so small, so seemingly insignificant, yet so powerful that it shapes destinies and guards the fragile citadel of the soul. This word, barely more than a breath, is no. How often it sits at the edge of our lips, trembling, unsure whether to emerge or retreat in silence, while around us the clamoring voices of demand and expectation rise like a storm. And so, we find ourselves in a paradox: though we have mastered the art of language, we often stumble over this one syllable, as though it were a stone too heavy to lift.

But saying no—ah, it is an art form, a dance of discernment, a declaration of personal sovereignty. To say no is to draw a sacred circle around oneself, not out of selfishness, but out of a profound understanding that the finite hours of life, the delicate threads of energy that weave our days, must be honoured. In a world that praises yes as the currency of kindness and virtue, no is often seen as a rebellion, a rejection. Yet, what if saying no is not the closing of a door, but the opening of another—a door that leads to greater freedom, clarity, and authenticity?

Let us consider the labyrinth of human interaction, that web of connections which stretches across the landscape of our days. It is through this web that the demands of the world reach us, sometimes softly, like a feather landing on our shoulder, and sometimes with the weight of a thousand expectations. "Will you do this?" "Can you come here?" "Could you help me with that?" Each request is a thread, tugging at us, binding us more tightly into the fabric of other people's desires and needs. And though many of these threads are woven with good intentions, we must ask ourselves: at what point does the fabric become too dense? At what point do we lose the ability to breathe within it?

To say no is to begin the unraveling of this web. It is to untangle oneself from the expectations of others and reclaim the freedom to move through life on one's terms. But this untangling is not a severing of relationships or a withdrawal from the world—it is an act of care, both for oneself and for those around us. For how can we give fully, how can we be present and engaged, if we are constantly stretched beyond our capacity, constantly saying yes when our hearts long to say no?

There is a quiet violence in the unexamined yes. It is a violence done to the self, a subtle erosion of boundaries, a giving away of one's life bit by bit until there is nothing left but a hollow echo of what once was. And so, the word no becomes a shield, not to ward off others, but to protect the self from dissolution, from the slow, insidious theft of time and energy that occurs when we fail to set boundaries.

But why, then, do we struggle so mightily to say no? Why does the mere thought of refusal fill us with guilt, anxiety, or fear? The answer lies deep within the architecture of our social conditioning, within the unspoken rules that govern human interaction. From a young age, many of us are taught that to be good, to be kind, to be loved, we must say yes. Yes to helping, yes to pleasing, yes to every request that comes our way. We learn to equate yes with acceptance, and no with rejection—both of others and of ourselves. To say no, we fear, is to risk alienation, to risk being seen as selfish, cold, or unfeeling.

Yet this fear, like so many fears, is a mirage—a distortion of reality. To say no is not to reject the other, but to honour oneself. It is to recognise that one's time, energy, and well-being are finite resources, and that to deplete them without care is not an act of generosity, but of self-neglect. The art of saying no, then, is the art of discerning where one's energy is best spent, and where it must be protected. It is the art of choosing with intention, rather than reacting out of fear or obligation.

The Nature of Boundaries: A Sacred Geometry

Let us pause for a moment to consider the nature of boundaries, those invisible lines that define the space in which we exist as autonomous beings. Boundaries are often misunderstood as barriers—walls erected to keep others out. But true boundaries are not walls; they are the contours of the self, the shape of our lives drawn in relation to the world around us. They are permeable, flexible, and yet firm. They are not meant to isolate, but to protect, to ensure that we remain whole even as we engage with the world.

Imagine, if you will, a garden. Within this garden, flowers bloom, trees stretch toward the sky, and the air is filled with the gentle hum of life. The garden is a sanctuary, a place of beauty and peace. But what happens if this garden has no fence, no boundary? Over time, weeds may creep in, animals may trample the delicate flowers, and the once-thriving sanctuary may become overgrown, chaotic, and unrecognizable. A boundary is not a rejection of the world outside the garden; it is a way of ensuring that the garden can flourish, that it can remain a place of beauty and vitality.

In much the same way, boundaries in our lives are not rejections of others, but affirmations of the self. They are the fences that protect our inner gardens, allowing us to cultivate the things that matter most—peace, creativity, rest, and meaningful relationships. Without boundaries, we risk becoming overwhelmed by the demands of the outside world, losing sight of our own needs and desires.

The word no is the gatekeeper of these boundaries. It is the tool we use to decide what enters our garden and what remains outside. To say no is to be the steward of one's life, to guard the gates with wisdom and care. But this stewardship requires discernment. Not every request is a threat to our well-being, and not every yes is a surrender. The art of saying no is the art of knowing when to open the gate and when to keep it closed.

The Emotional Landscape of Saying No

It is a strange thing, how a single word can carry such emotional weight. To say no is not merely to refuse a request; it is to engage with a complex web of emotions—guilt, fear, relief, and sometimes even joy. These emotions are not to be dismissed or ignored; they are part of the process of setting boundaries, and they deserve our attention.

Guilt is perhaps the most common emotion associated with saying no. We feel guilty because we fear that by refusing someone's request, we are causing them harm or disappointment. We imagine that our no will be met with resentment or anger, and we internalize this imagined reaction as evidence of our own inadequacy or selfishness. But guilt, like any emotion, is a signal. It is not a reflection of reality, but a reflection of our beliefs about ourselves and the world. If we believe that we are only worthy of love and acceptance when we say yes, then guilt will arise whenever we dare to say no.

The key to overcoming guilt is to recognise that our worth is not tied to our ability to please others. We are not obligated to meet every demand, nor are we responsible for the emotional reactions of others. To say no is not an act of cruelty; it is an act of self-care. And self-care, far from being selfish, is a necessary foundation for living a balanced and fulfilling life. When we care for ourselves, we are better able to care for others, not out of obligation, but out of genuine love and compassion.

Fear is another powerful emotion that can arise when we contemplate saying no. We fear rejection, conflict, or loss of approval. We fear that by setting boundaries, we will push others away or damage our relationships. But this fear, like guilt, is based on a misunderstanding. True relationships are not built on compliance or people-pleasing; they are built on mutual respect, honesty, and authenticity. When we say no with clarity and compassion, we are not weakening our relationships—we are strengthening them. We are creating space for true connection, for relationships that are based on respect for each person's boundaries and needs.

There is also relief in saying no, though we often fail to recognise it. When we say no to something that does not serve us, we create space for something that does. We free ourselves from the burden of overcommitment, from the stress of trying to do too much, and from the exhaustion that comes from constantly stretching ourselves thin. In this relief, we find the joy of living with intention, of choosing how we spend our time and energy, and of aligning our actions with our values.

No as a Declaration of Freedom

The word no, when spoken with intention, is a declaration of freedom. It is a refusal to be bound by the expectations of others, a reclaiming of one's time and energy, and a commitment to living in alignment with one's values. To say no is to step off the treadmill of endless doing and into the stillness of being. It is to reject the idea that our worth is measured by our productivity or by how much we can give to others. It is to embrace the truth that our worth is inherent, that we are enough as we are, and that we have the right to protect our well-being.

But this declaration of freedom does not come without cost. To say no is to risk disapproval, to face the possibility that others may not understand or accept our boundaries. It is to confront the discomfort of standing apart, of choosing a path that may be different from the one expected of us. But this discomfort is temporary, and the freedom that comes from saying no is lasting. For when we live in alignment with our values, when we honour our boundaries, we experience a sense of peace and fulfillment that cannot be found in the endless pursuit of external approval.

The Power of No in the World

Saying no is not only an act of personal liberation; it is also a powerful force for change in the world. When we say no to what is harmful, unjust, or untrue, we take a stand for what is right. No is the word that has fueled revolutions, ended oppressive regimes, and brought about social progress. It is the word that refuses to accept the status quo, that challenges the structures of power, and that demands a better way.

Consider the great movements of history—the fight for civil rights, for women's suffrage, for the end of colonialism. Each of these movements began with a no—a refusal to accept the injustices of the world as inevitable. The leaders of these movements said no to oppression, no to inequality, no to the forces that sought to diminish their humanity. And in saying no, they created the conditions for a new reality to emerge.

In our own lives, we may not be leading revolutions, but we are still called to say no to the things that do not align with our values. We are called to say no to the forces that seek to diminish our humanity, to the demands that would deplete us, and to the systems that perpetuate harm. When we say no with intention, we are not only protecting ourselves; we are contributing to a world in which boundaries are respected, in which people are valued for who they are, not for what they can do, and in which freedom is honoured.

The Joy of Saying Yes to Life

Paradoxically, it is through the art of saying no that we learn to say a deeper yes to life. For when we say no to what does not serve us, we create space for what does. We open the door to opportunities, relationships, and experiences that are in alignment with our values and desires. We create the conditions for joy, fulfillment, and peace.

Saying yes to life is not about saying yes to every request, every demand, or every opportunity. It is about saying yes to what matters most—to our well-being, to our growth, to our purpose. It is about living with intention, about choosing how we spend our time and energy, and about creating a life that reflects our deepest values.

When we master the art of saying no, we free ourselves from the tyranny of obligation, from the guilt of people-pleasing, and from the fear of rejection. We step into a place of clarity, where our actions are guided by our inner compass, rather than by the expectations of others. And in this place, we discover the joy of living in alignment with our truth.

The Silent Symphony of No

There is a quiet, almost imperceptible beauty in the art of saying no—a beauty that arises from the depths of personal integrity and the courage to honour oneself. In a world that often demands too much, that pulls us in a thousand directions, no is the word that brings us back to centre. It is the word that reminds us that our time, our energy, and our well-being are sacred, and that we have the right to protect them.

To say no is not to reject others, but to embrace oneself. It is an act of self-love, a way of creating space for what truly matters, and a path to greater freedom, joy, and fulfillment. The art of saying no is, ultimately, the art of saying yes to life.

CHAPTER 4: PATIENCE

The Hidden Superpower

In the quiet, almost imperceptible hum of existence, where the cycles of day and night weave their ceaseless dance and the seasons turn with unhurried grace, there lies a force so subtle, so understated, that its true power often goes unrecognised. This force is patience, a virtue sung of in hushed tones, revered by the wise, yet often dismissed by those caught in the frenetic rhythms of the modern world. It is a power unlike the fiery burst of determination or the sharp edge of ambition; it is instead a slow, steady flame, a whispering wind that shapes mountains, a river that carves its way through stone.

Patience is a superpower cloaked in humility, unadorned by the grandiosity that marks the more celebrated virtues of courage, passion, or brilliance. Yet, it is patience that underpins every lasting achievement, every meaningful transformation, every pursuit of a worthy goal. To master the art of patience is to unlock the secret to enduring success—not the fleeting, ephemeral success that burns brightly and quickly fades, but the deep, abiding success that stands the test of time.

And yet, patience is a quality at odds with the pulse of contemporary life, a life that glorifies immediacy, that prizes the instant gratification of our desires, and that rewards the swift over the slow. We live in an age of acceleration, where every moment is measured, where speed is equated with efficiency, and where the slow unfolding of time is often viewed as an inconvenience. But in our rush to achieve, to acquire, to attain, we forget the quiet, unyielding power of patience—the power that builds empires not overnight, but over decades; the power that cultivates wisdom not in a single epiphany, but in the slow accumulation of lived experience.

To understand patience is to understand time itself—not as an adversary to be conquered, but as an ally, a companion on the journey toward our deepest aspirations. Patience teaches us to trust in the process, to honour the unfolding of our efforts, and to believe in the slow, deliberate progress that leads us toward our goals. It is the antidote to the restless urgency that so often drives us, the balm for the anxiety that comes from wanting too much, too soon.

The Quiet Strength of Patience

There is a quiet strength in patience, a strength that does not demand attention or recognition but simply is. It is the strength of a tree standing firm in the face of the storm, its roots deep and unseen, holding it steady as the winds rage around it. The tree does not resist the storm, nor does it bend to its will; it simply waits, trusting in the resilience of its roots and the passing of time.

So too is the strength of patience. It is the ability to remain steadfast in the face of adversity, to endure the discomfort of waiting without losing sight of the goal, and to trust that progress, however slow, is still progress. Patience is not passivity; it is not the absence of action or ambition. Rather, it is the recognition that some things—perhaps the most important things—cannot be rushed. It is the understanding that growth, whether personal, professional, or spiritual, unfolds in its own time, and that to force it is to risk undermining its very essence.

Consider, for a moment, the process of planting a seed. One does not plant a seed and expect a tree to sprout overnight. The gardener knows that the seed must first be buried in the darkness of the earth, where it will lie dormant for a time, unseen and untouched by the light.

It will germinate slowly, its roots reaching down into the soil long before its shoots break through the surface. The gardener must wait, tending to the soil, watering the ground, but never rushing the process. And when the seed finally emerges, it is still only the beginning of a long journey—a journey of seasons and years, of growth and dormancy, of blossoming and withering, all in their time.

The lesson of the seed is the lesson of patience. It is a reminder that the most profound transformations —the kind that endure—are not the result of sudden bursts of effort, but of consistent, patient tending. Whether we are nurturing a dream, a relationship, or our own personal growth, we must learn to embrace the slow, steady work of progress, trusting that the fruits of our labor will come not in a single moment, but over the course of time.

Patience as a Mastery of Time

To cultivate patience is to cultivate a mastery of time— not in the sense of controlling or manipulating it, but in the sense of aligning oneself with its natural rhythms. Time is not the enemy; it is the great teacher, the force that reveals all things in their fullness if we are willing to wait, to observe, and to allow.

But how often do we rebel against time, treating it as something to be overcome, rather than embraced? We race against the clock, believing that the faster we move, the more we will achieve. We measure our days by how much we have accomplished, rather than by the quality or depth of our experiences. We become impatient with ourselves and with the world, frustrated by the gap between where we are and where we want to be.

Yet, the mastery of patience lies not in speeding up, but in slowing down. It lies in the ability to be present in the moment, to appreciate the small steps we take toward our goals, and to trust that the journey is as important as the destination. Patience teaches us to embrace the process, to find meaning in the daily rituals of our work, and to let go of the need for immediate results.

There is a profound wisdom in the phrase, good things take time. It is a reminder that the most valuable achievements—those that truly matter—are rarely the result of haste. Whether we are building a career, cultivating a talent, or pursuing a dream, the process of growth is one that unfolds over years, sometimes decades. And it is in the patience required to stay the course that we develop the resilience, the wisdom, and the depth needed to sustain success when it finally comes.

The Dance of Patience and Consistency

Patience and consistency are twin virtues, each dependent on the other for their full expression. Patience without consistency is idle waiting, a passive surrender to time. Consistency without patience is frantic effort, a restless striving for results that come too slowly. But when the two are combined, they form a powerful alchemy—a force that can move mountains, shape lives, and bring even the most distant dreams within reach.

Consistency is the steady beat that accompanies

patience's long, slow rhythm. It is the daily practice, the small, seemingly insignificant actions that, when repeated over time, lead to extraordinary results. It is the act of showing up, day after day, even when progress is invisible, even when the goal seems impossibly far away. It is the belief that each step, no matter how small, brings us closer to where we want to be.

In the pursuit of long-term goals, consistency is the bridge between where we are and where we want to go. But consistency without patience is unsustainable. Without patience, we become frustrated by the slow pace of progress; we lose sight of the bigger picture and become consumed by the day-to-day struggles. We may start strong, but without the steadying influence of patience, we risk burning out before we ever reach our destination.

Patience, then, is the sustaining force that allows us to remain consistent over the long haul. It is the quiet confidence that, though the journey may be long, we will arrive in time. It is the recognition that true growth is incremental, that it happens not in sudden leaps but in the accumulation of small victories over time. And it is this slow, steady progress that leads to mastery, to the fulfillment of our deepest ambitions.

Consider the sculptor, who spends hours, days, even years chiseling away at a block of stone. Each strike of the chisel is a small, seemingly insignificant action, but over time, these actions accumulate, and the stone begins to take shape. The sculptor does not rush the process, for to do so would risk damaging the work. Instead, they proceed with patience, trusting in the power of consistency to reveal the form that lies within.

So too must we approach our own lives—with patience and consistency, trusting that the small actions we take each day will, in time, lead to the realization of our goals. Whether we are building a career, mastering a skill, or pursuing a dream, the path to success is not one of sudden breakthroughs, but of steady, deliberate progress. And it is in the cultivation of patience that we find the strength to stay the course, even when the road is long and the progress is slow.

The Inner Landscape of Patience

To cultivate patience is not merely to learn to wait; it is to cultivate a certain inner stillness, a quiet confidence in the unfolding of life. It is to develop a deep trust in the rhythms of the world, to understand that everything has its season, and that there is a time for sowing and a time for reaping. This trust is not a passive resignation to fate, but an active engagement with the present moment, a willingness to be fully present in the process of becoming.

Patience requires us to confront our desire for control, to let go of the need to dictate the terms of our progress. It asks us to surrender to the unknown, to embrace the uncertainty of the journey, and to trust that the steps we are taking will lead us where we need to go. This surrender is not an abdication of responsibility, but a recognition that there are forces at work beyond our control, and that true growth happens not through force, but through alignment with these forces.

In this sense, patience is deeply connected to faith—not necessarily in a religious sense, but in the sense of a deep, abiding belief in the process of life. It is the faith that our efforts, though they may seem small or insignificant, are contributing to something larger, something that we may not yet be able to see. It is the faith that, in time, the fruits of our labor will come to fruition, and that we need not rush or force the process.

But this faith is not always easy to maintain. There are times when the journey feels endless, when the progress is so slow that it seems as though we are moving backward. There are times when we question whether our efforts are worth it, whether we are on the right path, or whether we should abandon our goals altogether. In these moments, patience is not just a virtue—it is a lifeline, the thread that keeps us connected to our purpose, even when the way is unclear.

The Paradox of Patience and Urgency

There is a paradox at the heart of patience—a paradox that reveals the true depth of this hidden superpower. Patience does not negate urgency; it does not ask us to abandon our goals or to become complacent in the pursuit of our dreams. Rather, it asks us to hold urgency and patience in balance, to cultivate a sense of urgency in our actions while maintaining patience in our expectations.

Urgency without patience leads to burnout, frustration, and disappointment. It is the relentless drive to achieve, to attain, to arrive, without regard for the process. It is the impatience that demands immediate results, that seeks shortcuts and quick fixes, and that ultimately leads to disillusionment when the desired outcomes do not materialize as quickly as we would like.

But patience without urgency can lead to stagnation, to a passive waiting for life to unfold without our active participation. It is the kind of patience that becomes an excuse for inaction, a way of avoiding the discomfort of growth by convincing ourselves that we are simply "waiting for the right time."

The mastery of patience lies in holding both urgency and patience in harmony. It is the ability to act with purpose and intention, to pursue our goals with dedication and focus, while also trusting in the slow, steady unfolding of time. It is the recognition that, though we must act with urgency in the present moment, the results of our efforts will come in their own time.

This balance is not easy to achieve, but it is essential for long-term success. It requires us to be fully engaged in the present, to take consistent action toward our goals, while also cultivating a deep trust in the process of growth. It is the ability to plant seeds with urgency, but to wait for them to grow with patience.

The Rewards of Patience

The rewards of patience are not always immediate, but they are profound. Patience teaches us to value the process, to find meaning in the journey, and to appreciate the small, incremental steps we take toward our goals. It teaches us to let go of the need for constant validation, to trust in our efforts, and to find satisfaction in the daily work of becoming.

When we cultivate patience, we free ourselves from the

constant pressure to achieve, to attain, to arrive. We become more present, more engaged, and more at peace with the unfolding of our lives. We learn to appreciate the beauty of the process, to find joy in the small victories, and to trust that, in time, the larger goals will be realized.

Patience also teaches us resilience. When we are patient, we are better able to weather the inevitable setbacks, challenges, and disappointments that come with any meaningful pursuit. We learn to see these obstacles not as failures, but as opportunities for growth, as part of the process of becoming.

The rewards of patience are not just the achievement of our goals, but the person we become in the process. Patience shapes us, molds us, and deepens us in ways that no other force can. It teaches us to trust in ourselves, to believe in the value of our efforts, and to find peace in the slow, steady unfolding of time.

The Hidden Superpower

Patience is the hidden superpower that underlies all great achievements, the quiet force that sustains us in the pursuit of our deepest goals. It is the strength to endure, the wisdom to wait, and the faith to trust in the process of becoming. To master patience is to master time itself, not by controlling it, but by aligning ourselves with its rhythms.

In a world that glorifies immediacy, patience asks us to slow down, to appreciate the journey, and to trust that the fruits of our labor will come in their own time. It is the superpower that allows us to stay the course, to remain consistent in our efforts, and to achieve success not in a single moment, but over the course of a lifetime.

To cultivate patience is to cultivate a deeper relationship with time, with ourselves, and with the world around us. It is the key to lasting success, to true mastery, and to a life lived in alignment with our highest aspirations. And so, as we move forward on our journey, let us remember the quiet, unyielding power of patience—the hidden superpower that makes all things possible.

CHAPTER 5: COURAGE OVER CONFIDENCE

In the symphony of human virtues, courage and confidence often find themselves mistaken for one another, their melodies entwined in the minds of those who seek strength in the face of life's uncertainties. Yet, while confidence strikes a bold and certain chord, it is courage that plays the deeper, more resonant note, a note forged not in the absence of fear, but within its very heart. It is courage that allows us to step forward, trembling yet determined, when the shadows of doubt linger at the edge of every decision. And it is courage, not confidence, that transforms lives, shapes destinies, and dares us to be vulnerable in a world that demands certainty.

To speak of courage is to speak of an inner alchemy, a quiet rebellion against the forces of fear that would otherwise keep us shackled in place. Courage does not roar; it whispers. It does not demand applause or recognition; it simply is. It exists in the still moments before action, in the split-second where we decide to leap despite the yawning abyss beneath us, where we resolve to speak when silence would be more comfortable, or where we choose to stand our ground when retreat seems the safer course.

Confidence, by contrast, often wears a brighter mask. It is confidence that strides boldly into the room, chest high and eyes unflinching, declaring its place in the world with assured certainty. Confidence, in its purest form, is the outward expression of competence, a belief in one's ability to navigate a particular domain with skill and ease. And while confidence is not without its value—it can indeed open doors, inspire trust, and propel us forward—it is often hollow when divorced from its quieter, more essential counterpart: courage.

For confidence thrives on certainty, on the assurance that the path ahead is clear, that the skills we possess will be sufficient to meet the challenges we face. But life, in its infinite complexity, rarely offers such assurances. It is in these moments of uncertainty, when the ground beneath us shifts and the way forward is obscured by fog, that courage emerges as the truer, deeper virtue. It is courage, not confidence, that enables us to act in the face of the unknown, to risk failure, rejection, or loss, and to persist even when the outcome is anything but guaranteed.

The Illusion of Confidence

The world often teaches us to prize confidence above all else, to cultivate the appearance of certainty, even when doubt gnaws at the edges of our resolve. We are told to "fake it till you make it," to project confidence even when it is absent, as though the mere appearance of assuredness could somehow conjure competence out of thin air. And to some extent, this works. There is a certain magic to confidence—others are drawn to it, doors open more readily for those who walk with conviction, and opportunities seem to gravitate toward those who believe they are worthy of them.

But confidence, when worn as a mask to hide inner uncertainty, is fragile. It shatters easily under the weight of real adversity, leaving us exposed and vulnerable, our insecurities laid bare. Confidence, when built on the shaky foundation of outward appearance rather than inner conviction, cannot withstand the storm. It is a facade, a mirage that dissolves the moment it is tested by the forces of fear, failure, or doubt.

Courage, on the other hand, does not rely on such illusions. It does not need to project strength, because courage is strength. It is the strength to move forward even when every fiber of our being trembles with fear. It is the strength to acknowledge our vulnerability, to admit that we do not have all the answers, and to act anyway. Courage is the quiet resolve that sustains us when confidence falters, the inner flame that burns steadily even when the winds of doubt threaten to extinguish it.

The Dance of Fear and Courage

At the heart of courage lies an inextricable relationship with fear. For without fear, there can be no courage. Courage is not the absence of fear, but the ability to act in spite of it, to step into the unknown with trembling hands and a beating heart. Fear, in all its many forms —fear of failure, fear of rejection, fear of the unknown —serves as the crucible in which courage is forged. It is the pressure that shapes us, that demands we confront our limitations, and that offers us the opportunity to grow beyond them.

Yet, fear is often misunderstood. We are taught to see it as an adversary, something to be conquered or eliminated, as though fear were a weakness to be overcome. But fear is not a sign of weakness; it is a natural, human response to the uncertainty of life. It is the mind's way of protecting us from danger, of signaling that we are stepping into territory that is unfamiliar or risky. To feel fear is to be alive, to be awake to the reality that life is fraught with uncertainty and risk. To deny fear, to pretend it does not exist, is to deny a fundamental aspect of our humanity.

Courage, then, is not the absence of fear, but the ability to sit with it, to acknowledge its presence without allowing it to dictate our actions. It is the willingness to feel the fear fully and to choose to move forward regardless. This is the essence of true bravery—not the absence of fear, but the decision to act in spite of it.

In this way, courage and fear are not enemies, but dance partners. They move in tandem, each shaping and defining the other. Without fear, courage would have no meaning, no reason to exist. It is in the face of fear that courage finds its fullest expression, that it rises up from the depths of our being and propels us forward when every instinct tells us to retreat.

The Vulnerability of Courage

To be courageous is to embrace vulnerability, to step into the world without the armor of certainty or invulnerability. It is to allow oneself to be seen, to risk failure, embarrassment, or rejection, and to do so with the full awareness that these outcomes are possible—perhaps even likely. Courage does not seek to shield itself from the possibility of pain; rather, it opens itself to the full spectrum of experience, knowing that growth and transformation often come through the very challenges we fear most.

There is a raw beauty in vulnerability, a beauty that is often hidden beneath the layers of protection we build around ourselves. We are taught to equate vulnerability with weakness, to believe that to be open is to be exposed, and to be exposed is to be at risk. And indeed, there is risk in vulnerability—the risk of being hurt, of being judged, of falling short. But there is also profound strength in the willingness to be vulnerable, in the courage it takes to show up fully and authentically in a world that often demands perfection and certainty.

When we embrace vulnerability, we are not simply opening ourselves to pain; we are also opening ourselves to connection, to growth, and to the possibility of something greater than what we can currently imagine. It is through vulnerability that we build deep, meaningful relationships, that we create art and ideas that resonate with others, and that we take the kinds of risks that lead to true fulfillment.

Courage is the force that allows us to step into this vulnerability, to move forward even when we feel exposed or uncertain. It is the quiet voice that whispers, "You are enough, as you are, in this moment," and encourages us to act, even when the outcome is unknown.

Courage in the Face of Failure

One of the greatest tests of courage comes in the face of failure. To fail is to experience the sting of defeat, to confront the gap between our aspirations and our reality. It is a humbling experience, one that forces us to reckon with our limitations, our mistakes, and our humanity. But it is also an opportunity—an opportunity to learn, to grow, and to cultivate resilience.

Courage in the face of failure is not about ignoring the pain or pretending that failure does not hurt. It is about acknowledging the pain, feeling it fully, and choosing to rise again. It is about refusing to be defined by our failures, but rather using them as stepping stones toward growth and eventual success. Courage allows us to pick ourselves up after a fall, to dust ourselves off, and to try again—perhaps with a new perspective, a new approach, or a renewed sense of determination.

There is a certain grace in the ability to fail well, to embrace failure not as a reflection of our worth, but as a natural part of the journey toward mastery. Those who succeed in life are not those who never fail, but those who have learned to fail with courage, to see each setback as a learning experience, and to continue forward with resilience and grit.

Courage in Everyday Acts

While we often think of courage in grand, heroic terms—images of soldiers in battle, revolutionaries standing up against tyranny, or individuals risking their lives for a cause—the truth is that courage exists in the small, everyday acts that shape our lives. It is the courage to speak up when something feels wrong, even if we are the only one doing so. It is the courage to be honest with ourselves and others, even when the truth is uncomfortable. It is the courage to pursue a dream, to take a risk, to venture into the unknown, even when success is not guaranteed.

Courage is found in the mother who wakes up every day to care for her children, despite her exhaustion. It is found in the artist who continues to create, even when the world does not yet recognise their talent. It is found in the person who shows up to therapy, to the gym, to the difficult conversation, because they know that growth requires discomfort.

These small acts of courage, though often unseen and uncelebrated, are the building blocks of a life well-lived. They are the moments in which we choose to act with integrity, to align our actions with our values, and to move toward the person we wish to become.

The Courage to Be Imperfect

At the core of courage is the willingness to be imperfect, to embrace the messiness of life and of ourselves. We live in a world that often demands perfection, that tells us we must have it all figured out, that we must be flawless in our execution, in our appearance, in our achievements. But this is an impossible standard, one that leads only to frustration, burnout, and a sense of inadequacy.

Courage, by contrast, allows us to let go of the need for perfection. It gives us permission to be human, to make mistakes, to learn, and to grow. It reminds us that we are enough, not because we are perfect, but because we are willing to show up, to try, and to continue moving forward in the face of imperfection.

This is the heart of Brené Brown's teaching in Daring Greatly—that vulnerability, far from being a weakness, is the very source of our strength. It is in our willingness to be imperfect, to risk failure, and to embrace uncertainty that we find the courage to live fully and authentically.

The Courage to Dare Greatly

To dare greatly is to live a life of courage, to step into the arena of life with our hearts wide open, knowing that we will be tested, that we will stumble, and that we will face challenges along the way. It is the willingness to pursue our dreams, to stand up for what we believe in, and to live with integrity, even when it is difficult.

Daring greatly requires us to move beyond the superficial markers of success—confidence, competence, and certainty—and to embrace the deeper, more meaningful qualities of courage, vulnerability, and resilience. It asks us to let go of the need for approval, for external validation, and to trust in our own worth, even when the world does not yet recognise it.

To dare greatly is to live with purpose, to align our actions with our values, and to pursue the things that matter most to us. It is the courage to take risks, to embrace failure, and to continue moving forward, even when the path is unclear.

In the end, courage is not about the absence of fear, but about the presence of something greater—a commitment to living fully, authentically, and with integrity. It is the ability to act in the face of uncertainty, to embrace vulnerability, and to dare greatly in the pursuit of a life that is meaningful and true.

Choosing Courage Over Confidence

As we move through life, we are faced with a choice: to seek confidence, the outward appearance of assuredness, or to cultivate courage, the inner strength that sustains us in the face of fear and uncertainty. Confidence, while valuable, is often fleeting and fragile. It is courage that endures, that allows us to act in the face of doubt, and that gives us the strength to pursue our dreams, even when the path is difficult.

It is courage that matters most—not the kind of courage that demands attention or recognition, but the quiet, steady courage that allows us to show up, to risk vulnerability, and to live fully and authentically. It is the courage to embrace imperfection, to dare greatly, and to continue moving forward, no matter the challenges we face.

Courage is not a superpower reserved for the fearless; it is a choice available to each of us, in every moment. And when we choose courage over confidence, we choose a life of depth, meaning, and true greatness.

CHAPTER 6: THE POWER OF ACTIVE LISTENING

In the intricate dance of human relationships, there exists an overlooked, often underestimated force—a force that holds the key to deeper connections, profound understanding, and the forging of bonds that transcend the superficial. It is not found in the eloquence of speech or the persuasiveness of words, though the world often reveres these qualities. Rather, it lies in the art of silence, in the simple yet profound act of listening. And not just listening, but active listening, a type of attention so rare in its purity that it has the power to transform conversations, heal rifts, and draw souls closer together.

Active listening is not a passive absorption of sounds, nor is it a mere waiting for one's turn to speak. It is an act of generosity, a surrendering of the self to the other, an offering of presence and attention without expectation or interruption. In a world that often prioritizes speaking, arguing, and asserting, true listening emerges as an almost radical act of humility and empathy. It is in listening, more than in speaking, that we touch the hearts of others, that we communicate our respect and understanding, and that we build the foundations of trust upon which all meaningful relationships rest.

To listen actively is to go beyond the surface of words, to hear not only what is spoken but what is left unsaid—the nuances of tone, the pauses, the emotions that ripple beneath the conversation's surface like currents beneath still water. Active listening requires patience, curiosity, and a genuine desire to understand, to connect, and to reflect without judgment or agenda. In this chapter, we will explore the profound power of active listening, drawing upon its hidden strengths, and unveiling the ways in which it can transform both personal and professional relationships.

The Silent Power of Listening

There is a quiet strength in listening that is often misunderstood in a culture that prizes assertiveness and the ability to articulate one's thoughts with precision. We are encouraged, from a young age, to speak up, to make ourselves heard, to contribute to the conversation. And while these are important skills, they often overshadow the more subtle, more potent power of listening. To listen is to give. It is to offer one's time, one's attention, and one's empathy, without demanding anything in return.

True listening requires us to set aside our own need to be heard, our impulse to respond, and our desire to assert our views. It asks us to step out of the spotlight and into the shadows, where the other person's voice can take centre stage. In this way, listening is an act of humility, a recognition that the thoughts, feelings, and experiences of another are just as valuable—if not more so—than our own.

But why is listening so powerful? Why does it carry the ability to deepen relationships, to resolve conflicts, and to inspire trust? The answer lies in the fundamental human need to be understood. At the core of every conversation, beneath the words and arguments, lies a yearning for connection. We speak not only to convey information but to share a part of ourselves, to invite others into our inner world, and to feel seen and acknowledged. When we listen—truly listen—we fulfill this need for understanding, and in doing so, we create a space in which the other person feels valued, respected, and heard.

Listening, then, is not a passive act; it is an active engagement with the other person's reality. It requires us to put aside our assumptions, our judgments, and our desire to control the conversation. It demands that we be fully present, that we attune ourselves not only to the words being spoken but to the emotions and intentions behind them. And when we listen in this way, we offer something far more valuable than advice or solutions—we offer the gift of presence, of being there with and for the other person in a way that transcends words.

The Art of Active Listening

To master the art of active listening is to cultivate a set of skills that go beyond hearing what someone says. It is to engage with their words, to immerse oneself in the flow of the conversation, and to respond in ways that encourage deeper communication. Active listening is a practice of mindfulness, of staying in the moment and resisting the temptation to let one's thoughts wander, to plan one's response, or to anticipate the direction of the conversation.

At its core, active listening involves several key elements:

- Presence: To be fully present is to focus entirely on the speaker, without distraction or preoccupation. This means setting aside the phone, the mental to-do list, and the urge to interrupt. It means offering one's undivided attention, both mentally and physically, and allowing the conversation to unfold without rushing or steering it toward a particular outcome.

- Empathy: Empathy is the ability to understand and share the feelings of another. In the context of listening, it means putting oneself in the speaker's shoes, imagining what they are experiencing, and responding in a way that reflects that understanding. Empathy is not about agreeing with the other person, but about acknowledging their perspective and validating their emotions.

- Curiosity: Active listening is fueled by genuine curiosity. It is the desire to learn more, to dig deeper, to explore the layers of meaning behind the words being spoken. Curiosity encourages open-ended questions, prompts for elaboration, and an openness to being surprised by what the speaker has to say.

- Reflection: Reflecting the speaker's words back to them is a powerful way to demonstrate understanding.

This can take the form of summarizing what the speaker has said, asking clarifying questions, or simply acknowledging the emotions behind their words. Reflection shows that you are not only hearing the speaker but engaging with their message on a deeper level.

- Patience: Active listening requires patience. Conversations, especially difficult ones, often unfold slowly, and it can be tempting to jump in with solutions, advice, or conclusions. But to listen actively is to allow the speaker the space to express themselves fully, without interruption or haste. It is to honour the natural pace of the conversation and to resist the urge to fill every silence.

In mastering these elements, we transform listening from a passive, automatic act into an intentional, meaningful practice. We move from simply hearing words to truly understanding the person behind them, and in doing so, we create the conditions for deeper, more authentic communication.

The Role of Listening in Building Relationships

Relationships—whether personal or professional—are built on a foundation of trust, mutual respect, and understanding. And at the heart of these qualities lies the ability to listen. Listening is not just a tool for communication; it is the bedrock upon which relationships are formed and maintained. When we listen, we communicate that we value the other person, that their thoughts and feelings matter, and that we are willing to invest the time and attention required to understand them.

In personal relationships, listening fosters intimacy and connection. It allows us to see the other person not as an extension of ourselves, but as a unique individual with their own thoughts, feelings, and experiences. It helps us to navigate conflict, to resolve misunderstandings, and to offer support in a way that is truly meaningful. When we listen to our partners, our friends, or our family members, we offer them a space to be fully themselves, without judgment or expectation.

In professional relationships, listening is equally important. It is the key to effective collaboration, to building trust with colleagues, clients, or customers, and to creating a work environment where people feel respected and valued. Leaders who listen are able to understand the needs and concerns of their teams, to inspire loyalty, and to create a culture of open communication. Employees who listen are able to work more effectively with others, to resolve conflicts, and to contribute to a positive and productive work environment.

But listening is not only about fostering positive relationships; it is also a powerful tool for influence. As Dale Carnegie points out in How to Win Friends and Influence People, one of the most effective ways to win people over is to show a genuine interest in them—and the best way to do this is by listening. People are naturally drawn to those who listen to them, who take the time to understand their perspective, and who make them feel heard. Listening builds rapport, deepens trust, and creates a sense of connection that is far more powerful than any persuasive argument or well-crafted speech.

Listening Beyond Words

While words are the primary medium through which we communicate, they are only one part of the equation. Much of what we communicate—our emotions, our intentions, our true feelings—lies beneath the surface of words, in the realm of body language, tone, and nonverbal cues. To be an active listener is to tune in not only to the words being spoken but to the full spectrum of communication, including the unspoken elements.

Body language is a rich source of information, revealing much about what a person is truly feeling, even when their words suggest otherwise. A person's posture, facial expressions, and gestures can convey openness, discomfort, excitement, or hesitation. When we listen actively, we pay attention to these nonverbal signals, allowing us to gain a deeper understanding of the speaker's emotional state.

Tone of voice is another crucial element of communication. The way something is said often carries more meaning than the words themselves. A statement that sounds neutral on the surface can carry a world of emotion—frustration, sarcasm, fear, or joy—depending on the tone in which it is delivered. By attuning ourselves to the speaker's tone, we gain insight into their emotional landscape and can respond in a way that reflects our understanding.

Silence, too, is a form of communication. It is in the pauses between words, in the moments of stillness, that we often find the most profound meaning. Silence can indicate hesitation, reflection, or a deep emotional response. It can signal that the speaker needs more time to gather their thoughts, or that they are inviting us to reflect on what has been said. In active listening, we honour these silences, allowing them to exist without rushing to fill them. We recognise that silence is not a void, but a space in which deeper understanding can emerge.

The Barriers to Active Listening

If active listening is so powerful, why is it so rare? The answer lies in the many barriers—both internal and external—that prevent us from fully engaging in the act of listening. These barriers can take many forms, from distractions and preoccupations to our own internal biases and assumptions.

One of the most common barriers to active listening is the desire to respond. All too often, we listen not to understand, but to formulate our own response. While the other person is speaking, our minds are busy crafting our rebuttal, preparing our next point, or waiting for an opportunity to insert our own thoughts. This is particularly true in conversations where there is disagreement or conflict. In these situations, we are often more focused on defending our own position than on truly hearing what the other person has to say.

Another barrier is distraction. In today's world, we are constantly bombarded by stimuli—phones, emails, notifications—that compete for our attention. Even when we are physically present in a conversation, our minds may be elsewhere, pulled away by thoughts of what we need to do later or by the pull of the digital world. Distraction prevents us from being fully present, from offering our complete attention to the speaker, and from engaging with their words on a deeper level.

Our assumptions and biases also act as barriers to active listening. We come into conversations with preconceived notions about the speaker, about the topic, or about the outcome. These assumptions color the way we interpret the speaker's words, leading us to filter their message through our own lens. When we listen through the lens of our assumptions, we are not truly hearing the other person; we are hearing only what we expect to hear.

Finally, there is the barrier of emotional reactivity. When a conversation touches on sensitive topics—whether personal, political, or professional—it can trigger strong emotions. These emotions can cloud our ability to listen, causing us to become defensive, reactive, or dismissive. When we are emotionally reactive, we are no longer listening; we are reacting. In these moments, it is important to recognise our emotional state and to take a step back, allowing ourselves the space to process our feelings before re-engaging in the conversation.

Overcoming Barriers to Active Listening

Overcoming these barriers requires both awareness and practice. The first step is to recognise when we are not fully listening, whether due to distraction, assumptions, or emotional reactivity. Once we are aware of the barriers, we can take steps to address them.

One of the most effective ways to overcome the desire to respond is to cultivate curiosity. Instead of focusing on what we will say next, we can shift our attention to the speaker, asking ourselves: What can I learn from this person? What are they really trying to say? This shift in focus allows us to engage more fully with the speaker's words and to respond from a place of understanding rather than defense.

To combat distraction, we can practice mindfulness, bringing our attention back to the present moment whenever we notice our minds wandering. This may involve putting away distractions—turning off the phone, closing the laptop—and reminding ourselves that the person in front of us deserves our full attention.

To address assumptions and biases, we can practice open-mindedness, approaching each conversation with the willingness to be surprised, to hear something new, or to have our perspective challenged. This requires humility—the recognition that we do not have all the answers, and that we can learn from others, even when we disagree with them.

Finally, to manage emotional reactivity, we can practice emotional regulation, recognizing when our emotions are clouding our ability to listen and taking steps to calm ourselves before re-engaging in the conversation. This may involve taking a deep breath, pausing before responding, or even taking a break from the conversation if necessary.

The Transformative Power of Listening

Active listening, when practiced consistently, has the power to transform not only our relationships but our entire approach to communication. It allows us to move beyond surface-level interactions and to engage with others on a deeper, more meaningful level. It fosters empathy, understanding, and connection, and it creates the conditions for trust and mutual respect to flourish.

In a world that often feels divided, where conversations are more likely to be battles of opinion than opportunities for connection, active listening offers a path forward. It reminds us that beneath the differences, beneath the arguments and the noise, we are all seeking the same thing: to be heard, to be understood, and to be valued.

By cultivating the art of active listening, we become better friends, partners, colleagues, and leaders. We create spaces where people feel safe to share their thoughts and feelings, where they know they will be met with respect and empathy. And in doing so, we build relationships that are not only stronger but more meaningful and fulfilling.

Listening is not a passive act; it is a choice. It is a choice to set aside our ego, our assumptions, and our distractions, and to offer our full attention to the person in front of us. It is a choice to engage with their words, to reflect on their meaning, and to respond with empathy and curiosity.

The power of active listening lies not in what we say, but in what we choose to hear. It lies in the space we create for others to be fully themselves, in the connections we forge through our presence and attention, and in the relationships we build through the simple, yet profound, act of listening.

CHAPTER 7: BUILDING TRUST

The Foundation Of All Relationships

In the grand architecture of human connection, trust stands as the keystone, holding the intricate structure of relationships together, unseen yet indispensable. It is the invisible currency that flows between individuals, silently weaving its way through conversations, gestures, promises, and shared experiences. Trust is the unseen thread that binds souls together, creating bridges of understanding and intimacy where before there were only chasms of uncertainty and doubt.

Yet, trust is both fragile and enduring—a paradox that defies simple comprehension. It takes time to build, yet can be shattered in an instant. It is earned, never given, and once broken, it is far harder to repair than it was to forge. Trust is the foundation upon which all meaningful relationships are built, whether personal or professional, and without it, even the most well-intentioned efforts at connection crumble like a house of cards.

But what is trust, truly? It is more than just reliability or dependability. Trust is an alchemical mixture of faith, belief, vulnerability, and respect. It is the act of placing a piece of one's heart, one's reputation, or one's livelihood into the hands of another, with the hope—but never the certainty—that it will be handled with care. Trust requires vulnerability because to trust someone is to expose oneself to the possibility of betrayal or disappointment. Yet, without trust, there can be no real connection, no true collaboration, and no lasting bond.

Trust is the cornerstone of every interaction that moves beyond the superficial. It is the foundation of all relationships—be they personal friendships, romantic partnerships, familial ties, or professional collaborations. Without trust, relationships remain shallow, transactional, and riddled with doubt. With trust, they flourish into something more profound, something rooted in shared respect, understanding, and mutual growth.

The Silent Power of Trust

Trust operates in the background of our lives, unnoticed until it is lost. It is the silent power that governs our interactions, allowing us to navigate the world with a sense of safety and assurance. When we trust someone, we open ourselves up to them; we allow ourselves to be vulnerable, to share our thoughts, fears, and dreams without the fear of judgment or exploitation. Trust is what makes intimacy possible, and intimacy, in turn, deepens trust, creating a virtuous cycle that strengthens relationships over time.

In professional contexts, trust is the lubricant that keeps the wheels of collaboration and teamwork turning smoothly. It allows for the free exchange of ideas, the delegation of responsibilities, and the confidence that everyone is working toward a common goal. Without trust, organizations grind to a halt, mired in micromanagement, suspicion, and miscommunication. Stephen M.R. Covey, in his seminal work The Speed of Trust, eloquently articulates this principle, noting that trust accelerates everything. When trust is present, decisions are made more quickly, tasks are completed more efficiently, and innovation flourishes. Conversely, when trust is absent, everything slows down, as people second-guess each other's intentions, double-check each other's work, and hesitate to take initiative for fear of reprisal.

Trust, then, is not only a moral or emotional necessity; it is a practical one. It is the invisible currency that drives not just relationships, but success in every endeavor that requires collaboration, communication, and partnership. And yet, despite its central importance, trust is often taken for granted—until it is broken.

The Fragility of Trust

Trust, as essential as it is, remains one of the most fragile aspects of human relationships. Like a delicate glass sculpture, it can be painstakingly crafted over time, yet can be shattered in an instant by betrayal, deceit, or even neglect. The breaking of trust is a moment of profound rupture, one that leaves both parties reeling—one in the sharp pain of betrayal, the other in the shame of having failed to live up to expectations.

The fragility of trust lies in its inherent vulnerability. To trust is to take a risk. It is to believe that another person will act in good faith, even when circumstances test their integrity. When that faith is betrayed, the wound cuts deep, often leaving scars that never fully heal. And unlike other aspects of relationships that can be mended with time and effort, trust, once broken, is difficult—sometimes impossible—to fully restore. This is because trust is not built on words or promises, but on consistent actions, on the lived reality of shared experience. To rebuild trust after it has been broken requires a level of commitment and sincerity that few are willing—or able—to muster.

This fragility is what makes trust so precious. It is why we guard it so closely, why we hesitate to extend it to those we do not know well, and why we feel such intense gratitude toward those who have earned it. Yet, despite its fragility, trust is also resilient. It can endure hardships, misunderstandings, and conflicts, as long as both parties are committed to nurturing and maintaining it. Trust is not a static quality, but a dynamic one—something that must be continually cultivated through honesty, transparency, and mutual respect.

The Building Blocks of Trust

Trust is not something that can be demanded or expected; it must be earned. And like any structure, it is built upon a foundation of smaller, interconnected elements. To build trust, whether in personal relationships or professional environments, requires attention to these building blocks:

- Integrity: Integrity is the cornerstone of trust. It is the quality of being honest, reliable, and consistent in one's actions and words. People trust those who demonstrate integrity because they know that these individuals will act in accordance with their values, even when it is difficult or inconvenient. Integrity is not about perfection; it is about authenticity—about showing up as one's true self and being willing to stand by one's commitments.

- Transparency: Trust thrives in the light of transparency. When we are open and honest about our intentions, our feelings, and our actions, we create a space where trust can grow. Transparency does not mean oversharing or revealing every thought and emotion, but it does mean being clear and direct in our communication, especially when it comes to difficult or sensitive issues. In professional settings, transparency about goals, expectations, and performance helps to build trust between colleagues, managers, and teams.

- Consistency: Trust is built over time through the repetition of trustworthy behaviour. It is not enough to act with integrity once; one must do so consistently. When people see that we are reliable, that we do what we say we will do, and that we can be counted on in times of need, they begin to trust us more deeply. Consistency is what transforms a single act of honesty into a lasting bond of trust.

- Vulnerability: Trust requires vulnerability on both sides. To trust someone is to open oneself up to the possibility of being hurt, and to be trusted is to bear the responsibility of caring for another's vulnerability. When we allow ourselves to be vulnerable, we invite others to do the same, creating a reciprocal exchange of trust that deepens over time. In personal relationships, vulnerability is the key to intimacy, while in professional settings, it fosters collaboration and innovation.

- Empathy: Trust is built on the foundation of understanding. When we empathize with others—when we take the time to listen to their concerns, to understand their experiences, and to acknowledge their emotions—we build trust. Empathy allows us to connect with others on a deeper level, to see the world through their eyes, and to respond with compassion and respect.

These building blocks, when combined, form the foundation of trust. They are the principles that guide our actions and our interactions with others, and they are the qualities that others look for when deciding whether or not to trust us. But building trust is not a one-time effort; it is an ongoing process, one that requires constant attention and care.

The Speed of Trust

In his book The Speed of Trust, Stephen M.R. Covey introduces the idea that trust is not just a moral or ethical concept, but a practical one that has a profound impact on the speed and efficiency of relationships and organizations. When trust is high, things move quickly. Decisions are made with confidence, actions are taken without hesitation, and collaboration flows smoothly. But when trust is low, everything slows down. People second-guess each other's intentions, miscommunication abounds, and the cost of doing business—both in terms of time and resources—rises exponentially.

The concept of "speed" in trust is crucial to understanding why trust is so essential in both personal and professional relationships. In a high-trust environment, people are more willing to take risks, to share ideas, and to work together toward common goals. They do not waste time on suspicion or on double-checking each other's work, because they trust that everyone is acting in good faith. This creates a sense of momentum and synergy that propels teams, organizations, and even friendships forward at an accelerated pace.

Conversely, when trust is absent, everything grinds to a halt. People are hesitant to share information, for fear that it will be misused or misunderstood. Collaboration breaks down as individuals become more focused on protecting themselves than on working toward a collective goal. The absence of trust creates a culture of fear, where every action is scrutinized, and every mistake is magnified. In such environments, progress becomes nearly impossible, and relationships —whether personal or professional—suffer.

Trust, then, is not just a feel-good concept; it is a practical necessity. It is the invisible currency that drives relationships forward, allowing for speed, efficiency, and mutual success. Without it, even the most talented individuals and the most well-resourced organizations will find themselves struggling to achieve their goals.

The Cost of Broken Trust

If trust is the currency that drives relationships forward, then the breaking of trust is akin to a financial crisis. When trust is broken, the cost is immense —emotionally, psychologically, and, in professional settings, financially. The loss of trust can lead to the unraveling of relationships, the dissolution of partnerships, and the collapse of organizations.

In personal relationships, the breaking of trust often results in feelings of betrayal, hurt, and disillusionment. It can take years to build trust, but only a moment to destroy it. When someone betrays our trust—whether through dishonesty, infidelity, or negligence—the emotional impact can be devastating. The bond that once held the relationship together is weakened, and the path to reconciliation is fraught with difficulty.

In professional contexts, the breaking of trust can have equally severe consequences. When trust is lost between colleagues, teams, or leadership and employees, the entire organization suffers. Productivity declines as people become more focused on protecting themselves than on collaborating. Innovation stalls as individuals are reluctant to share ideas or take risks. And, in the worst cases, the breaking of trust can lead to the collapse of the organization itself, as customers, clients, or stakeholders lose faith in its integrity.

The cost of broken trust is not only emotional or financial; it is also social. When trust is broken, it can create a ripple effect, spreading distrust throughout the broader community. People who have been betrayed are less likely to trust others in the future, creating a cycle of suspicion and guardedness that undermines the potential for connection and collaboration.

Rebuilding Trust

While the breaking of trust is painful, it is not always irreparable. Trust can be rebuilt, though the process is long and difficult, requiring a level of honesty, humility, and commitment that few are willing to undertake. To rebuild trust after it has been broken, both parties must be willing to engage in the hard work of reconciliation.

- Acknowledge the breach: The first step in rebuilding trust is to acknowledge that it has been broken. This requires honesty on both sides—an admission of the betrayal and an acknowledgment of the hurt it has caused. Too often, people try to sweep breaches of trust under the rug, hoping that time will heal the wound.

But trust cannot be rebuilt without first addressing the rupture head-on.

- Take responsibility: The person who has broken the trust must take full responsibility for their actions. This means offering a genuine apology—not just for the sake of smoothing things over, but as a sincere expression of regret and a commitment to change. Responsibility also involves making amends, whether through actions or words, and demonstrating a willingness to repair the damage that has been done.

- Be patient: Rebuilding trust takes time. It cannot be rushed or forced. Both parties must be patient with the process, understanding that trust is rebuilt not through words, but through consistent actions over time. The person who has broken the trust must be willing to prove, through their behaviour, that they are worthy of trust once again. And the person who has been betrayed must be willing to give them the opportunity to do so.

- Establish new boundaries: Rebuilding trust often requires the establishment of new boundaries, both to protect the relationship and to prevent further breaches of trust. These boundaries may involve clearer communication, greater transparency, or new expectations for how the relationship will move forward. Establishing boundaries is not about punishment or control; it is about creating a framework within which trust can grow again.

- Forgive: Finally, rebuilding trust requires forgiveness. This does not mean forgetting the betrayal or pretending that it did not happen. Rather, it means letting go of the anger, resentment, and desire for retribution that often accompany broken trust. Forgiveness is a gift—to oneself as much as to the other person—and it is essential for moving forward.

While rebuilding trust is difficult, it is not impossible. Relationships that survive the breaking of trust can often emerge stronger, as both parties have demonstrated a commitment to growth, honesty, and mutual respect. However, it is important to acknowledge that not all breaches of trust can—or should—be repaired. In some cases, the damage is too great, and the healthiest course of action is to move on.

The Role of Trust in Leadership

Trust is not only the foundation of personal relationships; it is also the cornerstone of effective leadership. Leaders who inspire trust create environments in which people feel safe, valued, and empowered to contribute their best work. In contrast, leaders who fail to build trust create cultures of fear, suspicion, and disengagement, where people are more concerned with protecting themselves than with collaborating or innovating.

A leader's ability to build trust depends on several key qualities:

- Authenticity: People trust leaders who are genuine and authentic—who show up as their true selves, rather than hiding behind a facade of authority. Authentic leaders are willing to admit their mistakes, to share their vulnerabilities, and to be transparent about their intentions. They do not pretend to have all the answers, but they are committed to finding them together with their team.

- Consistency: Consistency is one of the most important qualities in a leader. People need to know that they can rely on their leader to be steady and predictable in their actions. A leader who is erratic, who changes their mind without explanation, or who plays favorites, undermines trust. Consistency builds confidence and allows people to feel secure in their leader's direction.

- Empathy: Leaders who listen to their teams, who take the time to understand their concerns and their experiences, build trust through empathy. Empathetic leaders demonstrate that they value the people they lead, not just as employees or followers, but as individuals with unique perspectives and needs. This creates a culture of mutual respect and fosters a deeper sense of loyalty.

- Integrity: Above all, leaders must act with integrity. This means being honest, ethical, and transparent in all dealings. People trust leaders who do what they say they will do, who make decisions based on principles rather than convenience, and who are willing to stand by their values, even when it is difficult.

Trust in leadership is not just about competence; it is about character. People are willing to follow leaders they trust, even into uncertainty or risk, because they believe in the leader's integrity, authenticity, and commitment to the greater good.

The Invisible Currency of Trust

Trust is the foundation of all relationships, the invisible currency that drives personal and professional success. It is built through integrity, transparency, and empathy, and it is sustained through consistency and vulnerability. Without trust, relationships remain shallow and transactional, but with it, they flourish into something more profound and lasting.

In a world where speed and efficiency are often prioritized over depth and connection, trust reminds us of the importance of taking the time to build meaningful relationships—relationships based on mutual respect, understanding, and shared values. Trust is not only the foundation of relationships; it is the foundation of a life well-lived, one in which we can truly connect with others, collaborate toward common goals, and create a legacy of integrity and kindness.

Building trust is not easy, nor is it quick. But it is worth every effort, for in trust, we find the true essence of what it means to be human—interconnected, interdependent, and committed to one another's growth and well-being.

CHAPTER 8: THE UNWRITTEN RULES OF NETWORKING

In the grand tapestry of existence, where threads of destiny intertwine and the fates of individuals are woven into a shared narrative, there is an unspoken truth that often escapes the eye: the finest opportunities, those that shape the contours of our lives, seldom arrive through talent alone. They emerge, instead, from the invisible bonds we form with others, from the vast and intricate network of human connections that lie beneath the surface of every encounter. Relationships, not just skill, are the conduits through which success flows. This is the essence of networking—a subtle and profound art, governed by unwritten rules that few understand but all are subject to.

Networking is not a transactional game of favors, nor is it a cold exchange of business cards and pleasantries. It is a human endeavor, a delicate dance of trust, reciprocity, and shared purpose. It is about cultivating genuine relationships that, over time, blossom into mutual support, collaboration, and opportunity. And yet, despite its importance, networking remains an elusive skill, often misunderstood as superficial or self-serving. The truth, however, is far more nuanced: real networking is not about what you can take, but about what you can give. It is the art of building relationships not for immediate gain, but for the long-term enrichment of both parties involved.

As Keith Ferrazzi emphasizes in Never Eat Alone, the most successful people in the world do not rise to prominence on talent alone—they rise because they understand the importance of human connection. They know that, in a world where opportunities are often hidden behind closed doors, relationships are the keys that unlock those doors. To navigate the intricate web of human connection is to understand that the road to success is not a solitary path; it is a journey that we take together, supported by the people we meet along the way.

The Hidden Power of Relationships

We live in a world that often glorifies individual achievement, where the narrative of the self-made person is celebrated as the pinnacle of success. Yet, this narrative is largely a myth. While talent, hard work, and perseverance are essential, they are rarely sufficient on their own. The truth, quietly acknowledged but seldom proclaimed, is that no one succeeds in isolation. Behind every successful individual is a network of relationships—mentors, colleagues, friends, and collaborators—who have provided guidance, support, and opportunity.

It is in this web of relationships that the true power of networking lies. Networking is not about meeting as many people as possible, nor is it about climbing a social ladder for personal gain. It is about creating meaningful connections, built on trust and mutual respect, that allow for the exchange of ideas, resources, and support. These relationships are the invisible infrastructure of success, providing access to opportunities that might otherwise remain out of reach.

Consider, for a moment, the difference between two individuals of equal talent. One is isolated, relying solely on their skills and knowledge to navigate the world. The other is connected, part of a vast network of people who offer advice, introduce them to new opportunities, and provide support when challenges arise. Over time, the second individual will likely find more doors open to them, not because they are more talented, but because they have cultivated the relationships that allow them to access those opportunities.

This is the hidden power of relationships: they multiply the possibilities available to us. Through our connections with others, we gain access to new perspectives, resources, and opportunities that we could never achieve alone. In this sense, networking is not about accumulating contacts—it is about building a community of mutual support and collaboration.

The Foundations of Authentic Networking

At the heart of authentic networking lies a simple yet profound principle: relationships are not transactions, but human connections. To build a meaningful network, we must approach each interaction with authenticity, generosity, and a genuine interest in the other person. This requires us to move beyond the superficial, beyond the idea of networking as a tool for personal gain, and toward a deeper understanding of the value of human connection.

Generosity as the Cornerstone: True networking begins with generosity—the willingness to give without expecting anything in return. This is perhaps the most important, and often overlooked, aspect of networking. When we approach relationships with the mindset of "what can I offer?" rather than "what can I get?", we open the door to genuine connection. People are naturally drawn to those who are generous with their time, knowledge, and resources, and they are more likely to reciprocate that generosity in the future.

Generosity in networking can take many forms. It may involve offering advice, introducing someone to a helpful contact, or simply being a supportive listener. The key is to approach each interaction with the intention of helping others succeed, rather than focusing solely on your own goals. This approach not only builds trust and goodwill but also establishes you as a person of integrity and value in the eyes of others.

Authenticity and Vulnerability: In a world that often prioritizes image and appearance, authenticity can be a rare and precious quality. Yet, it is authenticity that forms the foundation of lasting relationships. People are not drawn to perfection; they are drawn to those who are real, who are willing to show their true selves, including their imperfections. Authentic networking requires us to be vulnerable, to share our challenges and struggles, as well as our successes.

Vulnerability in networking is not about oversharing or seeking sympathy; it is about being honest and open about who we are. When we allow ourselves to be vulnerable, we create space for deeper connection, as others feel more comfortable sharing their own experiences. This mutual vulnerability fosters trust, which is the bedrock of any meaningful relationship.

Consistency and Long-Term Thinking: One of the most common misconceptions about networking is that it is a short-term endeavor, something to be done when we need something—whether it's a job, a favor, or an opportunity. However, the most successful networks are built over time, through consistent effort and a long-term perspective. Networking is not about making a connection and immediately asking for something in return; it is about cultivating relationships that will grow and evolve over the years.

Consistency is key in this process. Relationships require nurturing, and that means staying in touch, offering support, and being present even when there is no immediate benefit to be gained. This long-term approach allows relationships to develop organically, and when opportunities do arise, they are built on a foundation of trust and mutual respect.

The Art of Listening and Empathy in Networking

One of the most overlooked yet powerful aspects of networking is the art of listening. Too often, networking is approached as a performance, where the goal is to impress others with our accomplishments, ideas, or knowledge. But true networking is not about talking—it is about listening. When we listen deeply and empathetically to others, we demonstrate that we value them as individuals, not just as contacts or connections.

Listening is a form of generosity. It requires us to set aside our own agenda and focus entirely on the other person. This kind of active listening involves not just hearing words, but paying attention to body language, tone, and the emotions behind the words. It means asking thoughtful questions, showing genuine interest in the other person's experiences and perspectives, and responding with empathy.

Empathy is the bridge that connects us to others on a deeper level. When we listen with empathy, we are not just gathering information; we are seeking to understand the other person's feelings, challenges, and desires. This creates a space for meaningful connection, where the other person feels seen and heard.

In networking, empathy is particularly important because it allows us to identify opportunities to help others. When we truly understand someone's needs, we are better equipped to offer support, whether by introducing them to a helpful contact, sharing relevant advice, or simply offering encouragement. This kind of empathetic networking is far more valuable than any transactional exchange, as it fosters trust and goodwill, which are the foundations of long-lasting relationships.

Building a Network Through Shared Interests and Values

The most effective networks are not built randomly, but are cultivated through shared interests, values, and goals. While it is possible to network with anyone, the strongest connections are those that are based on common ground. When we connect with others who share our passions, values, or professional goals, we create a natural bond that makes collaboration and support more likely.

One of the most effective ways to build a network is by seeking out communities where these shared interests are present. This might involve joining professional organizations, attending conferences or workshops, or participating in online communities related to your field or interests. These environments provide opportunities to meet like-minded individuals with whom you can form meaningful connections.

However, it is important to approach these opportunities with an open mind and a spirit of curiosity. Networking is not about immediately identifying how someone can help you achieve your goals; it is about building relationships based on mutual respect and shared values. When we approach networking with this mindset, we create the conditions for authentic connections to flourish.

Reciprocity: The Cycle of Giving and Receiving

At the heart of networking is the principle of reciprocity—the idea that relationships are built on a cycle of giving and receiving. However, reciprocity in networking is not a quid pro quo exchange, where we give with the expectation of immediate return. Rather, it is a long-term process, where acts of generosity and support create a ripple effect that eventually comes back to us in unexpected ways.

When we give generously to others, whether by offering advice, making introductions, or providing support, we contribute to a culture of collaboration and mutual aid. Over time, this creates a network of individuals who are willing to help each other succeed. The key is to give without keeping score, trusting that the goodwill you generate will eventually return to you in ways you may not anticipate.

Reciprocity is not just about material or professional support; it is also about emotional support, encouragement, and the sharing of ideas. In a strong network, members uplift each other, celebrate each other's successes, and offer guidance during difficult times. This sense of mutual support creates a resilient network, where individuals are not just looking out for themselves, but for the collective well-being of the group.

The Importance of Follow-Up and Consistency

In networking, the initial connection is only the beginning. The real work of building relationships happens in the follow-up. It is not enough to meet someone once and exchange contact information; relationships must be nurtured through ongoing communication and engagement. Consistency is key to maintaining and strengthening these connections over time.

One of the most effective ways to follow up is by

expressing genuine gratitude for the other person's time and insights. A thoughtful thank-you note, an email, or a message on social media can go a long way in solidifying the initial connection. From there, it is important to stay in touch regularly, whether through casual check-ins, sharing articles or resources that might be of interest, or offering support when needed.

Consistency in networking also means being reliable and following through on promises. If you offer to make an introduction or aid, it is crucial to do so in a timely manner. Reliability builds trust, and trust is the foundation of any strong network.

Networking in the Digital Age: Leveraging Technology for Connection

In today's world, networking has expanded beyond face-to-face interactions to include a vast array of digital platforms. Social media, professional networking sites, and online communities provide unprecedented opportunities to connect with people across the globe. However, the principles of networking remain the same, whether in person or online: authenticity, generosity, and empathy are still the keys to building meaningful relationships.

Platforms like LinkedIn, Twitter, and industry-specific forums offer valuable opportunities to expand your network, share your expertise, and engage with thought leaders in your field. However, it is important to approach these platforms with the same level of care and intentionality that you would in a face-to-face interaction. Networking online is not about collecting followers or connections—it is about building relationships.

One of the most effective ways to network online is by contributing valuable content. This might involve sharing articles, writing thoughtful posts, or participating in discussions. By consistently offering insights and resources, you establish yourself as a knowledgeable and generous member of your community, which in turn attracts others who share your interests and values.

However, online networking should complement, not replace, in-person interactions. While digital platforms offer convenience and reach, face-to-face meetings remain a powerful way to build trust and deepen relationships. Whenever possible, it is important to transition online connections into real-world interactions, whether through coffee meetings, attending events, or participating in professional groups.

The Role of Mentorship in Networking

Mentorship is one of the most powerful forms of networking, offering a unique opportunity to build deep, meaningful relationships based on guidance, learning, and mutual respect. A mentor can open doors, provide valuable insights, and offer support as you navigate your career or personal growth. However, mentorship is not a one-sided relationship; it is a partnership that requires effort, commitment, and reciprocity from both parties.

Finding a mentor requires both initiative and humility. It often begins with seeking out individuals whose experience, values, and approach align with your own goals and aspirations. However, mentorship is not something to be requested outright. It is a relationship that evolves over time, often beginning with informal conversations and gradually deepening into a more formal mentorship as trust is built.

Once a mentorship is established, it is important to approach the relationship with gratitude and a willingness to learn. Mentorship is a two-way street, and while a mentor provides guidance and support, a mentee can also offer value through their perspective, energy, and dedication. The best mentor-mentee relationships are those in which both parties grow and benefit from the exchange.

Mentorship can also extend beyond traditional one-on-one relationships. In a strong network, mentorship often takes the form of a community, where individuals support and guide each other. Whether through peer mentorship, group discussions, or shared learning experiences, these collective forms of mentorship create a rich environment for growth and connection.

Overcoming Networking Anxiety: Building Confidence in Connection

For many people, networking can be a source of anxiety. The idea of approaching strangers, initiating conversations, or asking for help can feel intimidating or uncomfortable. However, building confidence in networking is not about changing who you are; it is about embracing your unique strengths and finding an approach to networking that feels authentic to you.

One of the most effective ways to overcome networking anxiety is to shift your mindset. Instead of viewing networking as a performance or a series of transactions, try to see it as an opportunity to build relationships and learn from others. Approach each interaction with curiosity and a genuine desire to connect, rather than focusing on what you need to say or how you will be perceived.

Preparation can also help ease anxiety. Before attending a networking event or meeting, take some time to research the people you might meet and think about the topics or questions you would like to discuss. Having a few conversation starters in mind can help you feel more confident and prepared.

Finally, it is important to remember that networking is not about perfection. It is about building relationships, and relationships take time. Not every conversation will lead to an immediate connection, and that's okay. The key is to be patient, consistent, and authentic in your approach, trusting that over time, meaningful connections will emerge.

The Unseen Path to Success

The unwritten rules of networking are simple yet profound: give before you take, listen more than you speak, and build relationships on a foundation of trust, empathy, and generosity. In a world that often emphasizes individual achievement, networking reminds us that success is not a solitary endeavor. It is the result of collaboration, support, and the relationships we cultivate along the way.

As we navigate our personal and professional journeys, it is important to recognise that the best opportunities do not come through talent alone. They come through the connections we make, the people we meet, and the networks we build. Networking is not just a skill—it is a way of being in the world, one that recognises the value of human connection and the power of relationships to shape our lives.

By embracing the principles of authentic networking, we open ourselves up to a world of possibility. We create a community of support, a network of relationships that not only enhance our own success but also contribute to the success of others. In the end, it is through these connections that we find our greatest opportunities and our deepest fulfillment.

CHAPTER 9: EMBRACING VULNERABILITY

In the shadowed corridors of the human heart, where fear and uncertainty often reign, there lies a hidden strength—a strength not born of power or control, but of surrender. It is the quiet courage that comes from letting go of perfection, from opening oneself up to the unknown, and from allowing others to see us as we truly are: imperfect, vulnerable, and beautifully human. This is the essence of vulnerability—a concept that, for many, conjures images of weakness, yet in truth, is the source of our greatest strength and connection.

Vulnerability is not the absence of fear, nor is it a reckless disregard for the potential of pain or rejection. Instead, vulnerability is the conscious choice to step into uncertainty, to embrace discomfort, and to expose the most tender parts of ourselves to others. It is the willingness to say, "Here I am, in all my imperfect glory," and to invite others into that space, trusting that in doing so, we open the door to deeper relationships, greater understanding, and a more authentic way of living.

Brené Brown, in her seminal work The Gifts of Imperfection, teaches that vulnerability is not something to be avoided, but rather something to be embraced. It is through vulnerability that we form meaningful connections with others, and it is through these connections that we find true belonging. In a world that often values invulnerability—where strength is equated with stoicism and perfection is held up as the ideal—embracing vulnerability becomes a radical act of self-acceptance and courage.

The Paradox of Vulnerability

To understand vulnerability, we must first confront a paradox: that which makes us feel most exposed, most at risk, is also the source of our greatest power. We are taught, often from a young age, to protect ourselves from emotional harm. We build walls, we put on masks, and we strive for perfection in an effort to avoid the sting of rejection or the shame of being seen as "less than." Yet, in doing so, we distance ourselves from the very thing we crave most: connection.

Connection is the lifeblood of the human experience. It is what gives our lives meaning and purpose, and it is through connection that we experience love, belonging, and joy. But connection cannot exist without vulnerability. To truly connect with others, we must be willing to let them see us as we are, to share our fears, our failures, and our imperfections. This is the paradox of vulnerability: while it feels like a risk, it is the key to unlocking the deeper, more meaningful relationships we seek.

When we allow ourselves to be vulnerable, we invite others to do the same. Vulnerability is contagious; when we see someone else open up and share their truth, it gives us permission to do the same. This creates a space where real connection can flourish, where we are not simply interacting on a surface level, but engaging with each other in a way that is raw, real, and deeply human.

The Mask of Perfection

Perfectionism is one of the greatest barriers to vulnerability. It is the armor we wear to protect ourselves from the pain of criticism, judgment, and rejection. We believe that if we can just be perfect—if we can present ourselves in the "right" way, achieve the "right" things, and say the "right" words—then we will be safe. We will be loved, accepted, and valued.

But perfection is a myth, a false ideal that is both unattainable and damaging. In our pursuit of perfection, we lose touch with our authentic selves, hiding the very aspects of our humanity that make us lovable. We present a polished exterior to the world, but inside, we feel disconnected, isolated, and unseen. The more we strive for perfection, the more we distance ourselves from the people and experiences that could bring us true connection and fulfillment.

Vulnerability, on the other hand, requires us to take off the mask of perfection and to embrace our imperfections as part of what makes us uniquely valuable. It asks us to stop performing for others, to stop trying to be what we think the world wants us to be, and to instead show up as we are—flawed, yes, but also worthy of love and belonging.

This is not easy. The fear of judgment, rejection, and failure is powerful, and it can feel safer to hide behind perfectionism than to risk being seen. But in truth, it is only by allowing ourselves to be vulnerable that we can experience true connection. Perfectionism isolates us; vulnerability brings us closer to others.

Vulnerability and Courage

Vulnerability requires an immense amount of courage. It is not the courage of the battlefield or the boardroom, but a quieter, more personal bravery. It is the courage to face ourselves, to confront our fears, and to risk being hurt in the pursuit of connection. It is the courage to admit that we don't have all the answers, that we make mistakes, and that we are still learning and growing. And it is the courage to let others see us in our raw, unpolished state, trusting that we are enough as we are.

This kind of courage is transformative. When we embrace vulnerability, we stop trying to control how others perceive us and start living from a place of authenticity. We stop seeking validation from external sources and begin to find our worth within ourselves. And, paradoxically, when we stop trying to be perfect, we often find that we are more loved and accepted than we ever were when we were striving for perfection.

Courage and vulnerability are inextricably linked. It is through vulnerability that we find the courage to take risks, to try new things, and to pursue our passions. Without vulnerability, we remain trapped in fear, unwilling to step outside of our comfort zone or to put ourselves out into the world. But when we embrace vulnerability, we open ourselves up to the full spectrum of life's experiences, both the joyful and the painful. We allow ourselves to be fully alive.

The Role of Vulnerability in Relationships

Relationships, whether romantic, familial, or platonic, thrive on vulnerability. It is through vulnerability that we create the intimacy and trust that are the foundation of any meaningful relationship. When we allow ourselves to be vulnerable with others, we create a space where they can do the same. This mutual vulnerability fosters a deep sense of connection and belonging, as both parties feel seen, heard, and accepted for who they truly are.

In romantic relationships, vulnerability is essential for emotional intimacy. It is the willingness to share our deepest fears, desires, and insecurities with our partner, trusting that they will hold those parts of us with care. It is the courage to express our needs and boundaries, even when it feels uncomfortable or risky. And it is the ability to listen and respond with empathy when our partner does the same.

Without vulnerability, relationships remain shallow and transactional. We may go through the motions of connection, but we never truly let the other person in. We hold back out of fear of rejection or judgment, and in doing so, we deny ourselves the full richness of intimacy. Vulnerability, though it may feel risky, is what allows relationships to deepen and flourish.

In friendships, vulnerability plays a similar role. It is through vulnerability that we move beyond small talk and surface-level interactions, and into the realm of true friendship. When we share our struggles, our joys, and our imperfections with a friend, we create a bond that is rooted in mutual trust and understanding. This kind of friendship is not just about companionship; it is about being fully known and accepted.

Even in professional relationships, vulnerability has a place. While we may not share our deepest fears or insecurities in a work context, vulnerability can still foster trust and collaboration. Leaders who are willing to admit when they don't have all the answers, or who are open to feedback and growth, create a culture of psychological safety where others feel empowered to do the same. In this kind of environment, teams can innovate, take risks, and support each other in a way that is only possible when vulnerability is embraced.

Vulnerability and Shame

One of the greatest barriers to vulnerability is shame. Shame is the deeply held belief that there is something fundamentally wrong with us, that we are not worthy of love, connection, or belonging. It is the voice in our heads that tells us we are not enough—smart enough, attractive enough, successful enough, or good enough. Shame thrives in secrecy and silence, and it is often the reason we resist vulnerability. We fear that if others see the "real" us, they will reject us, and so we hide behind perfectionism, bravado, or emotional distance.

But shame cannot survive in the light of vulnerability.

When we allow ourselves to be vulnerable, we break the cycle of shame by bringing our fears and insecurities into the open. We share our stories, our struggles, and our imperfections, and in doing so, we create a space for empathy and connection. Vulnerability is the antidote to shame because it allows us to see that we are not alone in our struggles. When we are vulnerable with others, we give them the opportunity to respond with compassion, and in that compassion, shame begins to lose its power.

This is not to say that vulnerability will always be met with empathy. There will be times when our vulnerability is met with judgment, criticism, or rejection. But even in these moments, vulnerability is a victory because it is a step toward living authentically. It is a declaration that we are no longer willing to live in the shadows of shame, and that we are choosing to embrace ourselves as we are.

The Gifts of Imperfection

Brené Brown refers to vulnerability as "the birthplace of love, belonging, joy, courage, empathy, and creativity." These are the gifts of imperfection—the rewards that come from embracing our humanity, rather than striving for an unattainable ideal of perfection. When we allow ourselves to be vulnerable,

we open the door to experiences that are richer, more meaningful, and more fulfilling than anything we could achieve through perfectionism.

Love and Belonging: At the core of the human experience is the need for love and belonging. We are wired for connection, and it is through vulnerability that we create the deep, meaningful relationships that fulfill this need. When we allow ourselves to be seen and accepted for who we truly are, we experience a sense of belonging that is far more powerful than the fleeting approval we seek through perfection.

Joy: Vulnerability is also the gateway to joy. When we are willing to embrace the full spectrum of our emotions—both the joyful and the painful—we allow ourselves to experience life more fully. Joy is not the absence of struggle or difficulty; it is the ability to find meaning and beauty in the midst of it. Vulnerability allows us to open our hearts to the present moment, to connect with others, and to savor the small, everyday moments of joy that make life worth living.

Courage: Vulnerability requires immense courage, and it is through this courage that we grow as individuals. When we take the risk of being vulnerable, we expand our capacity for resilience, empathy, and compassion. We learn to navigate the complexities of life with greater authenticity and grace, and we become more capable of facing challenges with an open heart.

Empathy: Vulnerability fosters empathy because it allows us to connect with the struggles of others. When we are vulnerable, we share our common humanity—the fact that we all experience pain, fear, and uncertainty. This shared experience creates a space for empathy, where we can offer support and understanding to those around us, and receive the same in return.

Creativity: Finally, vulnerability is the key to creativity.

True creativity requires the willingness to take risks, to experiment, and to fail. It is only by embracing vulnerability that we can push the boundaries of what is possible and tap into the wellspring of our creative potential.

Embracing Vulnerability in Everyday Life

Embracing vulnerability is not a one-time act; it is a practice that we must cultivate in our everyday lives. It requires us to show up, to be present, and to engage with the world in a way that is open, honest, and courageous. This may involve small acts of vulnerability, such as asking for help when we need it, admitting when we don't have all the answers, or sharing our feelings with a friend or partner. Or it may involve larger acts, such as pursuing a passion that feels risky, having a difficult conversation, or taking a leap of faith in a new relationship or career.

Whatever form it takes, embracing vulnerability is a commitment to living authentically. It is the choice to let go of perfectionism, to silence the voice of shame, and to step into the fullness of who we are. It is the understanding that true strength lies not in invulnerability, but in the willingness to be seen, to be imperfect, and to be human.

In the end, vulnerability is not about being weak or exposed; it is about being brave. It is the courage to live with an open heart, to engage with the world on a deeper level, and to create the kind of connections that make life meaningful. And it is through this courage that we find the gifts of imperfection—the love, joy, and belonging that we have been seeking all along.

CHAPTER 10: READING BETWEEN THE LINES

Understanding Social Cues

There exists a delicate dance in the realm of human interaction, an intricate choreography that extends far beyond the words spoken. This dance, rich with unspoken signals and subtle gestures, is governed by a language that is often more powerful than any uttered phrase—the language of social cues. Social cues form the invisible threads of communication, weaving together body language, tone, facial expressions, and the context of a situation. To master the art of reading these cues is to unlock a deeper, more intuitive understanding of the people around us, and to navigate the complex landscapes of human relationships with grace and sensitivity.

Much of what we communicate is unspoken, residing in the realm of the unsaid and the implied. As

Daniel Goleman explores in Social Intelligence, effective communication is not just about the transmission of information through words; it is about understanding the emotional undertones and psychological context that shape every interaction. By learning to read between the lines, by attuning ourselves to the subtle signals that accompany speech, we can connect more deeply with others, resolve conflicts more effectively, and foster relationships that are built on empathy and trust.

The Silent Language of Body and Gesture

The human body is an eloquent storyteller, often revealing truths that words may seek to conceal. Every movement, every posture, every glance conveys something of our inner state, whether we intend it or not. When we learn to read these physical signals, we gain access to a world of meaning that lies beneath the surface of spoken language.

Posture and Presence: The way a person holds themselves—whether they stand tall and open or slump inward with closed arms—can reveal volumes about their emotional state. An upright, expansive posture often conveys confidence, openness, and engagement, while a slouched or closed-off posture can suggest discomfort, insecurity, or disengagement. When someone crosses their arms, it might signal defensiveness or a desire for protection, whereas an open stance, with arms relaxed, conveys a readiness to engage. Posture is a nonverbal map of how a person feels in any given moment.

Facial Expressions: The Mirror of Emotion: The face is

a window to the soul, reflecting the entire spectrum of human emotion. A fleeting frown, the crinkle of a smile, a raised eyebrow—these micro-expressions often occur in the blink of an eye but are packed with emotional information. A smile can signal warmth, friendliness, or even an attempt to mask discomfort, while a furrowed brow may suggest confusion or concern. Learning to interpret these subtle expressions allows us to understand not only what someone is saying but how they feel about what they are saying.

The eyes, in particular, are powerful communicators. Eye contact, or the lack thereof, plays a pivotal role in conveying attention, interest, and honesty. Direct, sustained eye contact often signals confidence and engagement, while avoidance of eye contact may suggest discomfort, deception, or a lack of interest. However, cultural differences in eye contact should also be considered, as norms vary significantly from one society to another.

Gestures and Movement: Our hands and bodies often speak when our voices do not. Gestures, whether intentional or unconscious, punctuate our words and add layers of meaning to what we say. A nod of the head can signal agreement or understanding, while a rapid, impatient tapping of the foot may convey frustration or anxiety. The way we move through space—whether we lean in to listen more closely or pull away to create distance—also sends powerful signals about our comfort level and our engagement in the conversation.

These gestures, when read in conjunction with words, provide a fuller picture of what is truly being communicated. For example, if someone says they are fine but their body is rigid, their arms are crossed, and they avoid eye contact, their body language may tell a different story. Learning to tune into these physical signals helps us to "read between the lines" and respond to what someone is actually feeling, not just what they are saying.

Tone of Voice: The Sound Beneath the Words

While words carry meaning, it is often the tone in which they are spoken that reveals the emotional weight behind them. Tone of voice can transform the meaning of a sentence, turning a neutral statement into an expression of anger, sarcasm, or affection. For example, the phrase "I'm fine" can be a genuine statement of well-being, but when spoken with a sharp, clipped tone, it might carry frustration or irritation. Similarly, a phrase delivered with a warm, gentle tone can convey empathy and care, even if the words themselves are neutral.

Tone includes not just the pitch of the voice but also its rhythm, speed, and volume. A raised voice often signals anger or urgency, while a soft, slow tone might indicate sadness or exhaustion. People who speak quickly may be excited or anxious, while those who pause frequently might be uncertain or reflective. Paying attention to these vocal nuances allows us to understand the emotional context behind the words, helping us to respond in a way that is attuned to the speaker's true emotional state.

For instance, when someone apologizes, the sincerity of the apology often lies not in the words but in the tone. A genuine apology is usually spoken softly, with a sense of humility, while an insincere apology might be delivered quickly, with an undertone of frustration or indifference. By learning to listen to the sound beneath the words, we can discern whether someone is speaking from a place of truth or merely going through the motions of politeness.

Context: The Silent Architecture of Conversation

Social cues do not exist in isolation; they are always embedded within a larger context, and it is this context that gives them meaning. The same gesture, facial expression, or tone of voice can mean very different things depending on the situation, the relationship between the people involved, and the cultural or social environment in which the interaction takes place.

Situational Awareness: To fully understand social cues, we must develop situational awareness—the ability to read the context of a conversation and interpret cues accordingly. For example, in a formal business meeting, someone who is unusually quiet might be seen as disengaged or uninterested, whereas in a social gathering, that same silence might simply reflect a more introverted personality. Similarly, a joke made among close friends might be seen as light-hearted, but in a professional setting, it could be perceived as inappropriate or disrespectful.

Recognizing the broader situation helps us interpret cues in a way that is sensitive to the dynamics at play. It also allows us to adjust our own behaviour to fit the context, ensuring that we communicate effectively and appropriately.

Cultural Sensitivity: Social cues are also deeply influenced by cultural norms, which shape how people express emotions, communicate nonverbally, and interpret gestures. In some cultures, maintaining direct eye contact is a sign of confidence and respect, while in others, it might be seen as confrontational or disrespectful. Similarly, physical proximity during conversation can vary significantly across cultures; what is considered friendly closeness in one culture might feel invasive in another.

To navigate social cues across cultures, it is important to be aware of these differences and to approach interactions with curiosity and humility. By learning about the social norms of different cultures, we can avoid misinterpretations and foster more meaningful cross-cultural connections. Cultural sensitivity not only enhances our ability to read social cues but also demonstrates respect for the diverse ways in which people communicate and express themselves.

Relationship Dynamics: The nature of the relationship between the people involved also plays a crucial role in how social cues are interpreted. A casual comment between close friends may be understood as affectionate teasing, but the same comment between acquaintances could be taken as offensive or inappropriate. Similarly, body language that conveys comfort and closeness in a romantic relationship might be misinterpreted as overfamiliarity or boundary-crossing in a professional setting.

Understanding the dynamics of the relationship helps us navigate social cues with greater finesse, ensuring that our communication is appropriate for the level of familiarity and trust between the individuals involved. It also helps us to interpret the cues we receive from others more accurately, recognizing that their behaviour may be influenced by the nature of the relationship as much as by their emotional state.

Empathy: The Key to Understanding Social Cues

At the heart of reading social cues is empathy—the ability to understand and share the feelings of another. Empathy allows us to move beyond the literal meaning of words and gestures, and to connect with the underlying emotions that drive them. When we approach interactions with empathy, we become more attuned to the subtle signals that others send, and we are better equipped to respond in ways that acknowledge and honour their emotional experience.

Empathy is not simply about feeling what another person feels; it is about being present to their emotions, even if those emotions are different from our own. It involves listening deeply, not just to what is being said, but to what is being expressed nonverbally. It requires us to put aside our own assumptions and judgments, and to enter into the emotional world of the other person.

When we practice empathy in communication, we are better able to pick up on social cues that might otherwise go unnoticed. We become more sensitive to the nuances of tone, body language, and context, and we are more likely to respond in ways that foster connection and understanding. Empathy transforms communication from a transactional exchange of information into a meaningful interaction that honours the emotional needs of both parties.

For example, if someone expresses frustration during a conversation, an empathetic listener will not only hear the frustration but also recognise the underlying emotions—perhaps disappointment, fear, or confusion—that are driving it. By responding with empathy, the listener can address those deeper emotions, offering support and validation rather than simply reacting to the surface level of the conversation.

The Impact of Social Cues on Conflict Resolution

Social cues play a particularly important role in conflict resolution, where emotions often run high and misunderstandings are common. In moments of tension, the ability to read between the lines becomes even more critical, as people may struggle to articulate their feelings clearly or may express emotions indirectly.

When we are in conflict, we may say things we do not fully mean, or we may withhold our true feelings out of fear of escalation. In these moments, social cues become the primary way that our emotions are communicated. A clenched jaw, averted eyes, or a heavy sigh may tell us more about how someone is feeling than their words alone. By paying attention to these nonverbal signals, we can gain insight into the emotional undercurrents of the conflict and respond with greater understanding and compassion.

For example, during a heated argument, one person may insist that they are not angry, but their body language—tense posture, raised voice, and rapid breathing—tells a different story. An attentive listener will recognise these cues and respond in a way that acknowledges the unspoken anger, perhaps by offering a calming gesture or suggesting a break in the conversation to allow emotions to settle.

Similarly, in moments of reconciliation, social cues can signal a shift in the emotional tone of the conversation. A softening of the voice, a gesture of openness, or a relaxed posture may indicate that the other person is ready to move toward resolution. By tuning into these signals, we can navigate the conflict with greater emotional intelligence, ensuring that our responses are aligned with the changing dynamics of the interaction.

Developing Social Intelligence Through Practice

Like any skill, the ability to read social cues and understand the unspoken elements of communication can be developed through practice. Social intelligence is not an innate talent reserved for a select few; it is a skill that can be honed by anyone who is willing to observe, listen, and engage with others on a deeper level.

Mindful Observation: One of the most effective ways to develop social intelligence is through mindful observation. By paying close attention to the people around us—their body language, tone of voice, and facial expressions—we can begin to notice patterns in how emotions are communicated nonverbally. This kind of observation requires us to be present in the moment, setting aside distractions and focusing fully on the interaction at hand.

Reflective Listening: Reflective listening is another powerful tool for developing social intelligence. This involves not just hearing the words being spoken, but reflecting back what we have understood, both verbally and nonverbally. By paraphrasing what the other person has said and checking in with them to confirm that we have understood their emotions accurately, we demonstrate empathy and create a space for deeper connection.

Emotional Awareness: Finally, developing emotional awareness—both of ourselves and others—is key to understanding social cues. The more attuned we are to our own emotions, the better equipped we are to recognise similar emotions in others. By practicing emotional regulation and self-reflection, we can approach interactions with greater calm and clarity, allowing us to pick up on social cues with greater sensitivity.

The Art of Reading Between the Lines

In the intricate dance of human communication, words are just the surface of a much deeper exchange. It is the unspoken signals—the subtle shifts in body language, tone, and context—that reveal the true meaning of an interaction. By learning to read between the lines, by tuning into the social cues that surround us, we open ourselves up to a more profound understanding of others and of ourselves.

Social intelligence is not just about interpreting gestures or deciphering tone; it is about fostering empathy, connection, and emotional attunement. It is about creating spaces where people feel seen, heard, and understood, not just through words, but through the unspoken language of human interaction. As we cultivate this skill, we enhance our ability to navigate the complexities of relationships, resolve conflicts with grace, and build connections that are rooted in trust and mutual understanding.

In a world that often prioritizes speed and efficiency, the art of reading between the lines reminds us of the importance of slowing down, of listening deeply, and of engaging with others on a human level. It is through this art that we find the true power of communication —the power to connect, to heal, and to understand.

CHAPTER 11: TIME MANAGEMENT

Life's True Currency

In the intricate dance of life, where moments slip by like grains of sand through an hourglass, one resource stands above all others in its scarcity and value: time. Time, unlike money or material wealth, cannot be earned back once spent. It is the true currency of life, and how we choose to allocate it ultimately shapes the trajectory of our existence. To understand the value of time is to grasp the key to success, fulfillment, and purpose. This understanding is what Stephen Covey illuminated in his transformative work The 7 Habits of Highly Effective People—a lesson that time, not money, is the most precious asset, and that mastering its management is essential to achieving our highest goals.

While we often focus on financial gains or professional achievements, the deeper truth is that time is the foundation upon which all success is built. It is the silent architect of our lives, and how we manage it determines not only what we accomplish, but also the quality of our relationships, our well-being, and our overall sense of purpose. Yet, despite its critical importance, time is a resource we frequently squander, mismanage, or take for granted, believing that more can always be found tomorrow.

But tomorrow, like the horizon, is always just beyond reach. The moments we waste today cannot be reclaimed. Each minute that passes is a part of our life's currency spent—whether wisely or in vain. And so, to achieve true success—both professionally and personally—we must learn to manage time with the same care, strategy, and intention that we would devote to managing a fortune. Time management is not merely about being efficient or getting more done; it is about aligning our use of time with our values, our goals, and our deeper purpose.

The Illusion of Time Abundance

There is a pervasive illusion that time is abundant, that the days stretch before us in endless succession, offering infinite opportunities to achieve, to grow, and to realize our dreams. This illusion is both comforting and dangerous. It allows us to procrastinate, to delay our ambitions, to put off meaningful tasks in favor of fleeting distractions. It seduces us into believing that we can always begin tomorrow, that there will always be another chance, another day.

But this is an illusion, for time is finite, and its passage is relentless. The hours we lose to trivial pursuits or mindless distractions are hours we can never recover. Each day that slips by unused is a day we have surrendered to the void, a day that could have been spent moving closer to our goals, deepening our relationships, or enriching our lives.

In the realm of professional success, this illusion of time abundance is particularly dangerous. It encourages us to delay important tasks, to allow our schedules to be dictated by the urgent rather than the important, and to lose sight of our long-term objectives in the face of short-term distractions. To combat this illusion, we must cultivate a sense of urgency—not in the frantic, stress-driven sense, but in the recognition that time is a limited resource and that every moment carries weight and significance.

Stephen Covey speaks to this in The 7 Habits of Highly Effective People, where he distinguishes between the "urgent" and the "important." Urgency demands immediate attention, but importance is what leads us toward our ultimate goals. The key to effective time management is learning to prioritize the important over the urgent, to recognise that while some tasks may scream for our attention, it is the quiet, steady pursuit of our long-term goals that will lead to true success.

Time as an Investment: The Power of Prioritization

To manage time effectively, we must first understand that time, like money, is an investment. Every action we take is a decision to invest our time in a particular way. The challenge, then, is to ensure that we are investing our time wisely, in activities that align with our values, goals, and aspirations. This requires a shift in perspective—from seeing time as something to be spent, to seeing it as something to be invested with intention and purpose.

The concept of prioritization lies at the heart of time management. Not all tasks are created equal, and not every demand on our time is worthy of attention. Covey's time management matrix, a framework that categorizes tasks based on their urgency and importance, offers a powerful tool for making these decisions. The matrix divides tasks into four quadrants:

1. Quadrant I: Urgent and Important – These tasks are both time-sensitive and critical to our goals. They often include crises or pressing deadlines. While they must be addressed, living constantly in this quadrant leads to stress and burnout.

2. Quadrant II: Not Urgent but Important – These are the tasks that move us toward our long-term goals. They are not immediate or pressing, but they are the most valuable uses of our time. Investing in this quadrant leads to growth, achievement, and success.

3. Quadrant III: Urgent but Not Important – These tasks demand our attention, but they do not contribute significantly to our goals. They often include interruptions, minor requests, and activities that feel productive but are ultimately distractions.

4. Quadrant IV: Not Urgent and Not Important – These are the true time-wasters, the activities that neither require our attention nor contribute to our success. They include mindless distractions and activities that offer no long-term value.

The goal of effective time management is to spend as much time as possible in Quadrant II—the space where we can focus on our long-term goals, personal development, and meaningful relationships. This requires us to be proactive in our time management, to plan ahead, and to make deliberate choices about how we allocate our time.

But prioritization is not just about deciding what to do; it is also about deciding what not to do. We must learn to say no to the distractions of Quadrant III and Quadrant IV, to the tasks that pull us away from what truly matters. This may mean turning down requests that do not align with our goals, or it may mean setting boundaries around our time to protect it from unnecessary demands. By learning to prioritize the important over the urgent, we reclaim control over our time and begin to use it as the powerful resource that it is.

The Myth of Multitasking

In today's fast-paced, hyper-connected world, multitasking has become a badge of honour. We pride ourselves on our ability to juggle multiple tasks at once, to respond to emails while attending meetings, or to complete several projects simultaneously. Yet, the myth of multitasking is one of the greatest obstacles to effective time management. While it may feel productive in the moment, multitasking is, in reality, a drain on our focus, our creativity, and our efficiency.

The human brain is not designed to focus on multiple tasks at once. When we attempt to multitask, we are not truly doing two things at once; we are rapidly switching our attention back and forth between tasks. This constant switching not only reduces our effectiveness, but it also increases our cognitive load, leading to mental fatigue and decreased productivity. Studies have shown that multitasking can reduce efficiency by as much as 40%, as the brain struggles to reorient itself with each switch.

Effective time management requires us to resist the temptation of multitasking and instead embrace the power of single-tasking—the practice of focusing on one task at a time, giving it our full attention, and completing it before moving on to the next. Single-tasking allows us to work more deeply and more creatively, and it leads to higher-quality results. By focusing on one task at a time, we not only increase our efficiency, but we also engage more fully with the work we are doing, leading to a greater sense of accomplishment and satisfaction.

In professional settings, the pressure to multitask can be overwhelming, as we are bombarded with emails, messages, and interruptions throughout the day. But by setting clear boundaries around our time, we can protect our focus and create periods of uninterrupted work. This might mean turning off notifications during certain hours, setting aside specific times for email responses, or scheduling deep work sessions where we can focus on important projects without distraction. The key is to recognise that multitasking is not a sign of productivity; it is a barrier to it.

Proactivity: The Heart of Time Management

One of the central themes of Covey's work is the concept of proactivity—the idea that we are responsible for our own lives and that we have the power to shape our future through the choices we make today.

In the context of time management, proactivity means taking control of our time, rather than allowing it to be dictated by external forces. It means being intentional about how we use our time, planning ahead, and making deliberate decisions that align with our goals and values.

Proactive time management is not about rigidly scheduling every minute of the day, but about creating a framework that allows us to stay focused on what matters most. This requires us to be clear about our priorities, to set goals that are meaningful and achievable, and to create systems that support our efforts. It also means being adaptable and flexible, recognizing that life is unpredictable and that we must be willing to adjust our plans when necessary.

At the heart of proactivity is the concept of time blocking—the practice of scheduling specific blocks of time for important tasks and activities. By setting aside dedicated time for deep work, personal development, and relationships, we ensure that our most important priorities receive the attention they deserve. Time blocking also helps us to protect our time from distractions and interruptions, as it creates a structure that allows us to stay focused on our goals.

Proactivity also means recognizing that we are not at the mercy of time—we are its stewards. We have the power to choose how we spend our time, and by making intentional choices, we can create a life that is aligned with our deepest values and aspirations. This requires us to move beyond the reactive mode of responding to every demand and instead take ownership of our time, using it to build the life and career we truly desire.

Energy Management: The Overlooked Aspect of Time Management

While time is a finite resource, energy is the force that drives how effectively we use that time. Too often, we focus on managing our time without considering how our energy levels fluctuate throughout the day. Yet, time management without energy management is like trying to drive a car with an empty fuel tank—no matter how carefully we plan our route, we won't get far if we don't have the energy to sustain us.

Understanding and managing our energy levels is essential to maximizing our productivity and well-being. This involves recognizing when we are at our most energetic and focused, and scheduling our most important tasks during those peak periods. For some, this might mean tackling creative work first thing in the morning, while for others, it might mean reserving the afternoon for high-focus tasks.

Energy management also involves taking regular breaks to recharge and avoid burnout. The human brain is not designed to focus for long stretches without rest, and studies have shown that taking short breaks throughout the day can actually improve productivity. Whether it's a five-minute walk, a quick stretch, or a moment of mindfulness, these breaks allow us to refresh our minds and return to our work with renewed energy and focus.

In addition to physical energy, emotional and mental energy play a crucial role in time management. Negative emotions such as stress, anxiety, or frustration can drain our energy and reduce our ability to focus. By practicing emotional intelligence and learning to manage our emotions, we can conserve our energy and stay productive even in challenging situations. This might involve mindfulness practices, stress management techniques, or simply taking time to reflect on our emotional state and address any underlying issues.

Ultimately, effective time management is not just about scheduling tasks; it is about creating a sustainable rhythm that allows us to maintain our energy, focus, and well-being throughout the day.

The Importance of Reflection and Review

Time management is not a static skill; it is an ongoing process that requires regular reflection and adjustment. To manage our time effectively, we must take the time to reflect on how we are using it, to evaluate what is working and what is not, and to adjust as needed. This process of reflection allows us to stay aligned with our goals and to ensure that we are investing our time in ways that truly matter.

One of the most powerful tools for reflection is the weekly review, a practice that involves setting aside time at the end of each week to review our progress, assess our goals, and plan for the week ahead. During the weekly review, we can ask ourselves important questions: What did I accomplish this week? What challenges did I face? How can I improve my time management next week? By taking the time to reflect on our use of time, we gain valuable insights into our habits and patterns, and we can make more informed decisions about how to move forward.

The weekly review also provides an opportunity to celebrate our successes and to acknowledge the progress we have made, no matter how small. This sense of accomplishment is essential for maintaining motivation and momentum, as it reminds us that our efforts are moving us closer to our goals.

In addition to the weekly review, it is important to periodically assess our long-term goals and priorities. As we grow and evolve, our goals may change, and our time management strategies must adapt accordingly. By regularly revisiting our goals and ensuring that our use of time is aligned with our current values and aspirations, we can stay on the path to success.

Time as Life's True Currency

In the final analysis, time is not just a resource; it is life itself. Every moment we spend is a moment of our life that we can never get back. The choices we make about how we use our time determine not only our success in the professional world but also the quality of our relationships, our personal fulfillment, and our sense of purpose.

To manage time effectively is to honour the preciousness of life. It is to recognise that time is our most valuable currency and to invest it wisely in the things that truly matter. This requires us to be intentional, to prioritize the important over the urgent, and to align our use of time with our deepest values and goals.

But time management is not just about productivity; it

is about creating a life that is meaningful, balanced, and fulfilling. It is about making space for the things that bring us joy, for the people we love, and for the pursuits that nourish our souls. In this sense, time management is not just a skill—it is an art, one that allows us to live our lives with purpose, intention, and grace.

CHAPTER 12: MASTERING THE ART OF NEGOTIATION

Negotiation is often imagined as a battle of wills, where one party emerges victorious, having outmaneuvered their opponent in a zero-sum game. But this view is both limiting and reductive, for true negotiation is not a contest with winners and losers, but a collaborative process that seeks to satisfy the deeper needs of all involved. At its best, negotiation is an art—a delicate dance of communication, empathy, and strategy, where success is measured not by dominance but by the ability to find common ground. This lesson lies at the heart of Getting to Yes by Roger Fisher and William Ury, a groundbreaking book that redefined the rules of negotiation by introducing the idea that the goal is not to "win" but to reach a solution that benefits all parties —a win-win outcome.

Negotiation, then, is not about victory over another; it is about creating value, about expanding the scope of possibilities so that everyone involved leaves the table with their needs met. Whether in business, relationships, or everyday life, the ability to negotiate effectively is one of the most critical skills we can cultivate. It allows us to resolve conflicts, build stronger relationships, and create solutions that are sustainable and equitable. But to do this, we must move beyond the traditional mindset of competition and embrace a new approach—one that is rooted in mutual respect, creative problem-solving, and a commitment to finding common ground.

The Traditional Approach: A Zero-Sum Game

For many, negotiation is synonymous with compromise. It evokes images of tense standoffs, where each party tries to extract as much as they can from the other, giving away as little as possible in return. This is the classic zero-sum game—where one party's gain is seen as the other's loss. In this model, negotiation is a competitive process, where each side seeks to maximize their own benefit, often at the expense of the other.

While this adversarial approach may yield short-term gains, it is ultimately a flawed strategy for achieving long-term success. When negotiation becomes a battle, it breeds resentment, mistrust, and dissatisfaction. Even if one side "wins" in the moment, the relationship between the parties is often damaged, and the solution is rarely sustainable. This approach also limits creativity and flexibility, as both sides are focused on protecting their positions rather than exploring new possibilities.

Roger Fisher and William Ury challenged this traditional view of negotiation with their concept of principled negotiation—an approach that seeks to separate the people from the problem, focus on interests rather than positions, and work together to find solutions that benefit everyone. In this model, negotiation is not about competing for a fixed pie but about working collaboratively to expand the pie, creating value for both parties.

The Shift to Principled Negotiation: Interests Over Positions

At the heart of principled negotiation is a simple but profound shift: from focusing on positions to focusing on interests. In a traditional negotiation, each party enters the discussion with a fixed position—what they want or demand. For example, in a salary negotiation, one side may say, "I want a 10% raise," while the other side counters, "We can only offer a 5% raise." These are positions—specific outcomes that each side is attached to. When negotiation is framed in terms of positions, it often leads to deadlock, as each side becomes entrenched in their demands, unwilling to budge.

But positions are not the same as interests. While positions are the surface-level demands, interests represent the underlying needs, desires, and motivations that drive those demands. In the salary negotiation, for example, the employee's position may be a 10% raise, but their interest might be financial security, recognition of their contribution, or the desire for professional growth. Similarly, the employer's position might be a 5% raise, but their interest could be staying within budget, ensuring fairness among employees, or rewarding performance in a sustainable way.

By focusing on interests rather than positions, negotiators can move beyond the superficial demands and explore the deeper needs that underlie them. This shift opens the door to creative problem-solving, where both parties work together to find solutions that address their interests, rather than simply haggling over numbers. For example, in the salary negotiation, instead of fixating on the percentage increase, both sides might explore alternative ways to meet the employee's interest—such as offering additional benefits, opportunities for career development, or performance-based bonuses. By addressing the interests of both parties, the negotiation moves from a zero-sum game to a win-win solution.

The Importance of Empathy and Understanding

One of the most powerful tools in negotiation is empathy—the ability to understand the other party's perspective and to recognise their needs, concerns, and emotions. Empathy allows us to see the negotiation not as a battle to be won, but as a conversation between two human beings, each with their own interests, challenges, and desires. When we approach negotiation with empathy, we create a space for collaboration and trust, where both parties feel heard and respected.

Empathy in negotiation begins with active listening. Too often, negotiators are so focused on preparing their next argument or defending their position that they fail to truly listen to what the other party is saying. Active listening involves not just hearing the words, but understanding the emotions and interests behind them. It requires us to ask open-ended questions, seek clarification, and demonstrate that we are genuinely interested in the other party's perspective.

For example, imagine a negotiation between two colleagues over a project deadline. One colleague insists on extending the deadline by a month, while the other argues that the original deadline must be met. Instead of becoming entrenched in their positions, an empathetic approach would involve asking questions such as, "What challenges are you facing that make the original deadline difficult?" or "How can we ensure that the project is completed on time without sacrificing quality?" By seeking to understand the other person's concerns, both parties can work together to find a solution that addresses their interests—such as reallocating resources, adjusting the project scope, or providing additional support.

Empathy also involves acknowledging the emotions that may be present in the negotiation. Emotions such as frustration, fear, or anxiety can often cloud the discussion and make it difficult to reach a resolution. By recognizing and validating these emotions, we can help to diffuse tension and create a more constructive dialogue. For example, if one party expresses frustration during the negotiation, a simple acknowledgment—"I can see that this situation is frustrating for you"—can go a long way toward calming the conversation and showing that you are attuned to their feelings.

Separating People from the Problem

One of the key principles of Fisher and Ury's approach is the idea of separating the people from the problem.

In many negotiations, emotions run high, and personal feelings can become entangled with the issues being discussed. When this happens, it becomes difficult to address the problem objectively, as both parties become defensive or aggressive in response to perceived personal attacks.

By separating the people from the problem, negotiators can focus on the substantive issues at hand without allowing personal emotions to derail the conversation. This means recognizing that the other party is not an adversary to be defeated, but a partner in the process of finding a solution. It also means being mindful of how our own emotions and biases might be influencing the way we approach the negotiation.

To separate people from the problem, it is important to approach the negotiation with a mindset of collaboration rather than competition. Instead of viewing the other party as an opponent, we should see them as a partner in solving a shared problem. This shift in mindset allows us to engage in the negotiation with openness and curiosity, rather than defensiveness or hostility.

In a negotiation between a manager and an employee over a work assignment, the manager might feel frustrated that the employee is pushing back on the assignment, while the employee might feel overwhelmed by their workload. By separating the people from the problem, the manager can recognise that the employee's resistance is not a personal attack, but a response to the workload issue. This allows both parties to focus on the real problem—how to manage the employee's workload more effectively—rather than getting caught up in personal conflict.

The Power of Creative Problem-Solving

At the heart of successful negotiation is the ability to think creatively. When both parties become entrenched in their positions, it can feel as though the options are limited—either one side gives in, or the negotiation ends in a stalemate. But by approaching negotiation with a mindset of collaboration and openness, we can often discover creative solutions that satisfy both parties' interests.

Creative problem-solving in negotiation involves looking beyond the obvious options and exploring new possibilities. This requires us to break free from the traditional mindset of negotiation as a zero-sum game and to embrace the idea that the pie can be expanded. Instead of focusing on what each side has to lose, we can focus on what both sides have to gain by working together.

In a business negotiation over pricing, one side may insist on a lower price, while the other side argues that the price must remain high to cover costs. Instead of haggling over the price, both sides might explore creative alternatives, such as offering a longer-term contract at a discounted rate, bundling additional services, or creating a performance-based pricing model. By thinking creatively, both parties can find a solution that meets their needs without sacrificing the relationship.

Creativity in negotiation also involves being willing to explore trade-offs. Not every interest is equally important to both parties, and sometimes one side may be willing to give up something of lesser value in exchange for something that is more important to them. For example, in a contract negotiation, one party might be willing to compromise on the delivery timeline in exchange for more favorable payment terms. By identifying these trade-offs, both sides can make concessions that do not feel like losses but rather like steps toward mutual benefit.

BATNA: The Power of Walking Away

One of the most empowering concepts in negotiation is the idea of the BATNA—the Best Alternative to a Negotiated Agreement. The BATNA represents the course of action that a party can take if the negotiation fails to reach an agreement. It is, in essence, the fallback option—the next best thing to a successful negotiation.

Understanding your BATNA is critical because it gives you leverage in the negotiation. When you know that you have a viable alternative, you are less likely to feel pressured into accepting a bad deal. Your BATNA provides a safety net, allowing you to negotiate from a position of strength rather than desperation. If the terms of the negotiation do not meet your needs, you can walk away knowing that you have another option.

For example, in a job negotiation, your BATNA might be another job offer or the ability to stay in your current role. If the employer's offer does not meet your expectations, having a strong BATNA gives you the confidence to walk away from the negotiation if necessary, rather than feeling compelled to accept an unfavorable deal.

However, the BATNA is not just about walking away; it is also a valuable tool for guiding the negotiation itself. By knowing your BATNA, you can set clear boundaries around what you are willing to accept and what you are not. You can use your BATNA as a benchmark for evaluating the offers on the table, ensuring that any agreement is better than your alternative.

It is also important to understand the other party's BATNA. If you have a sense of what their alternatives are, you can tailor your negotiation strategy to create an offer that is more appealing than their BATNA, increasing the likelihood of reaching an agreement.

Negotiation as a Long-Term Investment

One of the key insights from Getting to Yes is that negotiation should be viewed not as a one-time event but as part of an ongoing relationship. In many cases, the people we negotiate with today are the same people we will work with or interact with in the future. Whether in business, family, or friendships, relationships are built over time, and each negotiation is an opportunity to strengthen—or weaken—that relationship.

This long-term perspective is critical to mastering the art of negotiation. When we approach negotiation with a short-term mindset, focused only on getting the best deal in the moment, we risk damaging the relationship and losing the opportunity for future collaboration. But when we negotiate with an eye toward the long term, we prioritize the relationship and work to create solutions that benefit both parties. This not only leads to more sustainable agreements but also builds trust and goodwill, laying the foundation for future success.

In a business negotiation between two companies, one side may be tempted to push for the most favorable terms, even if it strains the relationship with the other side. However, if both companies recognise that they will be working together on future projects, they may be more inclined to find a solution that benefits both sides, even if it means making some concessions in the short term. By focusing on the long-term relationship, both companies can build a partnership that is mutually beneficial and sustainable.

The Art of Finding Win-Win Solutions

Negotiation, at its core, is about finding solutions that meet the needs of all parties involved. It is not a contest of wills or a game of dominance but a collaborative process that requires empathy, creativity, and a commitment to fairness. By shifting our focus from positions to interests, by practicing active listening and empathy, and by approaching negotiation with a mindset of collaboration, we can move beyond the limitations of the zero-sum game and discover the power of win-win solutions.

Mastering the art of negotiation is not about learning to "win" every time; it is about learning to create value, build relationships, and find common ground. It is about recognizing that success in negotiation is not measured by how much we take, but by how much we can give and how much we can gain together.

As we navigate the many negotiations that life presents

—whether in the boardroom, the kitchen, or the classroom—let us remember that the true measure of success is not in the victory, but in the partnership we build, the trust we earn, and the solutions we create that allow everyone to thrive.

CHAPTER 13: THE UNSPOKEN ETIQUETTE OF THE WORKPLACE

In the intricate web of the modern workplace, where hierarchies, personalities, and ambitions collide, there exists an invisible but powerful force that governs the way we interact with one another—an unspoken etiquette. This etiquette, unwritten and often unnoticed, plays a crucial role in shaping the dynamics of any professional environment. It is not codified in handbooks or policies, but it is deeply ingrained in the fabric of workplace culture, influencing how we communicate, how we give and receive feedback, and how we navigate the often delicate boundaries of hierarchy.

At the heart of workplace etiquette is the understanding that professional relationships are built on trust, respect, and clear communication. It is not just about knowing when to speak up or when to stay silent, but also about how to balance honesty with empathy, assertiveness with humility, and ambition with the awareness of others. In her seminal work Radical Candor, Kim Scott explores these nuances of workplace communication, introducing the concept of "caring personally while challenging directly" as the key to effective leadership and teamwork.

This balance—between candor and compassion, assertiveness and tact—is the foundation of workplace etiquette. To master it is to cultivate not only a sense of professionalism but also the emotional intelligence necessary to thrive in complex social environments. Understanding when and how to deliver feedback, when to defer to hierarchy, and how to navigate the subtleties of workplace relationships is essential for anyone seeking not only to succeed but to foster a positive and collaborative work environment.

The Art of Speaking Up: Finding Your Voice

One of the most challenging aspects of workplace etiquette is knowing when to speak up and how to do so effectively. There is a delicate balance between assertiveness and overstepping, between contributing valuable ideas and dominating the conversation. This balance is particularly difficult to navigate in environments where power dynamics and hierarchies are at play.

Yet, speaking up is not only a professional necessity; it is a sign of engagement, confidence, and ownership. Whether it's offering a new idea, raising a concern, or providing feedback, knowing how to voice one's thoughts in a way that respects both the content and the context of the situation is a skill that can elevate an individual's standing in the workplace.

In Radical Candor, Kim Scott emphasizes the importance of speaking up with both clarity and care. The ability to challenge others, whether it's a colleague, manager, or subordinate, requires the confidence to articulate one's thoughts clearly, as well as the emotional intelligence to deliver them in a way that does not alienate or offend. This is where the balance of candor and compassion comes into play: to be radically candid is to speak truthfully, but always with the understanding that the goal is not to tear down but to build up—to help the other person improve, learn, or make better decisions.

Consider a scenario in which an employee notices inefficiencies in a team project. The employee might feel hesitant to speak up, fearing that they will be seen as confrontational or critical. However, if they remain silent, the inefficiencies will persist, and the team will suffer as a result. In this situation, the unspoken etiquette of the workplace encourages the employee to find the right moment to raise their concerns, framing the feedback not as a criticism but as a constructive observation meant to improve the team's performance. By choosing their words carefully and showing respect for their colleagues' efforts, the employee can speak up in a way that is both effective and respectful.

Delivering Feedback: Balancing Candor and Compassion

One of the most delicate aspects of workplace etiquette is the art of delivering feedback. Feedback, when given thoughtfully, can be one of the most powerful tools for growth and improvement. Yet, when handled poorly, it can breed resentment, defensiveness, and even conflict. The unspoken rules of the workplace dictate that feedback must be given with care, balancing honesty with empathy and directness with tact.

Kim Scott's concept of Radical Candor offers a valuable framework for understanding how to deliver feedback in a way that fosters both personal and professional growth. At the heart of Radical Candor is the idea that effective feedback must be both clear and caring. It must challenge the individual to improve, but it must do so from a place of genuine concern for their well-being and success.

This means that feedback should never be delivered as a personal attack or in a way that undermines the individual's dignity. Instead, it should be framed as an opportunity for learning and development. The goal is not to criticize for the sake of criticism but to help the other person see where they can improve and how they can achieve greater success.

Imagine a manager who notices that a team member consistently misses deadlines. The manager could choose to confront the employee harshly, pointing out their failures and demanding immediate improvement. However, this approach is likely to lead to defensiveness and resentment. Alternatively, the manager could approach the situation with Radical Candor, saying something like: "I've noticed that you've been struggling to meet some of the deadlines recently. I know you care about the quality of your work, and I want to help you find ways to manage your time more effectively so that you can meet these expectations without feeling overwhelmed. Let's talk about what's going on and how we can address it together."

In this example, the feedback is clear—the issue of missed deadlines is addressed directly—but it is also delivered with compassion, showing that the manager cares about the employee's well-being and is willing to offer support. This balance of candor and compassion creates an environment where feedback is not feared but valued as a tool for growth.

Respecting Hierarchy: Navigating Power Dynamics

In every workplace, there exists a hierarchy—a structure that defines roles, responsibilities, and lines of authority. Navigating this hierarchy is one of the most challenging aspects of workplace etiquette, as it requires a delicate balance of respect, assertiveness, and strategic thinking.

Respecting hierarchy does not mean blindly deferring to authority or suppressing one's ideas in the face of seniority. Rather, it means understanding the power dynamics at play and finding ways to communicate effectively within those dynamics. This often involves a nuanced understanding of when to assert one's opinions and when to defer, when to challenge authority and when to align with it.

One of the unspoken rules of workplace etiquette is that hierarchy should be respected, but not feared. Too often, employees hesitate to speak up or offer their insights because they are intimidated by the perceived authority of their superiors. This hesitation can stifle innovation, creativity, and problem-solving, as valuable ideas go unspoken. However, it is possible to challenge ideas or offer feedback to those in positions of authority, as long as it is done with respect and tact.

In Radical Candor, Scott advocates for challenging directly, even when it involves speaking to those in higher positions. The key, however, is to do so in a way that respects the role and responsibilities of the person in authority. This means framing challenges not as confrontations but as contributions to the broader success of the team or organization.

For instance, if a junior employee disagrees with a decision made by their manager, they can express their concerns in a way that shows respect for the manager's position while also offering their perspective. Instead of saying, "I think your decision is wrong," they might say, "I see the logic behind your decision, but I have some concerns about how it might impact the project timeline. Can we discuss some alternatives that might address these concerns?"

By framing the challenge as a collaborative conversation rather than a confrontation, the employee demonstrates respect for the hierarchy while also asserting their own expertise and perspective. This approach allows for productive dialogue and ensures that the employee's voice is heard without undermining the authority of the manager.

The Role of Emotional Intelligence in Workplace Etiquette

At the heart of workplace etiquette is emotional intelligence—the ability to recognise, understand, and manage one's own emotions, as well as the emotions of others. Emotional intelligence plays a critical role in navigating the complexities of workplace relationships, as it allows individuals to respond to situations with empathy, self-awareness, and tact.

One of the key components of emotional intelligence is self-regulation—the ability to control one's emotional responses in challenging situations. In the workplace, there are bound to be moments of frustration, disagreement, or disappointment. However, the unspoken etiquette of the workplace demands that we manage these emotions in a way that maintains professionalism and respect for others.

If a team member feels slighted by a colleague's actions, their initial emotional response might be anger or frustration. However, instead of reacting impulsively or allowing those emotions to dictate their behaviour, an emotionally intelligent individual would take a step back, reflect on the situation, and choose a response that addresses the issue constructively. This might involve having a calm, private conversation with the colleague to express how the situation made them feel and to seek resolution.

Empathy, another key component of emotional intelligence, is equally important in maintaining workplace etiquette. Empathy allows us to understand the perspectives, emotions, and motivations of others, which in turn helps us navigate complex social situations with greater sensitivity. For instance, when delivering feedback or addressing a conflict, an empathetic approach ensures that we consider the other person's feelings and needs, rather than simply asserting our own perspective.

Empathy also helps to build stronger relationships in the workplace, as it fosters a sense of connection and mutual respect. By taking the time to listen to others, show understanding, and offer support, we create an environment where people feel valued and respected, which in turn leads to greater collaboration and teamwork.

The Unspoken Rule of Accountability

One of the most fundamental principles of workplace etiquette is accountability—the responsibility to own one's actions, decisions, and mistakes. In a professional environment, where the success of the team or organization often depends on the contributions of individuals, accountability is critical to maintaining trust, credibility, and respect.

Yet, accountability is often an uncomfortable topic, as it requires individuals to acknowledge their mistakes, accept responsibility for their actions, and take steps to make amends. The unspoken etiquette of the workplace demands that accountability be embraced not as a punitive measure, but as a reflection of integrity and commitment to growth.

If a project falls behind schedule due to an oversight by one team member, the appropriate response is for that individual to acknowledge their mistake, take responsibility, and work with the team to address the issue. By doing so, they demonstrate professionalism and a commitment to the success of the project, rather than trying to deflect blame or make excuses.

In contrast, a failure to take accountability can erode

trust and damage relationships within the team. If the individual denies responsibility or shifts the blame onto others, it creates an environment of defensiveness and mistrust, where people are more focused on protecting themselves than on working collaboratively to solve problems.

Kim Scott's concept of Radical Candor reinforces the importance of accountability in the workplace. To challenge others directly, as Scott advocates, requires a willingness to hold both oneself and others accountable for their actions. This means not only being open to feedback but also being proactive in addressing issues and making improvements.

Navigating Office Politics with Integrity

Office politics is an inevitable part of any workplace, as individuals and teams navigate competing interests, power dynamics, and organizational priorities. While office politics can sometimes take on a negative connotation, the reality is that understanding and engaging with the political landscape of the workplace is an important aspect of professional success.

However, the unspoken etiquette of the workplace requires that we navigate office politics with integrity. This means avoiding manipulation, gossip, or underhanded tactics in favor of transparency, honesty, and fairness. It also means being aware of the impact of our actions on others and striving to build alliances and relationships that are based on mutual respect and shared goals.

For example, in a situation where two colleagues are

competing for the same promotion, it can be tempting to engage in office politics by undermining the other person or seeking to gain favor with influential decision-makers. However, the unspoken etiquette of the workplace encourages a more ethical approach —one where individuals focus on demonstrating their value through their work, building positive relationships with others, and contributing to the success of the team as a whole.

By navigating office politics with integrity, individuals not only protect their own reputation but also contribute to a healthier and more collaborative workplace culture. This, in turn, leads to greater trust, better teamwork, and more sustainable success.

The Subtle Art of Workplace Etiquette

The unspoken etiquette of the workplace is a subtle but powerful force that shapes the way we interact with others, build relationships, and navigate the complexities of professional life. It is rooted in respect, empathy, and emotional intelligence, and it demands that we approach our work with a sense of accountability, integrity, and care.

In Radical Candor, Kim Scott reminds us that effective communication—whether in the form of feedback, collaboration, or conflict resolution—requires a balance of candor and compassion. By embracing this balance, we can create an environment where people feel safe to speak up, where feedback is valued as a tool for growth, and where relationships are built on trust and mutual respect.

Workplace etiquette is not about following a rigid set of rules; it is about cultivating the emotional intelligence and self-awareness needed to navigate the ever-changing dynamics of the professional world. It is about knowing when to speak up and when to listen, how to deliver feedback with care, and how to respect hierarchy without losing one's voice. In mastering this unspoken art, we not only elevate our own professional success but also contribute to a workplace culture that is collaborative, respectful, and ultimately, more human.

CHAPTER 14: ADAPTABILITY

The Secret To Thriving In Any Career

In a world where change is the only constant, the ability to adapt is no longer just a valuable skill—it has become essential for survival and success. The rapid pace of technological advancements, shifting market trends, and evolving workplace dynamics mean that those who are unable or unwilling to adapt risk being left behind. In Who Moved My Cheese?, Spencer Johnson uses a simple yet profound allegory to illustrate this truth: life, like the proverbial cheese, is always moving, and those who cling to the past or resist change are doomed to frustration, while those who embrace flexibility and adapt to new realities will thrive.

Adaptability is more than just the ability to adjust to external changes; it is a mindset, a way of approaching life with curiosity, resilience, and openness. It is about letting go of rigid expectations, being willing to step into the unknown, and seeing change not as a threat but as an opportunity for growth. In the context of a career, adaptability means continuously evolving, learning new skills, and staying open to new ideas and possibilities. It is the secret ingredient that allows individuals to navigate uncertainty, seize opportunities, and ultimately, thrive in any professional environment.

The Nature of Change: Embracing the Unpredictable

At the heart of adaptability lies the recognition that change is inevitable. Whether it's a shift in workplace dynamics, a reorganization of responsibilities, or the sudden emergence of new technologies, the modern career landscape is one of perpetual flux. To resist this reality is to invite frustration and stagnation; to embrace it is to open oneself to a world of possibilities.

Change often feels threatening because it disrupts our sense of control and predictability. When we become accustomed to a certain way of doing things—whether it's a familiar routine, a particular role, or a stable working environment—it can be unsettling when that stability is suddenly upended. However, clinging to the past or resisting change only compounds the discomfort. As Johnson illustrates through his allegory of the mice and the little people in Who Moved My Cheese?, those who are willing to accept that the "cheese" (representing stability, success, or comfort) has moved are the ones who are able to move forward and find new opportunities.

In a career context, adaptability means recognizing that what worked yesterday may not work tomorrow. It means being willing to let go of outdated practices, to unlearn old habits, and to remain flexible in the face of new challenges. For example, a professional who has relied on a specific set of technical skills for years might suddenly find that those skills are no longer in demand due to advancements in automation or artificial intelligence. Rather than resisting the change or lamenting the loss of relevance, an adaptable individual will see this as an opportunity to learn new skills, to explore emerging fields, and to position themselves for success in the new landscape.

Adaptability is not just about survival; it is about thriving. Those who embrace change with a mindset of curiosity and growth are often the ones who discover new passions, unlock new opportunities, and achieve greater success than they ever could have imagined within the confines of the status quo.

The Adaptable Mindset: Flexibility as a Core Value

Adaptability begins in the mind. It is a mindset that prioritizes flexibility over rigidity, openness over certainty, and curiosity over complacency. In a world where change is constant, the most successful individuals are those who cultivate a mindset that is both resilient and fluid—able to bend without breaking and to adjust without losing sight of their goals.

At its core, the adaptable mindset is characterized by:

1. Curiosity: An adaptable person is always asking questions, seeking to understand new trends, technologies, and ideas. They are not content to remain within the confines of what they already know but are eager to explore new territory. Curiosity is the driving force behind growth and innovation, and it allows individuals to stay ahead of the curve in their careers.

2. Resilience: Flexibility does not mean the absence of challenges or setbacks. In fact, adaptability often involves navigating difficult transitions or unexpected obstacles. The key is resilience—the ability to bounce back from failure or disappointment, to learn from mistakes, and to keep moving forward. Resilient individuals are not derailed by setbacks; they use them as stepping stones toward future success.

3. Open-Mindedness: An adaptable person is open to new ideas, new ways of working, and new possibilities. They do not cling to old methods simply because "that's the way it's always been done." Instead, they are willing to challenge assumptions, question the status quo, and embrace change, even when it feels uncomfortable.

4. Proactivity: Adaptability is not a passive quality; it requires proactivity. Rather than waiting for change to happen and then reacting, adaptable individuals take the initiative to seek out opportunities for growth and improvement. They anticipate change, prepare for it, and position themselves to take advantage of it when it arrives.

Consider an employee working in a traditional retail environment during the rise of e-commerce. As online shopping grows, they could either lament the decline of brick-and-mortar stores or proactively seek out opportunities to transition into the digital realm, whether by learning about digital marketing, exploring e-commerce platforms, or developing skills in customer experience design. By adopting an adaptable mindset, they position themselves to not only survive the industry shift but to thrive in the new landscape.

Overcoming Fear: The Biggest Barrier to Adaptability

One of the greatest obstacles to adaptability is fear—fear of the unknown, fear of failure, and fear of losing control. These fears often manifest as resistance to change, as individuals cling to what is familiar and predictable, even when it is no longer serving them.

In Who Moved My Cheese?, the character of Hem represents this fear-based resistance to change. Hem refuses to acknowledge that the cheese is gone, preferring to stay in the empty maze rather than venture out into the unknown in search of new opportunities. This resistance is a metaphor for the way many of us react to change in our careers: we cling to outdated practices, resist learning new skills, or refuse to explore new industries because we are afraid of stepping outside of our comfort zones.

However, as Johnson's story illustrates, it is only by overcoming this fear that we can move forward. Haw, the character who eventually ventures out of the maze in search of new cheese, demonstrates the courage it takes to embrace change. While the journey is uncertain, it is ultimately rewarding, as Haw discovers new opportunities that would have been impossible to find had he remained stuck in the past.

In real life, fear of change can manifest in many ways—fear of leaving a stable job for a new opportunity, fear of learning a new technology that feels overwhelming, or fear of taking on a leadership role that comes with greater responsibility. But the truth is that growth and success often lie on the other side of fear. By facing our fears head-on and choosing to adapt, we not only overcome the immediate challenges but also build the resilience and confidence needed to navigate future changes.

Lifelong Learning: The Key to Staying Adaptable

In a rapidly evolving world, one of the most important aspects of adaptability is the commitment to lifelong learning. The days when professionals could rely on a fixed set of skills for their entire careers are long gone. Today, staying relevant and competitive means continuously acquiring new knowledge, learning new tools, and expanding one's expertise.

Lifelong learning is not just about formal education or professional development courses, though those can be valuable. It is also about staying curious, seeking out new experiences, and being willing to learn from both successes and failures. In many ways, lifelong learning is a mindset—a recognition that no matter how much we know, there is always more to learn, and no matter how skilled we are, there is always room for improvement.

This mindset is particularly important in industries that are being transformed by technology. In fields such as marketing, finance, healthcare, and even education, new tools and platforms are constantly emerging, and those who fail to keep up with these changes risk being left behind. For example, a marketing professional who does not take the time to learn about digital advertising, social media analytics, or data-driven strategies will find it increasingly difficult to remain competitive in a market where these skills are in high demand.

The commitment to lifelong learning also involves staying attuned to broader trends and shifts in the industry. This might mean reading industry reports, attending conferences, or engaging with thought leaders in the field. By staying informed about where the industry is headed, adaptable professionals can anticipate changes and position themselves to take advantage of new opportunities before others have even realized they exist.

Adapting to New Roles: Expanding Beyond Your Comfort Zone

Adaptability in a career context often involves taking on new roles or responsibilities that push us outside of our comfort zones. Whether it's moving into a leadership position, switching industries, or expanding into new areas of expertise, the willingness to adapt to new roles is essential for career growth.

One of the unspoken rules of career success is that opportunities often arise when we least expect them. A promotion might come with little warning, or a company might reorganize, placing us in a role that is unfamiliar and challenging. In these moments, adaptability is key. Rather than shying away from the new responsibilities, adaptable individuals embrace the challenge, recognizing that it is through these experiences that they will grow and develop.

Consider a mid-level manager who is suddenly asked to take on a leadership role in a different department. At first, the manager might feel overwhelmed by the new responsibilities, especially if they lack experience in the specific area. However, by approaching the role with a willingness to learn, a flexible mindset, and a commitment to developing new skills, the manager can not only succeed in the new position but also broaden their expertise and open the door to future opportunities.

Adapting to new roles also requires

a degree of humility. It means acknowledging that there will be a learning curve and that mistakes are inevitable. However, it is through these mistakes that we learn and grow. The key is to approach each new role with an open mind and a willingness to seek out support, mentorship, and feedback.

Flexibility in Leadership: Navigating Change with Grace

Adaptability is not just a skill for individual contributors; it is also a crucial quality for leaders. In fact, adaptability in leadership may be even more important, as leaders are often responsible for guiding their teams through periods of change and uncertainty. A leader who is rigid, resistant to change, or unwilling to adapt to new realities can quickly lose the trust and respect of their team. Conversely, a leader who demonstrates flexibility, resilience, and a willingness to embrace change sets a powerful example and inspires their team to do the same.

One of the hallmarks of adaptable leadership is the ability to remain calm and composed in the face of uncertainty. When unexpected challenges arise—whether it's a sudden shift in the market, a change in organizational structure, or a crisis situation—an adaptable leader does not panic or react impulsively. Instead, they take the time to assess the situation, explore options, and make informed decisions. This sense of stability and level-headedness is crucial for maintaining morale and focus within the team.

Adaptable leaders also recognise that different situations require different leadership styles. In times of stability, a more hands-off, delegative approach might be appropriate, allowing team members to take ownership of their work. However, in times of change or crisis, a more hands-on, directive approach might be necessary to provide clear guidance and support. The ability to switch between these leadership styles as needed is a key aspect of adaptability.

During the COVID-19 pandemic, many leaders were forced to adapt to a new reality of remote work, virtual collaboration, and shifting business priorities. Those who were able to embrace these changes with flexibility—implementing new technologies, adjusting workflows, and providing emotional support to their teams—were more successful in navigating the crisis than those who resisted or struggled to adapt.

Adapting to Failure: Turning Setbacks into Opportunities

Failure is an inevitable part of any career, but it is how we respond to failure that determines our long-term success. For adaptable individuals, failure is not a permanent setback but an opportunity to learn, grow, and improve. This mindset of resilience allows them to bounce back from challenges and emerge stronger on the other side.

One of the most important lessons of adaptability is that failure is not something to be feared but embraced as part of the process of growth. In Who Moved My Cheese?, the characters who are willing to venture out of the maze in search of new opportunities inevitably face obstacles and setbacks. However, it is through these experiences that they ultimately find success.

In a career context, adaptability means being willing to take risks, knowing that failure is a possibility. It means viewing failure not as a reflection of one's abilities but as a natural part of the learning process. For example, an entrepreneur who launches a new business venture might face setbacks in the form of financial losses or market challenges. However, by analyzing what went wrong, adjusting, and trying again, they increase their chances of eventual success.

Adapting to failure also requires a degree of self-compassion. It is easy to be hard on oneself after a failure, but adaptable individuals recognise that setbacks are not a reflection of their worth or potential. Instead, they approach failure with curiosity, asking, "What can I learn from this?" and "How can I improve next time?"

The Power of Adaptability

In a world that is constantly changing, adaptability is the key to not only surviving but thriving. Whether it's navigating new technologies, adjusting to shifting market demands, or taking on new roles and responsibilities, those who embrace change with an open mind and a flexible attitude will find that they are better equipped to seize opportunities and achieve long-term success.

As Spencer Johnson's Who Moved My Cheese? reminds us, the cheese is always moving. Those who cling to the past or resist change will find themselves stuck in a maze of frustration and stagnation. But those who are willing to let go of old habits, step into the unknown, and embrace the journey of growth and learning will discover that new opportunities are always waiting just around the corner.

The secret to thriving in any career is not to avoid change but to embrace it. By cultivating adaptability as a core value—through curiosity, resilience, and a commitment to lifelong learning—we position ourselves to succeed not just in the present but in the ever-evolving future.

CHAPTER 15: IMPOSTER SYNDROME

It's Okay Not To Know Everything

There is a silent companion that many successful professionals carry with them, a quiet yet persistent voice that whispers, "You don't belong here." This voice, which tells us that our accomplishments are merely the result of luck or deception, that we are frauds waiting to be exposed, has a name—Imposter Syndrome. It is an experience not of failure but of success, where even the most capable individuals feel as though they are perpetually on the verge of being "found out" for their supposed inadequacies.

Imposter Syndrome, explored through the lens of The Confidence Code by Katty Kay and Claire Shipman, is an affliction that does not discriminate by gender, age, or profession. It affects everyone, from the novice entering a new career to the seasoned leader at the pinnacle of their field. And while its effects can be crippling—undermining confidence, stalling growth, and diminishing the joy of success—it is also an experience that can lead to profound personal development. For the key to overcoming Imposter Syndrome lies not in denying it but in acknowledging it, understanding that the feeling of being an imposter is, paradoxically, a sign of growth and expansion.

To navigate the professional world is to come face to face with moments of uncertainty, with challenges that stretch the limits of our knowledge and skills. The belief that we must know everything, that we must be perfect and invulnerable, is not only unrealistic but detrimental. It is through the acknowledgment of our limitations, our willingness to admit what we do not know, and our courage to step forward in spite of these doubts, that true confidence and competence are born.

The Roots of Imposter Syndrome: A Universal Experience

At its core, Imposter Syndrome is the internalization of the belief that one's achievements are undeserved or fraudulent. It is the feeling that, despite external evidence of competence, we are somehow fooling everyone around us, and that it's only a matter of time before we are exposed as inadequate. This pervasive self-doubt often arises in moments of transition or challenge—when we step into new roles, take on greater responsibilities, or enter unfamiliar environments.

The irony of Imposter Syndrome is that it tends to affect those who are the most driven, the most accomplished, and the most successful. It is often the high achievers, those who push themselves to excel, who are most susceptible to feeling like imposters.

This is because their very ambition leads them into uncharted territory, where they are constantly pushing the boundaries of their knowledge and abilities. The further they rise, the more they feel as though they are in over their heads.

In The Confidence Code, Kay and Shipman explore how Imposter Syndrome is particularly prevalent among women, who, due to societal pressures and expectations, often internalize the belief that they must be perfect in order to succeed. However, Imposter Syndrome is not limited by gender—it is a universal experience that affects people of all backgrounds. The feeling of being an imposter is often exacerbated by environments that prioritize performance over learning, where failure is stigmatized and where asking for help is seen as a sign of weakness.

But the truth is that everyone feels like an imposter at times. Whether it's the new employee trying to navigate the complexities of a new job, the entrepreneur launching a startup, or the executive managing a multi-million-dollar project, the experience of feeling inadequate or unworthy is a shared human condition. The key to overcoming Imposter Syndrome is not to eliminate these feelings, but to recognise that they are a natural part of growth and learning.

The Myth of Perfection: Letting Go of Unrealistic Expectations

One of the primary drivers of Imposter Syndrome is the myth of perfection—the belief that we must know everything, that we must have all the answers, and that we must never make mistakes. This myth is particularly damaging because it sets an impossible standard. No one can be perfect, and no one can know everything. Yet, when we internalize the expectation of perfection, we set ourselves up for perpetual disappointment and self-criticism.

The truth is that growth and learning are inherently messy processes. They involve making mistakes, encountering failure, and facing moments of uncertainty. In fact, it is through these very experiences that we develop the resilience, adaptability, and problem-solving skills that lead to long-term success. The expectation of perfection, however, prevents us from fully embracing these learning opportunities. Instead of seeing mistakes as a natural part of the journey, we view them as evidence of our inadequacy.

In the workplace, this myth of perfection often manifests as an unwillingness to admit what we don't know. We fear that if we reveal our lack of knowledge or skill in a particular area, we will be judged or exposed as incompetent. This fear can lead to a reluctance to ask questions, to seek help, or to take risks. But the reality is that no one knows everything, and no one expects us to. In fact, the ability to acknowledge what we don't know —and the willingness to seek out the resources and support we need to fill those gaps—is a sign of strength, not weakness.

In The Confidence Code, Kay and Shipman emphasize the importance of embracing imperfection as a pathway to confidence. True confidence, they argue, is not the absence of doubt, but the willingness to act in spite of doubt. It is the recognition that we are constantly learning, growing, and evolving, and that it is okay to not have all the answers. Confidence comes from the acceptance of our limitations, not from pretending they don't exist.

Consider a manager who is promoted to a leadership role in a department outside their area of expertise. Instead of feeling pressure to immediately master every detail of the new role, an adaptable and confident leader will recognise the value of asking for guidance, delegating tasks to those with more expertise, and focusing on learning as they go. By letting go of the need to be perfect, they create an environment where growth, collaboration, and learning are prioritized over individual performance.

Embracing Vulnerability: The Path to Authentic Confidence

One of the greatest lessons in overcoming Imposter Syndrome is the power of vulnerability. Vulnerability, often misunderstood as weakness, is actually the foundation of authentic confidence. It is the willingness to be open about our uncertainties, to admit what we don't know, and to embrace the possibility of failure without allowing it to define us.

In many professional environments, vulnerability is seen as something to be avoided. We are taught to project confidence, to appear knowledgeable and in control, even when we are feeling uncertain or overwhelmed. But this projection of false confidence only deepens Imposter Syndrome, as it reinforces the gap between how we appear on the outside and how we feel on the inside. The more we try to hide our insecurities, the more isolated and fraudulent we feel.

Authentic confidence, on the other hand, comes from the willingness to be vulnerable. It comes from the recognition that it's okay not to know everything and that asking for help or admitting uncertainty does not diminish our competence or worth. In fact, it is through vulnerability that we build stronger connections with others, as it allows us to engage in honest, open dialogue and to seek out the support and resources we need to grow.

For example, a junior employee might feel hesitant to ask questions in a meeting, fearing that doing so will reveal their lack of knowledge. However, by embracing vulnerability and asking for clarification, they not only gain the information they need but also demonstrate their commitment to learning and improving. This willingness to be open and honest fosters an environment of trust and collaboration, where others feel comfortable sharing their own uncertainties and working together to find solutions.

In The Confidence Code, Kay and Shipman explore how vulnerability is closely linked to the concept of "self-compassion"—the ability to treat ourselves with kindness and understanding, especially in moments of failure or difficulty. Self-compassion allows us to acknowledge our imperfections without harsh self-judgment and to approach challenges with a sense of curiosity and resilience. By cultivating self-compassion, we create the emotional space to take risks, make mistakes, and learn from our experiences, all of which are essential for building true confidence.

Reframing Failure: A Necessary Step Toward Growth

Imposter Syndrome thrives on the fear of failure. Those who experience it often believe that any mistake or setback will expose them as incompetent or unworthy. This fear leads to a constant pressure to perform perfectly and to avoid any situation where failure might be a possibility.

But the reality is that failure is an inevitable part of growth. No one achieves success without encountering obstacles along the way. In fact, failure is often the greatest teacher, providing us with the insights and experiences that lead to improvement and innovation. To overcome Imposter Syndrome, we must reframe failure not as something to be feared, but as a necessary step toward growth and development.

In The Confidence Code, Kay and Shipman highlight how failure, far from reflecting our worth, is a natural part of the learning process. The most successful individuals are not those who avoid failure, but those who embrace it, learn from it, and continue moving forward. By reframing failure as an opportunity for learning, we can begin to let go of the fear that holds us back and instead approach challenges with a mindset of curiosity and growth.

Consider an entrepreneur who launches a new business venture only to see it fail after a few months. Rather than viewing this failure as evidence of their inadequacy, an adaptable entrepreneur will reflect on what went wrong, gather insights from the experience, and use that knowledge to refine their approach in the future. Each failure becomes a stepping stone toward eventual success, rather than a definitive judgment of their abilities.

Reframing failure also involves recognizing that mistakes are not a reflection of our intelligence or competence. They are simply part of the process of trying something new or challenging. By embracing a growth mindset—one that sees abilities and intelligence as qualities that can be developed over time—we can begin to see failure not as a personal shortcoming but as an essential part of the journey toward mastery.

Imposter Syndrome as a Sign of Growth

One of the most powerful reframes of Imposter Syndrome is to see it not as a sign of inadequacy, but as a sign of growth. The very fact that we feel like imposters often indicates that we are pushing ourselves beyond our comfort zones, taking on new challenges, and stepping into roles that stretch our abilities.

In The Confidence Code, Kay and Shipman emphasize that confidence is built through action, not through the elimination of self-doubt. Confidence grows when we step into uncertainty, take risks, and prove to ourselves that we are capable of handling the challenges we face. In this sense, Imposter Syndrome can be viewed as a natural part of the growth process, a signal that we are expanding our skills, knowledge, and experiences.

A young professional who is promoted to a leadership position might feel overwhelmed by the new responsibilities and experience Imposter Syndrome.

However, this feeling is not a sign that they are unqualified for the role; rather, it reflects the fact that they are stepping into a new and challenging phase of their career. By acknowledging these feelings and continuing to move forward, they will eventually grow into the role and develop the confidence that comes from experience.

Imposter Syndrome often arises when we are comparing ourselves to others—when we see the success of our peers or colleagues and assume that they have everything figured out, while we are struggling to keep up. But the truth is that everyone experiences moments of doubt, insecurity, and uncertainty. By acknowledging that Imposter Syndrome is a shared experience, we can begin to normalize it and remove the stigma that surrounds it.

The Confidence-Competence Loop: Building Confidence Through Action

One of the key insights from The Confidence Code is the idea of the "confidence-competence loop"—the idea that confidence and competence reinforce each other in a positive feedback loop. Confidence comes from acting, from stepping into uncertainty and proving to ourselves that we are capable. And as we build competence through these actions, our confidence grows, which in turn encourages us to take on even greater challenges.

Imposter Syndrome often disrupts this loop by preventing us from acting in the first place. When we feel like imposters, we may hold back, avoiding opportunities or challenges out of fear that we will fail or be exposed as inadequate. But the only way to build confidence is to act—to step forward even when we feel uncertain, to embrace the possibility of failure, and to trust that we have the ability to learn and grow from our experiences.

Take a professional who is offered the opportunity to lead a high-stakes project. If they are experiencing Imposter Syndrome, they might hesitate, doubting their ability to succeed. However, by accepting the challenge and acting, they gain valuable experience, develop new skills, and build the confidence that comes from proving themselves in a real-world scenario. Each step they take reinforces both their competence and their confidence, creating a positive cycle of growth.

Embracing Imperfection and Moving Forward

Imposter Syndrome is a common and natural part of the professional journey, but it does not have to hold us back. By acknowledging that it's okay not to know everything, by embracing vulnerability, and by reframing failure as an opportunity for growth, we can begin to break free from the grip of self-doubt and move forward with confidence.

In The Confidence Code, Kay and Shipman remind us that confidence is not about eliminating uncertainty; it is about acting in spite of it. It is about recognizing that we are always in the process of learning, growing, and evolving, and that it is through this process that true competence and confidence are built.

As we navigate the challenges of our careers, we must remember that it's okay to feel like an imposter at times.

It's okay to admit what we don't know, to ask for help, and to make mistakes. In fact, it is through these very experiences that we become stronger, more capable, and more confident. The secret to overcoming Imposter Syndrome is not to deny it but to embrace it as a sign of growth, a reminder that we are pushing the boundaries of our abilities and stepping into the unknown.

In the end, confidence is not the absence of doubt but the willingness to move forward in spite of it. And it is this willingness that will ultimately lead to success, fulfillment, and the realization that we do, indeed, belong.

CHAPTER 15: IMPOSTER SYNDROME

It's Okay Not To Know Everything

There is a silent companion that many successful professionals carry with them, a quiet yet persistent voice that whispers, "You don't belong here." This voice, which tells us that our accomplishments are merely the result of luck or deception, that we are frauds waiting to be exposed, has a name—Imposter Syndrome. It is an experience not of failure but of success, where even the most capable individuals feel as though they are perpetually on the verge of being "found out" for their supposed inadequacies.

Imposter Syndrome, explored through the lens of The Confidence Code by Katty Kay and Claire Shipman, is an affliction that does not discriminate by gender, age, or profession. It affects everyone, from the novice entering a new career to the seasoned leader at the pinnacle of their field. And while its effects can be crippling—undermining confidence, stalling growth, and diminishing the joy of success—it is also an experience that can lead to profound personal development. For the key to overcoming Imposter Syndrome lies not in denying it but in acknowledging it, understanding that the feeling of being an imposter is, paradoxically, a sign of growth and expansion.

To navigate the professional world is to come face to face with moments of uncertainty, with challenges that stretch the limits of our knowledge and skills. The belief that we must know everything, that we must be perfect and invulnerable, is not only unrealistic but detrimental. It is through the acknowledgment of our limitations, our willingness to admit what we do not know, and our courage to step forward in spite of these doubts, that true confidence and competence are born.

The Roots of Imposter Syndrome: A Universal Experience

At its core, Imposter Syndrome is the internalization of the belief that one's achievements are undeserved or fraudulent. It is the feeling that, despite external evidence of competence, we are somehow fooling everyone around us, and that it's only a matter of time before we are exposed as inadequate. This pervasive self-doubt often arises in moments of transition or challenge—when we step into new roles, take on greater responsibilities, or enter unfamiliar environments.

The irony of Imposter Syndrome is that it tends to affect those who are the most driven, the most accomplished, and the most successful. It is often the high achievers, those who push themselves to excel, who are most susceptible to feeling like imposters.

This is because their very ambition leads them into uncharted territory, where they are constantly pushing the boundaries of their knowledge and abilities. The further they rise, the more they feel as though they are in over their heads.

In The Confidence Code, Kay and Shipman explore how Imposter Syndrome is particularly prevalent among women, who, due to societal pressures and expectations, often internalize the belief that they must be perfect in order to succeed. However, Imposter Syndrome is not limited by gender—it is a universal experience that affects people of all backgrounds. The feeling of being an imposter is often exacerbated by environments that prioritize performance over learning, where failure is stigmatized and where asking for help is seen as a sign of weakness.

But the truth is that everyone feels like an imposter at times. Whether it's the new employee trying to navigate the complexities of a new job, the entrepreneur launching a startup, or the executive managing a multi-million-dollar project, the experience of feeling inadequate or unworthy is a shared human condition. The key to overcoming Imposter Syndrome is not to eliminate these feelings, but to recognise that they are a natural part of growth and learning.

The Myth of Perfection: Letting Go of Unrealistic Expectations

One of the primary drivers of Imposter Syndrome is the myth of perfection—the belief that we must know everything, that we must have all the answers, and that we must never make mistakes. This myth is particularly damaging because it sets an impossible standard. No one can be perfect, and no one can know everything. Yet, when we internalize the expectation of perfection, we set ourselves up for perpetual disappointment and self-criticism.

The truth is that growth and learning are inherently messy processes. They involve making mistakes, encountering failure, and facing moments of uncertainty. In fact, it is through these very experiences that we develop the resilience, adaptability, and problem-solving skills that lead to long-term success. The expectation of perfection, however, prevents us from fully embracing these learning opportunities. Instead of seeing mistakes as a natural part of the journey, we view them as evidence of our inadequacy.

In the workplace, this myth of perfection often manifests as an unwillingness to admit what we don't know. We fear that if we reveal our lack of knowledge or skill in a particular area, we will be judged or exposed as incompetent. This fear can lead to a reluctance to ask questions, to seek help, or to take risks. But the reality is that no one knows everything, and no one expects us to. In fact, the ability to acknowledge what we don't know —and the willingness to seek out the resources and support we need to fill those gaps—is a sign of strength, not weakness.

In The Confidence Code, Kay and Shipman emphasize the importance of embracing imperfection as a pathway to confidence. True confidence, they argue, is not the absence of doubt, but the willingness to act in spite of doubt. It is the recognition that we are constantly learning, growing, and evolving, and that it is okay to not have all the answers. Confidence comes from the acceptance of our limitations, not from pretending they don't exist.

A manager is promoted to a leadership role in a department outside their area of expertise. Instead of feeling pressure to immediately master every detail of the new role, an adaptable and confident leader will recognise the value of asking for guidance, delegating tasks to those with more expertise, and focusing on learning as they go. By letting go of the need to be perfect, they create an environment where growth, collaboration, and learning are prioritized over individual performance.

Embracing Vulnerability: The Path to Authentic Confidence

One of the greatest lessons in overcoming Imposter Syndrome is the power of vulnerability. Vulnerability, often misunderstood as weakness, is actually the foundation of authentic confidence. It is the willingness to be open about our uncertainties, to admit what we don't know, and to embrace the possibility of failure without allowing it to define us.

In many professional environments, vulnerability is seen as something to be avoided. We are taught to project confidence, to appear knowledgeable and in control, even when we are feeling uncertain or overwhelmed. But this projection of false confidence only deepens Imposter Syndrome, as it reinforces the gap between how we appear on the outside and how we feel on the inside. The more we try to hide our insecurities, the more isolated and fraudulent we feel.

Authentic confidence, on the other hand, comes from the willingness to be vulnerable. It comes from the recognition that it's okay not to know everything and that asking for help or admitting uncertainty does not diminish our competence or worth. In fact, it is through vulnerability that we build stronger connections with others, as it allows us to engage in honest, open dialogue and to seek out the support and resources we need to grow.

A junior employee might feel hesitant to ask questions in a meeting, fearing that doing so will reveal their lack of knowledge. However, by embracing vulnerability and asking for clarification, they not only gain the information they need but also demonstrate their commitment to learning and improving. This willingness to be open and honest fosters an environment of trust and collaboration, where others feel comfortable sharing their own uncertainties and working together to find solutions.

In The Confidence Code, Kay and Shipman explore how vulnerability is closely linked to the concept of "self-compassion"—the ability to treat ourselves with kindness and understanding, especially in moments of failure or difficulty. Self-compassion allows us to acknowledge our imperfections without harsh self-judgment and to approach challenges with a sense of curiosity and resilience. By cultivating self-compassion, we create the emotional space to take risks, make mistakes, and learn from our experiences, all of which are essential for building true confidence.

Reframing Failure: A Necessary Step Toward Growth

Imposter Syndrome thrives on the fear of failure. Those who experience it often believe that any mistake or setback will expose them as incompetent or unworthy. This fear leads to a constant pressure to perform perfectly and to avoid any situation where failure might be a possibility.

But the reality is that failure is an inevitable part of growth. No one achieves success without encountering obstacles along the way. In fact, failure is often the greatest teacher, providing us with the insights and experiences that lead to improvement and innovation. To overcome Imposter Syndrome, we must reframe failure not as something to be feared, but as a necessary step toward growth and development.

In The Confidence Code, Kay and Shipman highlight how failure, far from reflecting our worth, is a natural part of the learning process. The most successful individuals are not those who avoid failure, but those who embrace it, learn from it, and continue moving forward. By reframing failure as an opportunity for learning, we can begin to let go of the fear that holds us back and instead approach challenges with a mindset of curiosity and growth.

Take the example of an entrepreneur who launches a new business venture only to see it fail after a few months. Rather than viewing this failure as evidence of their inadequacy, an adaptable entrepreneur will reflect on what went wrong, gather insights from the experience, and use that knowledge to refine their approach in the future. Each failure becomes a stepping stone toward eventual success, rather than a definitive judgment of their abilities.

Reframing failure also involves recognizing that mistakes are not a reflection of our intelligence or competence. They are simply part of the process of trying something new or challenging. By embracing a growth mindset—one that sees abilities and intelligence as qualities that can be developed over time—we can begin to see failure not as a personal shortcoming but as an essential part of the journey toward mastery.

Imposter Syndrome as a Sign of Growth

One of the most powerful reframes of Imposter Syndrome is to see it not as a sign of inadequacy, but as a sign of growth. The very fact that we feel like imposters often indicates that we are pushing ourselves beyond our comfort zones, taking on new challenges, and stepping into roles that stretch our abilities.

In The Confidence Code, Kay and Shipman emphasize that confidence is built through action, not through the elimination of self-doubt. Confidence grows when we step into uncertainty, take risks, and prove to ourselves that we are capable of handling the challenges we face. In this sense, Imposter Syndrome can be viewed as a natural part of the growth process, a signal that we are expanding our skills, knowledge, and experiences.

For example, a young professional who is promoted to a leadership position might feel overwhelmed by the new responsibilities and experience Imposter Syndrome.

However, this feeling is not a sign that they are unqualified for the role; rather, it reflects the fact that they are stepping into a new and challenging phase of their career. By acknowledging these feelings and continuing to move forward, they will eventually grow into the role and develop the confidence that comes from experience.

Imposter Syndrome often arises when we are comparing ourselves to others—when we see the success of our peers or colleagues and assume that they have everything figured out, while we are struggling to keep up. But the truth is that everyone experiences moments of doubt, insecurity, and uncertainty. By acknowledging that Imposter Syndrome is a shared experience, we can begin to normalize it and remove the stigma that surrounds it.

The Confidence-Competence Loop: Building Confidence Through Action

One of the key insights from The Confidence Code is the idea of the "confidence-competence loop"—the idea that confidence and competence reinforce each other in a positive feedback loop. Confidence comes from acting, from stepping into uncertainty and proving to ourselves that we are capable. And as we build competence through these actions, our confidence grows, which in turn encourages us to take on even greater challenges.

Imposter Syndrome often disrupts this loop by preventing us from acting in the first place. When we feel like imposters, we may hold back, avoiding opportunities or challenges out of fear that we will fail or be exposed as inadequate. But the only way to build confidence is to act—to step forward even when we feel uncertain, to embrace the possibility of failure, and to trust that we have the ability to learn and grow from our experiences.

For example, consider a professional who is offered the opportunity to lead a high-stakes project. If they are experiencing Imposter Syndrome, they might hesitate, doubting their ability to succeed. However, by accepting the challenge and acting, they gain valuable experience, develop new skills, and build the confidence that comes from proving themselves in a real-world scenario. Each step they take reinforces both their competence and their confidence, creating a positive cycle of growth.

Embracing Imperfection and Moving Forward

Imposter Syndrome is a common and natural part of the professional journey, but it does not have to hold us back. By acknowledging that it's okay not to know everything, by embracing vulnerability, and by reframing failure as an opportunity for growth, we can begin to break free from the grip of self-doubt and move forward with confidence.

In The Confidence Code, Kay and Shipman remind us that confidence is not about eliminating uncertainty; it is about acting in spite of it. It is about recognizing that we are always in the process of learning, growing, and evolving, and that it is through this process that true competence and confidence are built.

As we navigate the challenges of our careers, we must

remember that it's okay to feel like an imposter at times. It's okay to admit what we don't know, to ask for help, and to make mistakes. In fact, it is through these very experiences that we become stronger, more capable, and more confident. The secret to overcoming Imposter Syndrome is not to deny it but to embrace it as a sign of growth, a reminder that we are pushing the boundaries of our abilities and stepping into the unknown.

Confidence is not the absence of doubt but the willingness to move forward in spite of it. And it is this willingness that will ultimately lead to success, fulfillment, and the realization that we do, indeed, belong.

CHAPTER 16: MONEY MYTHS YOU LEARNED TOO LATE

There is a quiet paradox that exists in the world of finance: although money is central to nearly every aspect of life, most of us are ill-prepared to understand and manage it. Despite years of formal education, many people enter adulthood with little to no financial literacy, unaware of the key principles that govern wealth building. Instead, we inherit a set of assumptions, habits, and myths about money—many of which are not only misguided but detrimental to our financial well-being. These money myths, passed down from generation to generation, often prevent us from achieving true financial independence.

In Rich Dad Poor Dad, Robert Kiyosaki explores this paradox by contrasting the financial philosophies of two father figures—his biological father ("Poor Dad") and the father of his best friend ("Rich Dad"). Through this lens, Kiyosaki highlights the profound differences between traditional financial wisdom and the principles that lead to wealth accumulation. The central lesson of the book is simple yet profound: what we think we know about money is often wrong, and the key to financial success lies in unlearning these misconceptions and adopting a new, more informed approach to wealth building.

This chapter delves into some of the most pervasive money myths—beliefs that we often learn too late—and replaces them with financial principles that foster real wealth and independence. By examining these myths and replacing them with sound financial knowledge, we can begin to take control of our financial future and move toward true independence.

The Myth of "Work Hard, Earn More": Why Effort Alone Is Not Enough

One of the most ingrained money myths is the belief that hard work is the primary ingredient for financial success. From an early age, we are told that if we work hard, we will earn more, achieve stability, and eventually accumulate wealth. This myth is tied to the deeply entrenched idea of the "American Dream," which suggests that anyone, regardless of their background, can rise to financial success through perseverance and effort alone.

While there is no doubt that hard work plays a crucial role in achieving success, this belief oversimplifies the realities of wealth-building. In Rich Dad Poor Dad, Kiyosaki challenges the notion that working harder is enough to become wealthy, highlighting that many people who work long hours—sometimes juggling multiple jobs—never escape the cycle of financial struggle. The truth is, hard work, without financial education, rarely translates into wealth.

This is because financial success is not merely about effort; it's about strategy. The myth of "work hard, earn more" overlooks the fundamental importance of financial intelligence—knowing how money works, how to make it grow, and how to use it to generate income without direct labor.

For example, many people believe that earning a high salary is the key to financial success. However, a high income without sound financial management can still lead to financial insecurity. Professionals who earn six-figure salaries may still live paycheck to paycheck because they do not understand how to allocate their earnings wisely or invest for the future. They may purchase expensive homes, cars, or vacations, mistakenly equating these things with wealth, but these are liabilities rather than assets.

True wealth comes from the ability to make money work for you. Instead of focusing solely on working hard to earn a paycheck, Kiyosaki advocates for building assets—investments that generate income over time, such as real estate, stocks, or business ownership. In contrast to liabilities (such as cars or consumer goods that drain your resources), assets grow in value and can provide a steady stream of passive income.

By focusing on financial literacy, individuals can shift from the mindset of "working for money" to "making money work for you." Wealth is not just a function of labor; it is the result of smart decisions about how to manage, invest, and grow money.

The Myth of Job Security: Why Relying on a Single Income Stream Is Risky

For decades, the notion of job security has been a cornerstone of personal financial planning. Traditional wisdom suggests that if you get a stable job, work hard, and stay loyal to your employer, you will be financially secure. In this model, the primary goal is to secure a well-paying job, advance up the corporate ladder, and eventually retire with a pension or retirement fund.

However, in today's economy, the concept of job security has become increasingly obsolete. As Kiyosaki points out in Rich Dad Poor Dad, the days of guaranteed pensions, long-term loyalty from employers, and predictable career paths are fading. Relying on a single job as your primary source of income exposes you to significant financial risks. Economic downturns, corporate restructuring, outsourcing, and automation can all lead to sudden job loss, leaving those who rely solely on a paycheck vulnerable to financial instability.

The COVID-19 pandemic, for instance, revealed just how fragile job security can be. Millions of people around the world lost their jobs or experienced reduced incomes as businesses shut down or downsized. Entire industries, such as hospitality and retail, were upended, forcing individuals to rethink their financial strategies. Those who had built multiple streams of income —through investments, side businesses, or passive income sources—were better positioned to weather the storm, while those reliant solely on their jobs faced tremendous financial pressure.

The traditional advice to "get a good job and stay there" fails to account for the rapidly changing nature of work in the 21st century. Technological advancements, globalization, and shifts in consumer behaviour have made many jobs less stable than they once were. To achieve true financial security, individuals must move beyond the idea of job security and diversify their income streams.

Kiyosaki emphasizes the importance of building passive income streams—money that flows in whether or not you are actively working. This can come from real estate investments, dividend-paying stocks, royalties from creative works, or revenue from a business you own. By creating multiple streams of income, you reduce your dependence on any one source of money, thereby protecting yourself from the financial fallout of job loss or economic downturns.

This shift from relying on a single paycheck to creating diversified income sources is critical for achieving financial independence. It requires a new mindset—one that embraces entrepreneurship, investment, and risk-taking as part of a broader financial strategy. In this way, financial independence becomes a function of multiple income streams, not just the security of a single job.

The Myth of Saving: Why Hoarding Cash Won't Build Wealth

Another pervasive money myth is the belief that saving money is the key to financial security. From a young age, we are often taught that saving diligently

—putting money in a savings account or under the proverbial mattress—will lead to long-term financial stability. While saving money is important, especially for building an emergency fund, the idea that saving alone will lead to wealth is misguided.

In Rich Dad Poor Dad, Kiyosaki explains that simply saving money, especially in low-interest savings accounts, is not enough to build wealth in today's economic environment. In fact, one of the greatest dangers to savers is inflation—the gradual erosion of purchasing power over time. When inflation outpaces the interest earned on savings accounts (which is often the case), the real value of your money decreases.

Consider the following scenario: A person diligently saves $10,000 over several years in a traditional savings account with an interest rate of 0.5%. After 10 years, they will have earned approximately $500 in interest, bringing their total savings to $10,500. However, if the inflation rate during that same period averages 2%, the purchasing power of their money will have diminished. What could have been bought for $10,000 at the beginning of the decade will now require more money, meaning their savings have effectively lost value.

In contrast, investing that same $10,000 in a diversified portfolio of stocks, bonds, or real estate could yield far higher returns. While investing comes with risks, it also offers the potential for growth that far outpaces inflation. The power of compound interest—the ability to earn returns on both your original investment and the returns it generates—can exponentially increase wealth over time.

For example, if that same $10,000 were invested in a stock market index fund with an average annual return of 7%, it would grow to over $19,000 in 10 years, even accounting for fluctuations in the market. This difference demonstrates the importance of moving beyond saving and into investing to build wealth.

This is not to say that saving is unimportant. Having an emergency fund is essential for financial stability, providing a cushion for unexpected expenses or life events. However, saving alone will not lead to wealth. To achieve financial independence, individuals must embrace investing—whether in stocks, real estate, or business ventures—as the key to growing their money over time.

The Myth of Debt: Understanding Good Debt vs. Bad Debt

Debt is often portrayed as a universally negative force, something to be avoided at all costs. For many people, the idea of going into debt is synonymous with financial ruin. However, as Kiyosaki explains in Rich Dad Poor Dad, not all debt is created equal. In fact, understanding the difference between good debt and bad debt is crucial for building wealth.

Bad debt, such as credit card debt or high-interest personal loans used to finance consumer purchases, is indeed dangerous. It drains financial resources, increases monthly obligations, and can lead to long-term financial hardship if not managed properly. Bad debt is often used to finance items that depreciate in value or do not generate income, such as cars, vacations, or luxury goods. This type of debt offers no financial return and should be avoided or paid off as quickly as possible.

However, good debt is debt that is used to acquire assets that generate income or appreciate in value. For example, taking out a mortgage to purchase rental properties that generate positive cash flow is considered good debt. The income from the rental properties can cover the mortgage payments while also providing additional income. Over time, as the property appreciates, the owner builds equity and generates wealth, all while leveraging the bank's money (the mortgage).

In this way, good debt can be a powerful tool for building wealth. It allows individuals to acquire assets that they might not be able to purchase outright, and it enables them to generate returns on those investments. Many of the world's wealthiest individuals and companies have used debt strategically to finance growth, expand operations, or invest in new ventures.

The key is to use debt responsibly and to ensure that it is tied to investments that generate a return. For example, borrowing money to start a business that has the potential to generate significant revenue can be a smart financial move. However, borrowing money to finance a lavish vacation, with no plan for how to repay the debt, is financially reckless.

Understanding the difference between good debt and bad debt allows individuals to leverage debt strategically to build wealth. It shifts the perspective from viewing debt as inherently bad to seeing it as a tool that, when used wisely, can accelerate financial success.

The Myth of Homeownership: A House Is Not Always an Asset

For generations, homeownership has been seen as the ultimate financial achievement—a symbol of success, stability, and the American Dream. The common belief is that owning a home is the key to building wealth and securing financial independence. However, as Kiyosaki argues in Rich Dad Poor Dad, the idea that a home is always an asset is a myth.

While homeownership can certainly be a wise financial decision under the right circumstances, it is important to understand that a personal residence is not always an asset in the traditional sense. An asset, as Kiyosaki defines it, is something that puts money in your pocket. A liability, on the other hand, is something that takes money out of your pocket. A personal home, while it may appreciate in value over time, typically requires ongoing expenses—mortgage payments, property taxes, maintenance, and repairs. These costs can make a home more of a liability than an income-generating asset.

Many people fall into the trap of becoming "house poor," meaning they stretch their finances to purchase a home, only to find that the ongoing expenses leave them with little money left over for saving or investing. In some cases, homeowners find themselves tied to mortgages that exceed the value of their home, particularly if the real estate market declines.

The belief that homeownership is a guaranteed path to wealth has also led many individuals to overlook other, potentially more lucrative investment opportunities. Instead of pouring all of their financial resources into a single property, individuals could diversify their investments into assets that generate income or offer higher returns, such as rental properties, stocks, or businesses.

This is not to say that owning a home is a bad decision —far from it. In fact, homeownership can be a valuable part of a broader wealth-building strategy, particularly if the property is purchased at the right time and in the right location. However, it is important to approach homeownership with a clear understanding of its financial implications. For many, the goal should be to build a portfolio of assets that generate income, rather than relying solely on a personal residence to provide long-term financial security.

The Myth of Retirement: Why Traditional Retirement Planning Falls Short

For much of the 20th century, the traditional retirement model was straightforward: work for 40 years, save diligently in a pension or retirement account, and retire comfortably in your 60s. This model assumed that job security, employer-sponsored pensions, and government benefits would provide a stable financial foundation for retirees.

However, as Kiyosaki points out in Rich Dad Poor Dad, the traditional retirement model is becoming increasingly outdated. With the decline of pensions, the uncertainty of Social Security, and the rising cost of living, many individuals are finding that their retirement savings are insufficient to provide the financial security they had expected. Additionally, longer life expectancies mean that people need more money to support themselves in retirement than previous generations did.

Relying solely on a 401(k) or similar retirement account is often not enough to ensure financial security in retirement. Market fluctuations, inflation, and unexpected medical expenses can all erode the value of retirement savings. To achieve true financial independence, individuals need to think beyond traditional retirement planning and focus on building multiple streams of income.

Kiyosaki advocates for a proactive approach to retirement—one that involves creating passive income streams through investments, real estate, and business ventures. By building a portfolio of income-generating assets, individuals can achieve financial independence long before traditional retirement age and reduce their reliance on savings alone.

This approach not only provides greater financial security but also allows for greater flexibility in how and when one chooses to retire. Instead of working for 40 years and relying on savings to last through retirement, individuals who build passive income streams can continue to generate income throughout their lives, providing financial freedom and peace of mind.

The Power of Financial Literacy: The Foundation of

Wealth Building

At the core of Kiyosaki's teachings is the concept of financial literacy—the understanding of how money works and how to use it to build wealth. Traditional education systems often fail to teach basic financial concepts such as investing, managing debt, or understanding assets and liabilities. As a result, many people enter adulthood with little knowledge of how to achieve financial independence.

Financial literacy is not just about understanding numbers or knowing how to balance a budget. It is about cultivating a mindset that prioritizes long-term wealth building over short-term gratification. It involves understanding the power of compound interest, the importance of investing in assets, and the risks and rewards of entrepreneurship.

In Rich Dad Poor Dad, Kiyosaki emphasizes that financial education is the key to breaking free from the cycle of working for money and instead learning to make money work for you. By educating yourself about money—through books, courses, mentors, and real-world experience—you can develop the financial intelligence necessary to make informed decisions and build lasting wealth.

For example, a financially literate person understands that wealth is not just about how much money you earn, but about how you manage, invest, and grow that money over time. They know the difference between good debt and bad debt, and they understand how to leverage assets to generate passive income. Financial literacy is the foundation upon which all wealth-building strategies are built, and it is essential for anyone seeking to achieve financial independence.

Replacing Money Myths with Financial Wisdom

The money myths we often learn too late—whether it's the belief in hard work alone, the illusion of job security, or the assumption that saving is enough to build wealth—are deeply ingrained in our society. These myths, passed down through generations, shape the way we think about money, work, and success. However, as Kiyosaki emphasizes in Rich Dad Poor Dad, the path to financial independence requires unlearning these myths and adopting a new approach to wealth building.

True financial wisdom is not about working harder, hoarding cash, or relying on outdated models of security. It is about understanding how money works, leveraging assets, and creating multiple streams of income. It is about replacing traditional money myths with a mindset of growth, learning, and strategic investing.

By embracing the principles of financial intelligence—investing in assets, understanding the difference between good debt and bad debt, and building a diversified portfolio—anyone can take control of their financial future and achieve true independence. The key is to break free from the money myths that hold us back and to start thinking like the "Rich Dad"—with a focus on creating wealth, not just earning it.

CHAPTER 17: DEBT IS NOT YOUR ENEMY, IGNORANCE IS

Debt has long been vilified in the realm of personal finance. For many, it conjures images of crushing obligations, sleepless nights, and endless payments stretching far into the future. However, the real enemy in most financial woes is not debt itself, but the lack of understanding about how to manage it. As Dave Ramsey emphasizes in The Total Money Makeover, debt, when misunderstood or misused, can indeed be destructive. However, Ramsey also champions a strict avoidance of debt in any form, adhering to a philosophy that prioritizes eliminating debt at all costs.

While the approach of paying off debt and living debt-free is certainly empowering and liberating for many, it's important to recognise that debt, in and of itself, is not inherently evil. When properly understood and wielded, debt can be a tool for wealth-building, growth, and opportunity. The true problem is not debt but financial ignorance—the inability to recognise when and how debt should be used, and more importantly, how to avoid the financial traps that come from mismanaging it.

This chapter takes a balanced approach, inspired by The Total Money Makeover but tempered with the understanding that debt, like any tool, can be useful when wielded with skill. Debt becomes dangerous only in the hands of those who lack the financial literacy to understand its consequences. By shedding light on the intricacies of debt, we can transform it from a feared enemy into a potentially valuable ally.

The Fear of Debt: Where It Comes From and Why It Persists

The fear of debt is deeply ingrained in many cultures, and for good reason. Stories of financial ruin, foreclosure, and bankruptcy abound, reinforcing the narrative that debt is a trap from which few can escape. This fear is often passed down through generations, with well-meaning parents and mentors warning against the dangers of borrowing money. Debt, in these narratives, is seen as a moral failing, a symbol of reckless spending or irresponsibility.

This fear is exacerbated by the experiences of millions of individuals who have found themselves ensnared in high-interest credit card debt, underwater mortgages, or burdensome student loans. In many cases, these individuals entered into debt without fully understanding the terms, the long-term consequences, or the strategies for managing it effectively. As a result, debt becomes a source of shame, anxiety, and resentment.

In The Total Money Makeover, Dave Ramsey advocates for a life free from debt, warning against the dangers of borrowing money and encouraging individuals to pay off all debts as quickly as possible. His approach is straightforward: eliminate debt, live within your means, and build wealth through consistent saving and investing. Ramsey's method has helped millions of people take control of their finances and escape the cycle of debt dependency. For many, it is a life-changing approach.

However, while Ramsey's strict avoidance of debt works well for those struggling to break free from the chains of consumer debt, it's important to acknowledge that not all debt is created equal. The issue isn't necessarily the existence of debt, but how it's used. Debt becomes dangerous when people enter into it blindly, without a plan, or when they take on too much, too quickly, without considering the broader context of their financial health.

Good Debt vs. Bad Debt: Understanding the Difference

One of the most important concepts in managing debt is understanding the difference between good debt and bad debt. In Ramsey's philosophy, any debt is considered a burden. However, many financial experts, including those who advocate for strategic investing and wealth building, argue that some types of debt can be used to one's advantage.

Bad debt, as the name suggests, refers to debt incurred to purchase depreciating assets or to fund a lifestyle that is not supported by income. Credit card debt, personal loans for consumer goods, and auto loans often fall into this category. These types of debt typically come with high interest rates, and the items purchased with them lose value over time or do not generate any financial return. This type of debt can quickly spiral out of control, leading to financial stress and long-term economic insecurity.

For example, if an individual uses a credit card to finance a lavish vacation, they may end up paying significantly more than the original cost of the trip due to high interest rates. In this case, the vacation provides no financial return, and the debt incurred represents a drain on future income.

Good debt, on the other hand, is debt that is used to acquire appreciating assets or to generate income. For instance, taking out a mortgage to purchase rental property can be considered good debt, as long as the rental income exceeds the mortgage payments and associated expenses. Similarly, borrowing money to invest in education or professional development can also be viewed as good debt if it leads to higher earning potential and career growth.

In this context, good debt is used strategically to create opportunities for wealth-building. The key difference between good and bad debt lies in the purpose of the loan and the financial return it generates. Borrowing money to invest in something that will grow in value or generate income can be a smart financial move, while borrowing to fund consumption is often a recipe for financial disaster.

In The Total Money Makeover, Ramsey argues that

even good debt should be avoided, suggesting that it's better to save up and pay cash for major purchases. While this approach has its merits, particularly for those who struggle with managing debt responsibly, it is important to recognise that good debt, when used wisely, can accelerate wealth-building and open doors to opportunities that might otherwise be out of reach.

Debt as a Tool: When and How to Use It Wisely

Debt, when used strategically, can be a powerful tool for building wealth, expanding opportunities, and achieving financial goals. However, using debt wisely requires a deep understanding of the terms, risks, and potential rewards involved. Entering into debt without a clear plan or understanding of how it will be repaid can lead to financial strain. But when debt is managed carefully, it can be a stepping stone to financial success.

Here are a few examples of how debt can be used effectively:

1. Real Estate Investments: One of the most common uses of good debt is in real estate. Many investors use mortgages to acquire rental properties, leveraging borrowed money to generate income. The key to using debt in real estate is ensuring that the property generates enough rental income to cover the mortgage payments, property taxes, insurance, and maintenance. Over time, as the property appreciates in value, the investor builds equity, and the rental income continues to provide cash flow.

For example, consider an investor who takes out a $200,000 mortgage to purchase a rental property. If the property generates $2,000 in rental income per month and the mortgage payment is $1,500, the investor is able to cover the mortgage and still pocket $500 each month. Additionally, as the property appreciates in value, the investor builds equity, creating long-term wealth.

2. Education and Career Development: Borrowing money to invest in education or professional development can also be considered good debt, as long as the investment leads to higher earning potential. For instance, taking out student loans to attend medical school or law school can be a smart financial decision if the resulting career provides a significant income boost.

However, it's important to approach student loans with caution. Not all educational programs offer the same return on investment, and individuals should carefully consider the potential income gains before taking on large amounts of student debt. For example, pursuing a degree in a high-demand field such as engineering or healthcare may offer a higher return than a degree in a field with fewer job opportunities or lower earning potential.

3. Business Financing: Many entrepreneurs use debt to finance the start or growth of their businesses. This can be a smart financial move if the borrowed funds are used to generate revenue and grow the business. However, business debt, like any debt, should be used carefully. It's important to have a clear plan for how the debt will be repaid and to ensure that the business has the potential to generate enough income to cover the loan payments.

For example, a small business owner might take out a loan to purchase equipment that will allow them to expand their production capacity. If the increased production leads to higher sales and greater profits, the loan can be considered a successful use of debt. However, if the business owner takes on too much debt without a clear plan for how to generate revenue, they may find themselves in financial trouble.

The key to using debt wisely is understanding the purpose of the loan, the terms of repayment, and the potential financial return. Good debt is used to acquire assets or opportunities that will generate income or appreciate in value, while bad debt is used to finance consumption. By recognizing the difference and using debt strategically, individuals can harness its power to achieve financial goals.

The Debt Snowball and Debt Avalanche: Two Approaches to Paying Off Debt

In The Total Money Makeover, Dave Ramsey advocates for the debt snowball method as a strategy for paying off debt. This method involves listing all of your debts from smallest to largest and focusing on paying off the smallest debt first, regardless of interest rate. Once the smallest debt is paid off, you move on to the next smallest debt, and so on, until all debts are eliminated. The idea behind the debt snowball is to create momentum and build confidence by quickly eliminating smaller debts, which can provide a psychological boost and motivate you to continue.

For many people, the debt snowball method is highly

effective because it offers quick wins. By paying off smaller debts first, individuals experience a sense of accomplishment and are more likely to stay committed to their debt repayment plan. This method has helped countless people achieve debt freedom and regain control of their finances.

However, there is another approach to paying off debt known as the debt avalanche method. This method focuses on paying off the debt with the highest interest rate first, regardless of the size of the debt. The rationale behind the debt

avalanche is that by tackling high-interest debt first, you save more money over time, as you reduce the amount of interest you pay on larger debts.

For example, if you have a credit card with a 20% interest rate and a personal loan with a 7% interest rate, the debt avalanche method would suggest paying off the credit card debt first, even if the balance is higher. This approach is mathematically more efficient because it minimizes the amount of interest paid over time.

Both the debt snowball and debt avalanche methods have their advantages. The debt snowball method is effective for those who need the psychological boost of seeing debts eliminated quickly, while the debt avalanche method is more cost-effective in the long run. Ultimately, the best approach depends on your personal preferences and financial situation. The important thing is to commit to a debt repayment strategy and stick to it, regardless of which method you choose.

Financial Traps: How to Avoid the Pitfalls of Mismanaging Debt

While debt can be a useful tool when managed wisely, it can also lead to financial disaster if misused. There are several common financial traps that people fall into when dealing with debt, and avoiding these pitfalls is essential for maintaining financial health.

1. Payday Loans and High-Interest Debt: One of the most dangerous forms of debt is payday loans. These short-term, high-interest loans are marketed as a quick fix for people in need of immediate cash, but they often come with exorbitant interest rates, sometimes exceeding 400%. Borrowers can quickly find themselves trapped in a cycle of debt, unable to repay the loan and forced to take out additional loans just to cover the interest.

To avoid falling into the payday loan trap, it's important to have an emergency fund in place to cover unexpected expenses. Building a cushion of savings can help you avoid the need for high-interest loans in times of financial difficulty.

2. Overleveraging: Overleveraging occurs when you take on too much debt relative to your income or assets. This can happen when individuals borrow more than they can reasonably afford to repay, often in pursuit of investments or lifestyle upgrades. While borrowing money to invest in real estate or a business can be a smart financial move, it's important to ensure that the debt is manageable and that the investment will generate enough income to cover the loan payments.

To avoid overleveraging, it's important to carefully evaluate your financial situation before taking on new debt. Consider factors such as your income, expenses, and existing debt obligations, and make sure that you have a clear plan for how the debt will be repaid.

3. Credit Card Debt: Credit card debt is one of the most common forms of consumer debt, and it can quickly spiral out of control due to high interest rates and minimum payment requirements. Many people fall into the trap of using credit cards to finance a lifestyle they can't afford, only to find themselves struggling to make even the minimum payments each month.

To avoid the credit card debt trap, it's important to use credit cards responsibly. This means paying off your balance in full each month, avoiding unnecessary purchases, and being mindful of your spending habits. If you're already carrying credit card debt, consider using the debt snowball or debt avalanche method to pay it off as quickly as possible.

4. Ignoring Interest Rates: One of the most common mistakes people make when dealing with debt is ignoring interest rates. Many borrowers focus solely on the size of their monthly payments without considering how much they are paying in interest over the life of the loan. High-interest debt can add thousands of dollars to the total cost of borrowing, making it difficult to get ahead financially.

To avoid this trap, it's important to pay attention to the interest rates on your loans and prioritize paying off high-interest debt first. Refinancing or consolidating high-interest loans can also be a good strategy for reducing your overall interest costs.

Building Financial Literacy: The Key to Managing Debt

At the heart of managing debt effectively is financial literacy—the knowledge and skills necessary to make informed financial decisions. Without financial literacy, debt can quickly become overwhelming and lead to long-term financial problems. However, with the right knowledge and strategies, debt can be managed effectively and even used as a tool for building wealth.

Financial literacy involves understanding key concepts such as interest rates, compound interest, credit scores, and loan terms. It also involves developing a budget, tracking expenses, and creating a plan for debt repayment. By educating yourself about how debt works and how to manage it responsibly, you can avoid financial traps and take control of your financial future.

One of the best ways to build financial literacy is to seek out educational resources, whether through books, courses, or financial advisors. The Total Money Makeover is a great starting point for those looking to gain a better understanding of personal finance and debt management. However, it's also important to seek out diverse perspectives on debt and finance, as there is no one-size-fits-all approach to financial success.

Debt as a Tool, Not an Enemy

Debt, in and of itself, is not the enemy. Ignorance—of how debt works, how to manage it, and how to use it wisely—is the real threat to financial well-being. While debt can be dangerous when misused, it can also be a powerful tool for building wealth, investing in opportunities, and achieving financial goals. The key is to approach debt with knowledge, understanding, and a clear plan for how it will be managed and repaid.

By understanding the difference between good debt and bad debt, using debt strategically, and avoiding common financial traps, individuals can harness the power of debt to build wealth and achieve financial independence. Debt does not have to be a source of fear or anxiety; with the right approach, it can be a stepping stone to financial success.

CHAPTER 18: THE UNSEEN COST OF LIFESTYLE INFLATION

In the modern world, the pursuit of wealth and success often comes with an unexpected trap: as income grows, so too does the pressure to elevate one's lifestyle. This phenomenon, known as lifestyle inflation, refers to the tendency for people to increase their spending as their earnings rise, often resulting in little to no real improvement in financial stability. While it seems natural to want to upgrade one's living standards as income rises, the unseen cost of lifestyle inflation can be far more damaging than it initially appears. The dream of financial freedom becomes elusive as the demands of a more expensive lifestyle swallow any gains in income.

In Your Money or Your Life by Vicki Robin and Joe Dominguez, the authors explore the relationship between money, time, and personal fulfillment, challenging readers to rethink their relationship with consumption. They emphasize that true wealth is not measured by material possessions or high income, but by the ability to live a life aligned with one's values, free from the pressures of financial stress. The book's lessons underscore the dangers of lifestyle inflation and highlight the importance of managing desires, not just income, in the quest for financial independence.

This chapter delves into the subtleties of lifestyle inflation, the hidden costs it incurs, and how to break free from the cycle of constantly upgrading one's lifestyle. By understanding the psychological and social drivers behind lifestyle inflation, we can learn to live more intentionally, make conscious financial choices, and redefine wealth beyond material accumulation.

What is Lifestyle Inflation?

Lifestyle inflation is the tendency to increase spending as one's income grows. As people earn more money, they often feel entitled to spend more—whether it's on a bigger house, a luxury car, more frequent vacations, or dining at expensive restaurants. What starts as a reward for hard work or success soon becomes a baseline expectation. The comforts and luxuries that were once out of reach quickly transform into necessities, and before long, even a substantial salary increase can disappear under the weight of new financial obligations.

The paradox of lifestyle inflation is that it often prevents people from achieving true financial security, despite the increase in earnings. Instead of saving, investing, or using the extra income to pay down debt, individuals find themselves living paycheck to paycheck, only at a higher level of consumption. As a result, the pursuit of financial freedom is replaced by the need to sustain an increasingly expensive lifestyle.

Imagine a young professional who receives a substantial promotion and salary increase. At first, they may choose to reward themselves with a few luxuries—a nicer apartment, a new wardrobe, or a better car. These changes might seem harmless, even reasonable, given the increase in income. However, over time, the individual may continue to upgrade their lifestyle, taking on more financial obligations like a mortgage, expensive vacations, and higher-end gadgets. What they fail to realize is that each new expense reduces their ability to save and invest for the future. The more their lifestyle inflates, the harder it becomes to step off the treadmill of ever-increasing consumption.

The Psychological Trap of "Deserving More"

At the heart of lifestyle inflation is the belief that success, particularly financial success, should be rewarded with an upgraded lifestyle. This mentality is fueled by societal expectations, advertising, and a culture that equates material wealth with happiness and fulfillment. We are constantly bombarded with messages that tell us that we "deserve" to have more—whether it's a bigger house, a fancier car, or the latest technology.

This sense of entitlement can be particularly strong after periods of financial struggle or hard work. Many people justify their increased spending by telling themselves that they have earned it. After years of sacrificing, they feel they finally deserve to enjoy the fruits of their labor. While there is nothing wrong with rewarding oneself for hard work, the problem arises when these rewards become habitual and lead to a permanent increase in spending.

Vicki Robin and Joe Dominguez, in Your Money or Your Life, argue that this cycle of consumption is a never-ending chase for happiness that ultimately leaves people unfulfilled. The desire for more is insatiable; as soon as one material need is met, another takes its place. This is the essence of the hedonic treadmill—the phenomenon where increases in income or material possessions lead to temporary spikes in happiness, but over time, people return to their baseline level of contentment. The more we have, the more we want, and the cycle continues.

The danger of this mindset is that it keeps individuals locked in a perpetual state of financial insecurity. The more they spend, the more income they require to sustain their lifestyle, leaving little room for savings or financial growth. What begins as a desire to enjoy life more fully ends up creating a financial burden that limits freedom and peace of mind.

The Social Pressure to Keep Up

Beyond personal desires, lifestyle inflation is often driven by social comparison—the pressure to keep up with the lifestyles of others. This is particularly true in today's world, where social media constantly exposes us to the curated, glamorous lives of friends, family, and celebrities. The desire to match or exceed the status of those around us can lead to financial decisions that are more about appearance than necessity.

Think about the phenomenon known as "keeping up with the Joneses." This phrase encapsulates the idea that people feel compelled to match the spending habits of their peers, neighbors, or colleagues. When someone in the social circle buys a new car, moves into a larger home, or takes an extravagant vacation, it can trigger a desire in others to do the same, regardless of whether they can afford it. The pressure to maintain appearances leads many people to stretch their finances, even taking on debt, in order to project a certain image of success.

Social pressure can also come from more subtle sources, such as workplace culture. In high-paying professions, there is often an unspoken expectation that employees will spend in line with their income level, whether it's through expensive suits, dinners at upscale restaurants, or luxury vehicles. Those who choose to live more frugally may feel out of place or judged for not conforming to the lifestyle of their peers.

The danger of social comparison is that it distorts our perception of what we truly need to live a fulfilling life. Instead of making decisions based on our own values and goals, we begin to make financial choices based on external validation. This leads to a cycle of consumption that is driven more by fear of judgment than by genuine desire.

The Unseen Cost: More Money, Less Freedom

One of the most insidious aspects of lifestyle inflation is the way it erodes financial freedom. At first glance, increasing one's spending as income rises seems harmless. After all, if you're earning more, shouldn't you be able to enjoy life more fully? However, the reality is that lifestyle inflation often leads to a higher cost of living without a corresponding increase in financial stability or freedom.

As people increase their spending, they become more dependent on their income to sustain their lifestyle. This dependence can limit their options, making them feel trapped in jobs they no longer enjoy or forcing them to maintain high levels of work-related stress in order to keep up with their financial obligations. Instead of creating freedom, higher income leads to greater financial pressure.

For example, an individual who purchases a larger home and takes on a higher mortgage may find themselves tied to a particular job because they need the income to cover their monthly payments. Similarly, someone who upgrades to a luxury car with high maintenance costs may feel the pressure to keep earning at the same level to support their lifestyle. Over time, these financial obligations can begin to feel like a burden, limiting the individual's ability to make choices that align with their personal values and long-term goals.

In Your Money or Your Life, Robin and Dominguez argue that true wealth is not about having more money but about having more control over your time and choices. They encourage readers to rethink the way they spend money, focusing on aligning their spending with their personal values rather than societal expectations. By breaking free from the cycle of lifestyle inflation, individuals can achieve financial independence and regain control over their lives.

Escaping the Lifestyle Inflation Trap: Practical Strategies

Breaking free from lifestyle inflation requires a shift in mindset, as well as practical strategies for managing income and spending. It's not about denying yourself the comforts of life, but about making conscious choices that prioritize long-term financial freedom over short-term gratification.

Here are some key strategies to escape the lifestyle inflation trap:

1. Define Your Values and Goals: The first step in escaping lifestyle inflation is to define what truly matters to you. What are your personal values and long-term financial goals? Do you value experiences over material possessions? Is your priority to achieve financial independence, retire early, or pursue a passion project? By clarifying your values, you can make spending decisions that align with your priorities rather than the expectations of others.

For example, if travel is one of your core values, you might choose to allocate more of your budget toward vacations while cutting back on unnecessary material purchases. By aligning your spending with your values, you can experience greater fulfillment without the need to constantly upgrade your lifestyle.

2. Live Below Your Means: One of the simplest and most effective ways to avoid lifestyle inflation is to live below your means. This means resisting the temptation to increase your spending as your income

rises. Instead, focus on saving and investing the extra income. By keeping your expenses steady while your income grows, you can build a solid financial foundation that allows you to achieve long-term financial independence.

For example, if you receive a raise at work, instead of upgrading your home or car, consider increasing your contributions to retirement accounts, building an emergency fund, or investing in assets that will generate passive income. This approach allows you to grow your wealth without falling into the trap of increased spending.

3. Set Boundaries on Spending: Another important strategy is to set clear boundaries on your spending. This can be done by creating a budget

that allocates money for necessities, savings, and discretionary spending. By setting limits on how much you spend in certain categories, you can avoid the gradual creep of lifestyle inflation.

You might decide to set a monthly budget for dining out, entertainment, or clothing. By sticking to these limits, you ensure that your spending remains in check, even as your income increases.

4. Embrace Minimalism: Minimalism is a philosophy that encourages individuals to focus on the things that truly bring value to their lives and to let go of excess material possessions. By embracing minimalism, you can break free from the cycle of consumption and focus on living more intentionally. This doesn't mean you have to live with the bare minimum, but it does mean

being more mindful of your purchases and avoiding the accumulation of unnecessary items.

Instead of upgrading to the latest smartphone every year, you might choose to keep your current phone until it no longer serves its purpose. By making mindful choices about what you buy and why, you can avoid the pressure to constantly upgrade your lifestyle.

5. Automate Savings and Investments: One of the most effective ways to ensure that you're building wealth rather than inflating your lifestyle is to automate your savings and investments. Set up automatic transfers from your checking account to a savings or investment account each month. This ensures that a portion of your income is being set aside for future financial goals, rather than being spent on lifestyle upgrades.

If you receive a 10% raise, consider automatically increasing your contributions to retirement accounts or investment funds by the same percentage. By automating this process, you take the decision-making out of the equation and ensure that your wealth is growing consistently over time.

Redefining Wealth: It's About Freedom, Not Stuff

At the core of Your Money or Your Life is the idea that true wealth is not about accumulating material possessions or living an extravagant lifestyle, but about having the freedom to live life on your terms. Robin and Dominguez emphasize that financial independence is achieved when you no longer need to trade your time for money, and when your financial choices are aligned with your personal values.

The problem with lifestyle inflation is that it often leads people further away from financial independence. The more you spend, the more income you need to sustain your lifestyle, and the less freedom you have to make choices that prioritize your well-being. By breaking free from the cycle of consumption and focusing on building wealth through intentional spending, saving, and investing, you can achieve true financial freedom.

For many, this may involve redefining what it means to be wealthy. Instead of equating wealth with material possessions or a high salary, wealth can be seen as the ability to control your time, pursue your passions, and live in alignment with your values. It's about having the freedom to choose how you spend your days, without being constrained by financial obligations or the need to keep up with societal expectations.

Escaping the Cycle of More

Lifestyle inflation is a subtle, insidious force that can erode financial security and keep people trapped in a cycle of consumption. While it's natural to want to improve your lifestyle as your income grows, the key to achieving financial independence lies in managing desires, not just income. By understanding the psychological and social drivers behind lifestyle inflation, and by adopting strategies to live intentionally and within your means, you can break free from the cycle of more.

In Your Money or Your Life, Robin and Dominguez remind us that the pursuit of wealth is not about accumulating more possessions, but about achieving freedom—freedom from financial stress, freedom to pursue your passions, and freedom to live a life that aligns with your values. By rethinking our relationship with money and consumption, we can redefine wealth in a way that prioritizes happiness, fulfillment, and true financial independence.

CHAPTER 19: THE ART OF INVESTING IN YOURSELF

In the world of finance, discussions often revolve around markets, stocks, bonds, and portfolios—strategies for building wealth and ensuring long-term financial success. But amid all these external opportunities, there lies an often-overlooked yet incredibly powerful form of investment: investing in yourself. Just as one might diversify a financial portfolio to optimize returns and manage risk, individuals must take a similar approach to personal development, understanding that self-investment is the foundation upon which all other success is built.

Inspired by The Intelligent Investor by Benjamin Graham, the classic text that introduced the concept of value investing, this chapter extends the principles of investing to the realm of personal growth. Graham's emphasis on prudent decision-making, careful analysis, and long-term planning translates seamlessly to the pursuit of self-improvement. By applying the same discipline and foresight to your personal development as you would to your financial portfolio, you create the potential for extraordinary returns that surpass mere monetary wealth.

Investing in yourself means prioritizing your physical, mental, and emotional well-being, developing skills, knowledge, and competencies that will serve you throughout your life. It is about building a foundation that increases your personal value over time, just as wise financial investments compound and grow. Unlike stocks or bonds, investing in yourself is a lifelong endeavor that continually pays dividends, whether through career advancement, personal fulfillment, or enhanced resilience in the face of challenges.

This chapter will explore the art of investing in yourself —why it's the most lucrative investment you can make, the principles that guide it, and practical ways to cultivate lifelong growth and self-improvement.

The Concept of Value Investing in Yourself

In The Intelligent Investor, Benjamin Graham introduces the concept of value investing, a strategy that emphasizes buying stocks or assets that are undervalued by the market but have strong fundamentals, thus offering the potential for long-term growth. The goal is not to chase quick returns or speculative gains, but to make careful, deliberate investments in companies with proven worth that will grow steadily over time.

Applying this philosophy to personal development, value investing in yourself means focusing on the areas of your life that may not yield immediate or flashy returns but that are essential for long-term growth and success. This includes areas such as education, skill acquisition, emotional intelligence, health, and relationships. Just as a savvy investor evaluates the intrinsic value of a stock, a person who invests in themselves must recognise their strengths, weaknesses, and areas for improvement. By identifying and nurturing your most valuable qualities, you build a foundation for enduring success.

Value investing in yourself requires patience and long-term thinking. Personal growth is not a sprint but a marathon, and the most meaningful gains often take time to materialize. While the external rewards—career advancement, financial success, or recognition—may take years to manifest, the internal benefits of self-investment, such as confidence, knowledge, and resilience, begin to accrue immediately.

For instance, consider an individual who decides to invest time and effort in learning a new skill, such as coding or digital marketing. The immediate impact may be subtle, perhaps even invisible, but over time, as they apply their new knowledge, they begin to see opportunities for career advancement or entrepreneurship. This type of investment builds lasting value, not only because of the tangible benefits it brings but because it cultivates adaptability, problem-solving, and confidence—qualities that remain invaluable regardless of market conditions or career changes.

The Compound Interest of Knowledge

One of the most profound ways to invest in yourself is through the acquisition of knowledge. Knowledge, like financial capital, compounds over time. The more you learn, the more you are able to synthesize, apply, and build upon that knowledge in meaningful ways. Just as Benjamin Graham advocates for understanding the fundamentals of a company before investing, one must continuously seek to understand the world, oneself, and the industries in which one operates to create lasting value.

Warren Buffett, one of Benjamin Graham's most famous disciples, famously said, "The best investment you can make is in yourself. The more you learn, the more you earn." This doesn't simply refer to formal education, though earning degrees or certifications can certainly enhance career prospects. It also refers to the habit of lifelong learning—the commitment to continually expanding your knowledge base and intellectual curiosity.

Here are a few ways that investing in knowledge compounds over time:

1. Breadth and Depth of Expertise: When you deepen your expertise in a particular field, you increase your value within that domain. For example, becoming an expert in a specific technology, like artificial intelligence or cybersecurity, can open doors to high-paying roles and opportunities. However, when you broaden your knowledge across multiple fields—such as combining technological expertise with business acumen—you create a rare and valuable combination of skills. This breadth and depth of knowledge make you more versatile, adaptable, and sought-after in a rapidly changing world.

2. Interdisciplinary Thinking: The ability to draw connections between seemingly unrelated fields is one of the hallmarks of true intellectual growth. For instance, a marketing professional who understands behavioural psychology can craft more compelling campaigns, while an engineer with a background in philosophy might bring a unique ethical perspective to technological innovation. The more diverse your knowledge, the better equipped you are to solve complex problems and think creatively.

3. Continuous Growth Mindset: When you view learning as an ongoing process rather than a finite goal, you cultivate a growth mindset—the belief that abilities and intelligence can be developed over time. This mindset fosters resilience, adaptability, and a willingness to take risks, all of which are critical for personal and professional success. Rather than fearing failure, those with a growth mindset see challenges as opportunities to learn and grow.

Knowledge compounds in the sense that each new piece of information builds on previous learning, creating a network of understanding that deepens and expands over time. This compounding effect can lead to breakthroughs, innovations, and insights that would be impossible without a foundation of accumulated knowledge. By making a commitment to lifelong learning—whether through reading, courses, mentorship, or practical experience—you continuously increase your personal value and create opportunities for growth.

Physical Health: The Foundation of All Success

While intellectual development is critical, it's equally important to invest in your physical health, which serves as the foundation for all other forms of success. Just as an investor carefully monitors the health of their financial portfolio, you must take care of your body, as it is the vehicle through which you experience and engage with the world.

Benjamin Graham's philosophy emphasizes protecting your investments against risk and loss, and this concept translates perfectly to the realm of health. Neglecting physical well-being can lead to significant "losses" in terms of productivity, energy, and quality of life. Moreover, health problems can deplete financial resources, as medical expenses and the inability to work take a toll on personal finances.

Here's how investing in your health can yield both immediate and long-term benefits:

1. Increased Energy and Productivity: Physical health is closely tied to energy levels and cognitive function. Regular exercise, a balanced diet, and adequate sleep all contribute to increased stamina, mental clarity, and focus. When you prioritize your health, you are better equipped to handle the demands of your career and personal life, leading to greater productivity and effectiveness in all areas of life.

2. Stress Management: Chronic stress is one of the greatest threats to long-term well-being. Regular exercise, mindfulness practices, and a healthy diet can help mitigate the effects of stress, reducing the risk of burnout, anxiety, and depression. By investing in your

physical health, you build resilience and the ability to cope with life's challenges, allowing you to maintain a sense of balance and well-being even in the face of adversity.

3. Longevity and Quality of Life: Just as investors seek to maximize the longevity of their portfolios, you should aim to maximize the quality and length of your life through healthy habits. A healthy lifestyle reduces the risk of chronic illnesses such as heart disease, diabetes, and cancer, allowing you to enjoy a higher quality of life for longer. This, in turn, provides you with more time and energy to pursue your personal and professional goals.

4. Confidence and Self-Esteem: Taking care of your body can also have a profound impact on your confidence and self-esteem. When you feel strong, fit, and healthy, you are more likely to approach challenges with a sense of capability and resilience. This sense of empowerment can extend to all areas of your life, from your career to your relationships.

Just as with financial investments, the key to reaping the benefits of investing in your health is consistency and long-term thinking. Small, incremental changes—such as incorporating more movement into your day, choosing healthier foods, or practicing mindfulness—can lead to significant gains over time. By viewing your health as an essential component of your personal portfolio, you prioritize long-term well-being over short-term gratification.

Emotional Intelligence: The Ultimate Social Currency

Another critical aspect of investing in yourself is developing emotional intelligence (EQ)—the ability to understand, manage, and navigate emotions, both your own and those of others. In The Intelligent Investor, Graham emphasizes the importance of temperament in making sound financial decisions, noting that the ability to remain calm and rational in the face of market volatility is often more valuable than pure intellectual ability. Similarly, emotional intelligence is crucial for personal and professional success, as it allows individuals to manage stress, build relationships, and make informed decisions in high-pressure situations.

Emotional intelligence is often referred to as the "ultimate social currency" because it enhances your ability to connect with others, build trust, and foster collaboration—all of which are essential for thriving in today's interconnected world. Whether you're leading a team, negotiating a deal, or navigating personal relationships, emotional intelligence can be the key to success.

Here's how investing in emotional intelligence can pay off:

1. Stronger Relationships: Emotional intelligence helps you build deeper, more meaningful connections with others. By understanding and empathizing with the emotions of those around you, you can foster trust and rapport, whether in the workplace or in your personal life. People with high emotional intelligence are often seen as more approachable, compassionate, and reliable, making them valuable partners and leaders.

2. Improved Communication: One of the hallmarks of emotional intelligence is the ability to communicate effectively. This means not only articulating your thoughts and feelings clearly but also listening actively and responding appropriately to the emotions of others. By improving your communication skills, you can resolve conflicts more effectively, collaborate more productively, and lead with greater impact.

3. Better Decision-Making: Emotions play a significant role in decision-making, and individuals with high emotional intelligence are better equipped to manage their emotions and avoid impulsive or irrational decisions. By cultivating emotional intelligence, you develop the ability to stay calm under pressure, weigh the consequences of your actions, and make choices that align with your long-term goals.

4. Resilience and Stress Management: Emotional intelligence also plays a crucial role in managing stress and building resilience. By understanding your emotional triggers and developing strategies for coping with difficult emotions, you can maintain a sense of balance and perspective, even in challenging situations. This resilience not only helps you navigate personal difficulties but also allows you to thrive in high-stress environments, such as competitive workplaces or entrepreneurial ventures.

Developing emotional intelligence is an ongoing process that requires self-reflection, practice, and feedback. It involves not only understanding your own emotions but also cultivating empathy and awareness of the emotions of others. By investing in your emotional intelligence, you enhance your ability to build strong relationships, communicate effectively, and make sound decisions—skills that are invaluable in both personal and professional contexts.

The Power of Mentorship and Networking

In The Intelligent Investor, Graham emphasizes the importance of seeking guidance from those who have experience and expertise in the field. Similarly, when it comes to personal development, surrounding yourself with mentors, role models, and a strong network is a critical investment in your success.

Mentorship provides you with the opportunity to learn from others who have walked the path you are on, offering valuable insights, advice, and support. A mentor can help you avoid common pitfalls, navigate challenges, and accelerate your personal and professional growth. Whether it's a career mentor, a life coach, or a trusted advisor, having someone in your corner who believes in your potential and helps you refine your goals is an invaluable asset.

Networking, too, is an essential component of investing in yourself. The relationships you build within your industry or field can lead to new opportunities, collaborations, and partnerships that might otherwise have been out of reach. A strong network can open doors to career advancement, business opportunities, and personal growth by connecting you with individuals who share your values and goals.

Here's how mentorship and networking can amplify your personal investment:

1. Access to New Opportunities: A well-cultivated network provides access to opportunities that may not be publicly available. Whether it's a job opening, a business partnership, or an invitation to speak at a conference, your network can help you stay connected to the latest developments in your field.

2. Personal Growth and Accountability: Mentors and peers can hold you accountable for your goals, providing constructive feedback and encouragement along the way. A mentor can challenge you to step outside of your comfort zone, set higher goals, and push yourself toward continuous improvement.

3. Learning from Experience: A mentor's experience can be a valuable resource as you navigate your own challenges and decisions. They can provide insight into how to handle setbacks, balance work and life, or make strategic career moves. Learning from someone else's successes and failures allows you to grow more quickly and avoid common mistakes.

Investing in relationships—whether through mentorship, networking, or collaboration—can have profound effects on your personal and professional success. It's a reminder that the path to growth is rarely walked alone, and that surrounding yourself with people who support and challenge you is one of the best investments you can make.

You Are Your Greatest Asset

Investing in yourself is the most important and lucrative investment you can make. It is an ongoing process that touches every aspect of your life—

from your knowledge and health to your emotional intelligence and relationships. Inspired by the principles of The Intelligent Investor, the art of self-investment is about long-term growth, careful analysis, and a commitment to making choices that enhance your personal value.

Just as a wise investor diversifies their portfolio and takes a measured approach to risk, you must approach personal development with intention, patience, and discipline. By focusing on knowledge, health, emotional intelligence, and relationships, you create a foundation that allows you to weather challenges, seize opportunities, and experience a life of fulfillment and purpose.

Ultimately, the greatest return on investment is not measured in dollars or possessions but in the quality of your life. When you invest in yourself, you increase your ability to achieve your goals, build meaningful connections, and live a life that reflects your values. In the art of self-investment, you are both the asset and the beneficiary—your growth and well-being are the true measures of success.

CHAPTER 20: FINANCIAL FREEDOM THROUGH MULTIPLE INCOME STREAMS

In a world where job security is becoming increasingly elusive and traditional retirement models are proving insufficient, the pursuit of financial freedom is more urgent than ever. For many, financial freedom represents not only the ability to cover expenses without worry but also the freedom to live life on one's terms—free from the constraints of working solely to pay bills. Yet, too often, the path to achieving this freedom is framed in narrow terms: get a good job, climb the corporate ladder, save diligently, and eventually retire comfortably. This traditional model, while secure for some, is no longer enough for those seeking not just survival but true independence.

In The Millionaire Fastlane by MJ DeMarco, the author challenges the conventional approach to wealth-building and financial independence, presenting an alternative: the fastlane to wealth through entrepreneurship, leverage, and diversification of income. DeMarco asserts that financial freedom is not about waiting until retirement to enjoy life; rather, it's about creating multiple streams of income that generate wealth quickly and sustainably, allowing you to break free from the slow and often unfulfilling "slowlane" of traditional career paths.

The secret to financial freedom lies not in relying on a single paycheck but in diversifying your income streams. Whether through side businesses, investments, royalties, or passive income, multiple income streams provide the flexibility, security, and growth potential that are essential for achieving lasting financial independence. This chapter explores how to build and manage multiple income streams, the mindset shift required to break free from conventional financial wisdom, and how diversification accelerates the path to true wealth.

The Myth of the Single Paycheck: Why Relying on One Income Source is Risky

One of the greatest misconceptions in the pursuit of financial freedom is the belief that a single, well-paying job is enough to ensure long-term security and prosperity. For decades, the conventional wisdom was clear: if you land a stable job with a good salary, save consistently, and invest wisely, you'll eventually accumulate enough wealth to retire comfortably.

However, this approach—what DeMarco calls the "slowlane"—is increasingly flawed in the face of modern economic realities.

The problem with relying on a single paycheck is twofold:

1. Vulnerability to External Shocks: A single source of income leaves individuals highly vulnerable to external disruptions. The COVID-19 pandemic illustrated this vulnerability starkly, as millions of people who relied on a single income stream found themselves unemployed or facing reduced hours almost overnight. Economic recessions, corporate downsizing, automation, and shifts in industry demand can all jeopardize even the most stable jobs. Relying on one paycheck means that if that source dries up, financial ruin is a real possibility.

2. Limited Scalability: A job, no matter how high-paying, has inherent limitations in terms of growth. Salary increases are often incremental, tied to promotions, raises, or company performance—factors largely outside your control. Moreover, a job usually requires trading time for money, which means that your income is capped by the number of hours you can work. Even with a significant salary, this structure limits your ability to scale your earnings beyond a certain point.

DeMarco emphasizes that financial freedom comes from breaking free from the dependency on a single source of income. He likens the traditional model to driving in the slow lane—progress is possible, but it's agonizingly slow, and external forces (like layoffs or economic downturns) can easily derail your progress. The "fastlane" to wealth involves diversifying income sources, creating opportunities that can grow exponentially, and building streams of income that work for you, even when you're not actively working.

The Power of Multiple Income Streams: Why Diversification is Key

Diversification is a well-known principle in the world of investing: spreading risk across multiple assets or sectors reduces the likelihood of losing everything if one investment fails. This same principle applies to income. Relying on a single paycheck is akin to putting all your eggs in one basket. The moment that basket falls, so does your financial stability. In contrast, having multiple income streams offers several key advantages:

1. Increased Financial Security: With multiple streams of income, losing one source doesn't spell disaster. If one stream dries up—such as a job loss or a dip in freelance work—you still have other sources of revenue to fall back on. This buffer provides peace of mind and greater resilience in the face of economic uncertainty.

2. Opportunities for Exponential Growth: While a traditional job may offer steady, linear growth, multiple income streams, especially those that are scalable, can generate exponential growth. For instance, a business, once established, has the potential to grow rapidly without being limited by the number of hours you work. Similarly, investments in stocks, real estate, or other assets can appreciate significantly over time, providing increasing returns without additional effort on your part.

3. More Freedom and Flexibility: With multiple income streams, you're not tied to a single employer or industry. This provides flexibility in how you manage your time and pursue your passions. You can choose which projects or opportunities to focus on, and as your streams of income become more passive, you gain more freedom to live life on your terms.

4. Reduced Dependence on Time: Many of the best forms of multiple income streams involve passive income—money that continues to flow in without requiring active effort on your part. Whether it's through investments, royalties, affiliate marketing, or automated business systems, passive income allows you to decouple your earnings from the hours you work. This is the true key to financial freedom: earning money while you sleep.

Types of Income Streams: Active, Passive, and Hybrid

When discussing multiple income streams, it's important to understand the different types of income and how they can be combined to create a robust financial ecosystem. Broadly speaking, income streams can be classified into three categories: active, passive, and hybrid.

1. Active Income: This is the most familiar form of income and includes wages, salaries, or earnings from freelance work. Active income requires you to trade your time, energy, or expertise for money. While active income can be lucrative, it has limitations, as it is dependent on the number of hours you can work. Nonetheless, active income is often the starting point

for building wealth and can be reinvested into other income streams.

Examples: Full-time jobs, consulting gigs, freelance projects, and service-based businesses.

2. Passive Income: Passive income is the holy grail of financial freedom. It refers to income that continues to flow in with little to no ongoing effort. While passive income often requires an initial investment of time, money, or energy, the goal is to create systems or assets that generate revenue automatically. Once established, passive income streams provide consistent earnings without requiring you to actively work for them.

Examples: Rental income from real estate, dividends from stocks, royalties from books or music, affiliate marketing, and automated e-commerce businesses.

3. Hybrid Income: Hybrid income streams blend elements of both active and passive income. These streams may require some ongoing effort or management but can still generate revenue without a direct exchange of hours for dollars. For instance, running an online course might require periodic updates and customer support, but the majority of the income is passive once the course is created and automated.

Examples: Online courses, subscription services, semi-passive business ventures (like managing a rental property with a property manager), and membership sites.

A key part of building multiple income streams is balancing these three types of income in a way that suits your lifestyle, skills, and financial goals. Most people start with active income and gradually transition to more passive or hybrid streams as they invest in assets or build businesses.

Practical Strategies for Building Multiple Income Streams

Building multiple income streams requires a strategic approach, focusing on areas where you can leverage your skills, capital, and time effectively. Here are some practical strategies to get started:

1. Leverage Your Expertise: One of the most accessible ways to create additional income streams is by leveraging the skills or knowledge you already possess. This could involve starting a consulting business, offering freelance services, or creating digital products, such as online courses or eBooks. By turning your expertise into a marketable product or service, you can create both active and passive income streams.

For example, if you're a skilled graphic designer, you might offer freelance design services (active income) while simultaneously creating and selling design templates on platforms like Etsy or Creative Market (passive income).

2. Invest in Real Estate: Real estate is a classic way to generate both active and passive income. Whether you purchase rental properties, invest in commercial real estate, or engage in real estate flipping, the potential for long-term appreciation and cash flow makes real estate one of the most reliable income streams. Rental income, in particular, can provide a steady passive income

stream while the property itself appreciates over time.

DeMarco emphasizes the importance of leveraging other people's money (OPM) in real estate, such as using mortgages to purchase properties that generate cash flow. By doing so, you can scale your portfolio without tying up all your capital, creating multiple streams of income from multiple properties.

3. Create an Online Business: The rise of the internet has opened up countless opportunities to build scalable, automated businesses. Whether through e-commerce, affiliate marketing, or digital products, online businesses allow for the creation of passive income streams with minimal overhead costs. Once an online business is established, it can run with little active involvement, generating revenue through automated systems, marketing funnels, and outsourcing.

An example of this would be starting an Amazon FBA (Fulfillment by Amazon) business, where you source or create products that Amazon stores and ships on your behalf. While this business requires upfront effort to set up, it can generate passive

income once it's automated.

4. Invest in the Stock Market: Investing in dividend-paying stocks, index funds, or bonds is a classic way to generate passive income. While there is risk involved, particularly with individual stock picks, a well-diversified portfolio can provide a steady stream of dividend income, which can be reinvested to compound over time. Dividend investing allows you to benefit from both capital appreciation and regular income.

Additionally, investing in REITs (Real Estate Investment Trusts) allows you to gain exposure to real estate without the hassles of property management. REITs pay regular dividends, making them a popular choice for income investors.

5. Build Intellectual Property: Another lucrative form of passive income comes from creating intellectual property that can be monetized over time. This includes writing books, composing music, developing software, or creating courses. Once these products are created, they can generate royalties or sales revenue indefinitely, often with minimal ongoing effort.

For example, an author who writes a best-selling book can continue to earn royalties for years, even decades, after the book is published. Similarly, a musician who composes a popular song can earn royalties from streaming services, radio plays, and licensing deals.

6. Side Hustles and Gig Economy Work: Many people start building multiple income streams through side hustles or gig economy work. Platforms like Uber, Lyft, Airbnb, and Upwork offer flexible opportunities to earn additional income without quitting your full-time job. While these opportunities typically provide active income, they can be an effective way to generate extra cash flow that can be reinvested into more passive income streams.

For instance, someone who rents out a spare room on Airbnb might use the income to invest in real estate or start a business, creating a more sustainable and scalable income stream over time.

The Mindset Shift: From Linear Income to Exponential Growth

The pursuit of multiple income streams requires a mindset shift—from viewing income as a linear function of time to seeing it as an opportunity for exponential growth. This shift involves moving away from the traditional paradigm of trading time for money and embracing the idea that income can—and should—be decoupled from the hours you work.

In The Millionaire Fastlane, MJ DeMarco emphasizes the importance of leverage—the ability to multiply your efforts and create exponential returns through automation, delegation, and scalable systems. Whether it's leveraging technology, capital, or other people's time, the goal is to create income streams that can grow independently of your direct involvement.

The key to this mindset shift is understanding that wealth is not just about how much you earn but about how you earn it. By creating systems and investments that work for you, rather than requiring constant effort, you unlock the potential for financial freedom. This freedom allows you to focus on the things that truly matter—whether it's spending time with loved ones, pursuing passions, or contributing to causes you care about.

The Path to Financial Freedom

Financial freedom is not a destination that is reached through a single job or a single income source. It is the result of carefully cultivating and managing multiple streams of income, each contributing to your overall financial security, flexibility, and independence. By diversifying your income streams—through active, passive, and hybrid sources—you not only increase your earning potential but also protect yourself from the risks of relying on a single source of income.

In The Millionaire Fastlane, MJ DeMarco reminds us that the road to wealth does not have to be slow. By embracing the fastlane mindset—leveraging multiple income streams, building scalable businesses, and investing wisely—you can accelerate your journey toward financial freedom. Ultimately, the goal is to create a life where your income works for you, rather than the other way around, allowing you to enjoy the freedom, security, and fulfillment that come from true financial independence.

CHAPTER 21: HANDLING REJECTION WITH GRACE

In life, rejection is inevitable. Whether it's a job application that doesn't result in an offer, a business pitch that falls flat, or a personal relationship that fails to blossom, rejection is a universal experience that can leave us feeling vulnerable, defeated, and sometimes, unworthy. Yet, the way we handle rejection can profoundly shape our personal and professional lives. Those who learn to face rejection with grace, resilience, and determination often find that each "no" is not a dead-end but a redirection—a step closer to a "yes."

Inspired by Rejection Proof by Jia Jiang, this chapter delves into the art of handling rejection and transforming it into a tool for personal growth. Jia Jiang's journey is one of courage in the face of rejection, as he embarks on a 100-day experiment of intentionally seeking out rejection to desensitize himself from the fear of it. Through his experiences, he discovers that rejection is not something to be feared but rather embraced as an opportunity for growth, learning, and, surprisingly, connection. In the same way, we too can develop the emotional resilience to face rejection head-on and learn from each experience, using each setback as a stepping stone toward eventual success.

The Nature of Rejection: Why It Hurts

Rejection stings for a reason—it taps into some of our most basic human fears and needs. Psychologically, humans are wired to seek acceptance and belonging. From an evolutionary perspective, acceptance into a group meant survival, while rejection often implied danger or exclusion. This primal fear of being cast out remains deeply ingrained in our psyches, and even minor rejections—such as a social slight or a declined invitation—can trigger feelings of insecurity and inadequacy.

However, it's important to recognise that rejection is not a reflection of our inherent worth. Rather, it's a natural part of navigating a world filled with differing opinions, preferences, and circumstances. Every rejection has a context, and understanding that context can help us detach our sense of self-worth from the outcome. A rejection often says more about the other party's needs, limitations, or perspectives than it does about our value as individuals.

The Fear of Rejection: Why It Holds Us Back

For many, the fear of rejection is paralyzing. It prevents people from taking risks, pursuing opportunities, or putting themselves out there. This fear often manifests as avoidance behaviour—we avoid asking for a promotion because we fear being told no, we hesitate to start a business because we dread the possibility of failure, or we shy away from expressing our feelings to someone because we don't want to be hurt. In each case, the fear of hearing "no" becomes a barrier to growth, holding us back from reaching our full potential.

The key to overcoming this fear lies in changing our relationship with rejection. Instead of viewing rejection as a final judgment or a personal failure, we can begin to see it as a natural part of life's process—a stepping stone to success. The truth is, rejection is often necessary for growth. Each "no" we encounter helps refine our approach, builds our resilience, and gets us closer to the "yes" we're ultimately seeking.

In Rejection Proof, Jia Jiang demonstrates that rejection, when viewed through the right lens, can be a powerful tool for learning and self-improvement. By intentionally seeking out rejection in his experiment, Jiang desensitizes himself to the pain of rejection and begins to see it as a normal, even valuable, part of life. This shift in perspective allows him to approach challenges with greater courage and tenacity, knowing that rejection is simply part of the process.

Reframing Rejection: Every "No" Is a Stepping Stone

One of the most powerful lessons in handling rejection with grace is the ability to reframe rejection—to see it not as a failure but as a stepping stone toward eventual success. Every rejection brings with it a lesson, an opportunity for growth, and a chance to refine your approach. When we reframe rejection in this way, we begin to see it not as a reflection of our inadequacy but as a necessary part of the journey.

An entrepreneur pitching their business idea to investors might face numerous rejections before securing funding. Each rejection, while disappointing, provides valuable feedback: the pitch may need refining, the market strategy may need adjusting, or the product might require improvement. By learning from each rejection and making the necessary adjustments, the entrepreneur increases their chances of eventually receiving a "yes." In this sense, rejection is not a dead-end but a detour—a chance to recalibrate and improve.

In Rejection Proof, Jia Jiang shares an illuminating experience where, after being rejected for a bizarre request (to borrow $100 from a stranger), he asks the person why they said no. The stranger's response opens a dialogue and provides insight into how he might have framed the request differently to get a different result. By seeking to understand the reason behind the rejection, Jiang turns what could have been a disheartening experience into a learning opportunity. This shift in mindset—from viewing rejection as final to seeing it as part of a feedback loop—empowers us to grow stronger with each "no" we encounter.

Building Emotional Resilience: Strengthening Your Rejection Muscle

Emotional resilience—the ability to bounce back from setbacks—is crucial in handling rejection with grace. Like a muscle, resilience can be developed and strengthened over time through practice and exposure. The more we face rejection, the more we build our capacity to handle it without being emotionally devastated. This resilience allows us to keep moving forward, even when the road is filled with obstacles.

One way to build emotional resilience is to gradually expose yourself to rejection in low-stakes situations. Just as Jia Jiang sought out rejection intentionally, you can practice facing rejection in areas of life where the stakes are not too high. For example, ask for a discount at a coffee shop or request a favor from a friend that you know might be declined. These small acts of seeking rejection help desensitize you to the fear of hearing "no," making it easier to handle more significant rejections in the future.

Another key to building resilience is to separate rejection from personal identity. It's essential to recognise that a rejection of your idea, proposal, or request is not a rejection of you as a person. This mental separation allows you to maintain your confidence and self-esteem, even in the face of multiple rejections. It also enables you to view rejection more objectively, as something to be analyzed and learned from, rather than a blow to your ego.

For example, an aspiring author who faces multiple rejections from publishers can choose to see each rejection as feedback on their manuscript, rather than as a personal indictment of their worth as a writer. By maintaining a growth mindset, they can refine their work, seek new opportunities, and continue pursuing their dream with resilience and grace.

Embracing Rejection as a Teacher

Rejection, when embraced, can be one of the greatest

teachers in life. Each rejection provides valuable insights that help us improve, whether it's in our professional pursuits, personal relationships, or creative endeavors. Instead of fearing rejection, we can learn to approach it with curiosity, asking ourselves: What can I learn from this experience? How can I improve? What adjustments can I make to increase my chances of success next time?

In many cases, rejection helps us clarify our goals and refine our approach. For instance, an individual who is rejected after applying for a promotion might take the opportunity to assess their skills and areas for improvement. The rejection could serve as a catalyst for professional development, prompting them to seek additional training, build new skills, or strengthen their network. In this way, rejection becomes a stepping stone to future success, guiding us toward the path of growth and self-improvement.

In Rejection Proof, Jia Jiang finds that many of the rejections he faced were not as final as they initially appeared. By simply engaging with the person who rejected him—asking follow-up questions, expressing curiosity, or reframing his request—he was able to turn some "no's" into "yes's." This experience highlights an important lesson: rejection is often not the end of the conversation, but the beginning of a new dialogue. By staying open, flexible, and willing to learn, we can transform rejection into an opportunity for growth and connection.

The Power of Persistence: Turning "No" into "Yes"

Perhaps the most critical lesson in handling rejection

with grace is the power of persistence. Many of the world's most successful individuals faced countless rejections before achieving their goals. Their success was not defined by the absence of rejection but by their ability to persevere despite it. Each "no" became a stepping stone on the path to a "yes."

Consider the story of J.K. Rowling, who faced multiple rejections from publishers before Harry Potter was finally accepted for publication. Had she given up after the first rejection, the world would never have experienced one of the most beloved literary series of all time. Her persistence in the face of rejection is a testament to the power of resilience and determination.

In the same way, each of us has the capacity to persist in the face of rejection. By embracing the "no's" as part of the journey, we can continue moving forward, learning, and improving until we reach the "yes" that will change everything. Persistence, combined with a willingness to learn from rejection, is the key to turning setbacks into stepping stones for success.

Practical Strategies for Handling Rejection

While building emotional resilience and reframing rejection are essential components of handling rejection with grace, there are also practical strategies that can help you navigate rejection more effectively:

1. Seek Feedback: After experiencing rejection, don't be afraid to ask for feedback. Understanding the reasons behind the rejection can provide valuable insights into how you can improve or adjust your approach in the future. Feedback turns rejection into a learning

opportunity.

2. Detach from the Outcome: Instead of focusing solely on the outcome (whether it's a "yes" or "no"), focus on the process. By detaching your self-worth from the result, you free yourself from the emotional rollercoaster of rejection and can approach each situation with a sense of curiosity and growth.

3. Celebrate the Attempt: Each time you put yourself out there, you are demonstrating courage. Whether the outcome is positive or negative, celebrate the fact that you had the bravery to try. Each attempt, regardless of the result, is a victory in itself.

4. Practice Self-Compassion: Rejection can be painful, and it's important to treat yourself with kindness in the aftermath. Instead of criticizing yourself for the rejection, practice self-compassion by acknowledging that rejection is a normal part of life and a necessary part of growth. Treat yourself as you would treat a close friend who experienced a setback—with understanding, encouragement, and support.

5. Reframe Your Thinking: When faced with rejection, remind yourself that it's not a reflection of your worth. Reframe rejection as an opportunity to grow, improve, and move closer to success. Each "no" is one step closer to the "yes" you're seeking.

Turning Rejection into Opportunity

Handling rejection with grace is a skill that can transform not only how we approach challenges but also how we navigate life itself. Every "no" is not a final judgment but an opportunity to learn, grow, and refine our approach. By reframing rejection, building emotional resilience, and embracing persistence, we can turn setbacks into stepping stones toward success.

Inspired by Rejection Proof by Jia Jiang, this chapter reminds us that rejection is not something to be feared —it is something to be embraced. Each rejection carries with it a valuable lesson, and every "no" brings us one step closer to the "yes" that will change everything. By handling rejection with grace, we unlock the power to grow stronger, wiser, and more resilient in the face of life's challenges.

CHAPTER 22: THE POWER OF EMOTIONAL CONTROL

Emotions are powerful forces that shape our decisions, influence our behaviour, and define how we experience life. They can propel us to great heights or, when left unchecked, lead us down paths of regret and self-sabotage. Learning to master our emotions is not about suppressing or denying them but about understanding and harnessing their energy in a way that serves us, rather than hinders us.

Inspired by The Chimp Paradox by Dr. Steve Peters, this chapter delves into the art of emotional control—how to recognise the emotions that drive our thoughts and actions, and how to manage them effectively to achieve mental stability and success. Dr. Peters uses the metaphor of a "chimp" to describe the emotional, impulsive, and sometimes irrational part of our brain. This "chimp" is a natural part of who we are, but if left unchecked, it can dominate our decision-making processes, often leading us to act in ways that do not align with our rational, long-term goals.

By learning to recognise when our "chimp" is in control and by developing strategies to manage it, we can cultivate emotional intelligence, resilience, and clarity of thought. The power of emotional control lies not in eliminating emotions but in gaining mastery over how we respond to them, using them to fuel positive action rather than being driven by impulse or fear. In doing so, we unlock a path to greater mental well-being and success in both our personal and professional lives.

The Emotional Brain: Understanding the "Chimp" Within

At the heart of The Chimp Paradox is the idea that our brain is divided into two key systems: the "human" brain (the rational, logical part) and the "chimp" brain (the emotional, impulsive part). The "chimp" represents the emotional brain, which is responsible for our fight-or-flight responses, immediate reactions, and gut feelings. It is driven by primal instincts and emotions like fear, anger, and desire. The "human" brain, on the other hand, is responsible for logical thinking, planning, and decision-making based on long-term goals and values.

While the "chimp" brain is essential for survival—responding quickly to danger and helping us react to immediate threats—it is not always well-suited for the complexities of modern life. In many situations, the emotional brain can lead us to make impulsive decisions that we later regret or to react in ways that are disproportionate to the circumstances. The key to emotional control is recognizing when our "chimp" brain is in control and learning to manage its impulses.

Think of a situation where a colleague criticizes your work. Your "chimp" brain may immediately react with anger, interpreting the criticism as a threat to your self-worth or professional reputation. In this moment, you might feel the urge to lash out, defend yourself, or dismiss the feedback entirely. However, if you allow your "human" brain to take over, you can pause, assess the situation more objectively, and recognise that the criticism may be constructive. By managing the initial emotional reaction, you are better able to respond in a way that supports your long-term goals—improving your work and maintaining professional relationships.

Dr. Peters emphasizes that the "chimp" is not inherently bad; it plays an important role in protecting us and guiding us through life's challenges. However, it must be managed. When we allow the "chimp" to take control in situations where rational thought is needed, we risk making decisions that are emotionally charged, short-sighted, and often counterproductive.

Emotional Hijacking: When the "Chimp" Takes Over

One of the most important aspects of emotional control is recognizing when we are experiencing an emotional hijack—a situation where the "chimp" brain takes over, leading us to react impulsively or irrationally. Emotional hijacking occurs when emotions like anger, fear, or anxiety overwhelm the rational brain, making it difficult to think clearly or make sound decisions. In these moments, we often say or do things we later regret, acting out of emotion rather than reason.

For example, think of a time when you were stuck in traffic, running late for an important meeting. Your "chimp" brain likely took over, causing frustration, anger, and possibly even road rage. In that moment, the emotion of being late for the meeting became the focus, and your emotional brain reacted as though you were in danger—flooding your system with adrenaline and stress hormones. This reaction, while natural, is not helpful. It leads to increased stress, anxiety, and often poor decision-making.

Similarly, in high-stakes situations like job interviews, presentations, or public speaking, the "chimp" can trigger fear and self-doubt, leading to nervousness or a loss of confidence. Emotional hijacking in these moments can undermine your ability to perform at your best, as your emotional brain focuses on potential threats rather than the task at hand.

The first step in managing emotional hijacks is awareness. By recognizing the signs that your "chimp" brain is in control—such as rapid heartbeat, tense muscles, or a surge of emotion—you can begin to take steps to calm the "chimp" and regain control over your thoughts and actions.

Taming the "Chimp": Techniques for Emotional Control

Learning to manage the "chimp" requires practice, patience, and a set of strategies that help you regain control in moments of emotional intensity. Here are several techniques, inspired by The Chimp Paradox, that can help you tame your emotions and stay in control:

1. Pause and Reflect: When you feel your emotions rising, take a moment to pause before reacting. This simple act of delaying your response gives your "human" brain time to catch up with your "chimp" brain. By pausing, you can assess the situation more objectively and decide how you want to respond, rather than reacting impulsively.

For example, if you receive a frustrating email at work, instead of firing off an angry response, take a few minutes to step away, breathe deeply, and reflect on the best way to handle the situation. This pause can prevent you from saying something you'll later regret and allows you to respond with clarity and professionalism.

2. Acknowledge Your Emotions: Rather than trying to suppress or ignore your emotions, acknowledge them. Recognise that your "chimp" is reacting and that it's okay to feel angry, frustrated, or scared. By acknowledging your emotions, you give yourself permission to experience them without letting them dictate your actions. This self-awareness helps you separate your feelings from your behaviour.

For example, if you feel nervous before giving a presentation, say to yourself, "I'm feeling nervous because my 'chimp' is worried about how others will perceive me." By naming the emotion, you gain distance from it, making it easier to manage.

3. Challenge Irrational Thoughts: The "chimp" brain often generates irrational or exaggerated thoughts, such as "I'm going to fail" or "Everyone will think I'm incompetent." These thoughts can fuel negative

emotions and lead to self-sabotage. One way to regain control is to challenge these irrational thoughts by asking yourself, "Is this really true?" or "What evidence do I have to support this thought?"

If your "chimp" is telling you that you'll fail a test or perform poorly at an interview, ask yourself, "What preparation have I done to succeed?" By focusing on the facts rather than your fears, you can reframe the situation and reduce the emotional intensity.

4. Breathe and Relax: Deep breathing is one of the most effective ways to calm the emotional brain and activate the body's relaxation response. When you feel your emotions escalating, take several slow, deep breaths, focusing on the sensation of the breath entering and leaving your body. This simple practice helps lower your heart rate, reduce stress, and create a sense of calm.

Additionally, progressive muscle relaxation—tensing and then relaxing each muscle group in your body—can help release physical tension that often accompanies emotional stress. By physically relaxing your body, you send signals to your brain that it's safe to calm down, which can help bring your emotions under control.

5. Shift Your Focus: When the "chimp" brain is in control, it tends to focus on negative outcomes or potential threats. One way to regain emotional control is to shift your focus to something more positive or constructive. This could involve thinking about a past success, visualizing a positive outcome, or redirecting your attention to a task that requires focus.

If you're feeling overwhelmed by a challenging project, take a few moments to remind yourself of previous projects you've successfully completed. Shifting your focus to past achievements can boost your confidence and help you approach the current challenge with a more balanced perspective.

The Benefits of Emotional Control: Mental Stability and Success

Mastering your emotions offers a wide range of benefits, from improved mental stability to greater success in both personal and professional endeavors. When you are in control of your emotions, you are better equipped to navigate life's challenges with grace, resilience, and clarity. Here are some of the key benefits of emotional control:

1. Improved Decision-Making: Emotional control allows you to make decisions based on logic and long-term thinking, rather than being driven by immediate emotions. Whether in your personal life or career, the ability to think clearly under pressure leads to better outcomes and more informed choices.

A business leader who can remain calm and rational during a crisis is more likely to make decisions that benefit the company in the long run, rather than reacting impulsively to short-term pressures.

2. Enhanced Relationships: Emotions play a significant role in how we interact with others, and uncontrolled emotions can strain relationships. By managing your emotions, you can communicate more effectively, resolve conflicts more calmly, and build stronger

connections with others.

For instance, when disagreements arise in a relationship, those who can manage their emotions are better able to listen to the other person's perspective, avoid escalating the conflict, and work toward a resolution that benefits both parties.

3. Increased Resilience: Emotional control builds resilience, allowing you to bounce back from setbacks and challenges. When you can manage your emotions, you are less likely to be derailed by failure, rejection, or criticism. Instead, you can view challenges as opportunities for growth and keep moving forward with determination.

4. Greater Confidence: When you are in control of your emotions, you are more confident in your ability to handle difficult situations. This confidence stems from knowing that, no matter what life throws your way, you have the tools to stay calm, focused, and effective.

An athlete who has mastered emotional control can maintain their composure under pressure, whether they're facing a critical game or dealing with the frustration of a bad performance. This mental fortitude allows them to perform at their best, even in high-stakes situations.

5. Mental Well-Being: Emotional control is essential for maintaining mental well-being. By managing your emotions, you reduce stress, anxiety, and negative thought patterns, creating a more balanced and positive mental state. Over time, this leads to greater overall happiness and a sense of fulfillment.

Individuals who practice emotional control are better equipped to handle life's ups and downs, maintaining a sense of peace and stability even in the face of adversity.

Mastering the "Chimp" for Success and Stability

The power of emotional control lies not in denying or suppressing our emotions but in understanding and managing them. Inspired by The Chimp Paradox by Dr. Steve Peters, this chapter has explored the metaphor of the "chimp" brain—our emotional, impulsive side—and how learning to manage this part of ourselves is key to mental stability and success.

By recognizing when our "chimp" brain is in control, practicing techniques to regain emotional balance, and cultivating emotional intelligence, we can navigate life's challenges with greater clarity, resilience, and grace. Emotional control not only enhances our ability to make sound decisions but also strengthens our relationships, boosts our confidence, and promotes mental well-being.

In mastering the art of emotional control, we unlock the potential to live more purposefully, achieve our goals, and experience life with a sense of peace and fulfillment. Just as a skilled investor manages their portfolio with care and discipline, we too can manage our emotions in a way that leads to lasting success and happiness.

CHAPTER 23: MINDFULNESS FOR THE MODERN WORLD

In a society that races forward at breakneck speed, constantly multitasking and overloaded with digital distractions, the simple act of being present may seem like a forgotten art. Yet, as the modern world continues to accelerate, it's precisely mindfulness—the ability to be fully present and engaged in the moment—that offers a potent antidote to the stress, anxiety, and sense of disconnection many people experience today.

Inspired by The Power of Now by Eckhart Tolle, this chapter explores how mindfulness—the deliberate act of bringing attention to the present moment—can transform our mental and emotional health. Tolle teaches that our mental and emotional struggles often stem from our inability to live in the present. We either dwell on past regrets or future worries, thus missing the depth and peace that are only accessible in the now. This obsession with what was or what will be distracts us from the essence of life—the current moment, which is the only true reality we can ever experience.

In our hyper-connected world, where we are constantly inundated with notifications, demands for attention, and the ever-growing pressure to perform and produce, mindfulness is not just a retreat from the chaos but an active engagement with life. It is about reclaiming our attention, grounding ourselves in the here and now, and finding peace amidst the noise.

The more we understand and practice mindfulness, the better equipped we become to handle the complexities of modern life. We shift from being reactive to reflective, from being overwhelmed by external pressures to living with intentionality and awareness.

The Allure of the Present: Why Mindfulness Matters

Mindfulness—commonly understood as the state of being fully aware of the present moment without judgment—has deep roots in various philosophical and spiritual traditions, from Buddhism to Stoicism. However, it has gained significant traction in modern psychological and therapeutic contexts for its powerful effects on mental health, emotional resilience, and overall well-being.

At its core, mindfulness teaches us to quiet the mental chatter that often dominates our lives. Whether it's ruminating over past mistakes or catastrophizing about future outcomes, our minds are constantly pulled away from the present moment. This leaves us in a perpetual state of unease, as though we're living life in a fog, always chasing something just out of reach.

But why does mindfulness matter, especially in the

modern world?

1. Mindfulness Reduces Stress: Chronic stress is a hallmark of the modern age. From professional pressures to personal demands, many people feel as though they are constantly on edge. Mindfulness interrupts the cycle of stress by pulling us out of the reactive mode—where we are constantly responding to external stimuli—and into a reflective state. When we are mindful, we are better able to see situations clearly and avoid being swept up in the stress response.

A 2011 study published in Health Psychology revealed that mindfulness not only reduces perceived stress but also decreases levels of cortisol, the body's primary stress hormone. By engaging with the present moment, the body's natural relaxation response is activated, allowing us to manage stress more effectively.

2. Mindfulness Improves Focus and Clarity: In a world full of distractions, the ability to focus is a rare and valuable skill. The constant barrage of emails, messages, and social media notifications fractures our attention, making it difficult to engage deeply with any one task. Mindfulness strengthens our ability to concentrate by training the mind to focus on a single point of attention—whether it's the breath, a task, or a sensation. Over time, mindfulness improves cognitive function and helps us maintain clarity amidst the mental clutter.

3. Mindfulness Promotes Emotional Regulation: Emotions can often feel like a rollercoaster—one minute we're calm, the next we're overwhelmed by

frustration, fear, or anger. Mindfulness helps us develop the ability to observe our emotions without being swept away by them. Instead of reacting impulsively, we learn to respond thoughtfully. This emotional regulation leads to greater resilience, as we become less influenced by the highs and lows of daily life.

4. Mindfulness Cultivates Compassion and Connection: Mindfulness not only improves our relationship with ourselves but also with others. When we are fully present with another person—listening to them without judgment or distraction—our connections deepen. We become more attuned to the needs, emotions, and experiences of others, fostering greater empathy and compassion. In a world where meaningful connection is often sacrificed for digital interaction, mindfulness reintroduces genuine, human presence.

5. Mindfulness Enhances Mental Health: Numerous studies have shown that mindfulness is highly effective in treating anxiety, depression, and other mental health disorders. By grounding us in the present, mindfulness helps us break free from the cycles of negative thought patterns that fuel these conditions. In fact, mindfulness-based therapies such as Mindfulness-Based Stress Reduction (MBSR) and Mindfulness-Based Cognitive Therapy (MBCT) are now widely used in clinical settings to help individuals manage mental health challenges.

Breaking Free from the Time Trap

A fundamental teaching in The Power of Now is the idea that time is one of the primary sources of human suffering. We are either lost in the past, replaying old wounds, or anxiously anticipating the future. Rarely do we allow ourselves to simply be in the present moment, where life is actually unfolding.

This "time trap" can be likened to a mental prison. When we dwell on the past, we often experience guilt, shame, or regret—emotions that keep us tethered to experiences we can no longer change. Conversely, when we project ourselves into the future, we are consumed by anxiety, fear, and the constant sense that something is missing. This focus on time keeps us in a state of dissatisfaction, forever seeking happiness somewhere other than where we are.

Tolle's message is clear: The past is gone, and the future is not yet here. The only moment that truly exists is the present. By learning to fully inhabit the now, we free ourselves from the mental burden of time and open ourselves to the peace that is always available in the present moment.

One of the ways we can practice mindfulness is by paying attention to the body's sensations—a powerful way to anchor ourselves in the present. When our thoughts start racing, we can turn our attention to something simple, like the sensation of the breath entering and leaving the body or the feeling of our feet on the ground. These physical sensations are always present and serve as a reliable touchstone for bringing our awareness back to the now.

When we find ourselves ruminating over a past event, we can notice how that thought affects our body. Are our shoulders tensing up? Is our breath becoming shallow? By bringing attention to these physical reactions, we create space between ourselves and the thought, allowing us to return to the present without being consumed by the past.

Similarly, when we feel overwhelmed by the future—whether it's an upcoming deadline, a financial worry, or a health concern—we can gently bring our focus back to the current moment. What is happening right now? Can we give our full attention to the task or situation at hand, rather than being pulled into imagined scenarios that may never come to pass?

Mindfulness in the Digital Age: Reclaiming Our Attention

The digital age presents a unique challenge to mindfulness. With the rise of smartphones, social media, and constant connectivity, our attention has become one of the most valuable commodities. Tech companies and advertisers compete for every spare moment of our attention, bombarding us with notifications, ads, and content designed to keep us engaged and distracted. As a result, many of us struggle to maintain focus, stay present, and avoid the pull of endless digital distractions.

Mindfulness offers a way to reclaim our attention in this digital age. It helps us become more intentional about how we use technology and reminds us that we have the power to choose where our attention goes.

Here are a few strategies for practicing mindfulness in the digital age:

1. Set Boundaries Around Technology: One of the simplest ways to cultivate mindfulness in a hyper-

connected world is to set clear boundaries around technology. This might mean designating certain times of the day when you unplug from devices, such as during meals or before bed. Creating technology-free zones in your home can also help reduce the constant temptation to check your phone or computer.

Many people find that practicing a morning mindfulness ritual before checking their phones sets a calm and intentional tone for the day. Instead of immediately diving into emails or social media, you might spend the first 10–15 minutes of your day in silence, practicing meditation, mindful breathing, or journaling.

2. Practice Mindful Digital Consumption: Instead of mindlessly scrolling through social media or watching videos, bring mindfulness to your digital consumption. Before opening an app or website, ask yourself: Why am I doing this? What do I hope to gain from this experience? By becoming more intentional about how and why you engage with technology, you can break the habit of mindless consumption and focus on what truly matters.

If you find yourself mindlessly scrolling through Instagram, pause and ask yourself: Is this serving me? What am I looking for? If the answer is that you're simply trying to distract yourself or fill time, consider redirecting your attention to a more meaningful activity, such as reading, spending time with loved ones, or going for a walk.

3. Create Digital Mindfulness Practices: Mindfulness doesn't have to mean completely disconnecting from

technology. In fact, you can bring mindfulness to your digital interactions. For instance, when writing an email, take a few moments to pause, breathe, and focus on the intention behind your message. When having a video call, try to be fully present with the person you're speaking to, rather than multitasking or checking other tabs.

By bringing mindfulness into your digital life, you can transform even mundane tasks into opportunities for presence and awareness.

4. Practice Digital Minimalism: Digital minimalism is the practice of intentionally reducing digital clutter and simplifying your online life. This might involve decluttering your social media feeds, unsubscribing from emails that no longer serve you, or limiting the number of apps on your phone. By simplifying your digital environment, you create more mental space and reduce the constant bombardment of information that pulls you away from the present moment.

You might choose to delete apps that you rarely use or that contribute to feelings of anxiety or comparison. Instead, focus on curating a digital environment that supports mindfulness and well-being, such as apps for meditation, learning, or creativity.

The Power of Now: Cultivating Presence in Everyday Life

Mindfulness is not just a practice for quiet meditation or moments of stillness; it is a way of being that can be cultivated in every aspect of life. Whether you are at work, spending time with loved ones, or simply going about your daily routines, mindfulness invites you to engage fully with the present moment and experience life with greater depth, clarity, and joy.

Here are some simple ways to bring mindfulness into your everyday life:

1. Mindful Breathing: One of the simplest and most effective mindfulness practices is mindful breathing. Throughout the day, take moments to focus on your breath. Notice the sensation of the air entering and leaving your body. This practice helps ground you in the present moment and creates a sense of calm and clarity, even in the midst of a busy day.

2. Mindful Eating: Instead of rushing through meals or eating while distracted, practice mindful eating. Pay attention to the flavors, textures, and aromas of your food. Notice the sensations of chewing and swallowing. By eating mindfully, you not only enhance your enjoyment of food but also cultivate gratitude and awareness in the present moment.

3. Mindful Walking: Whether you're walking to the store, commuting to work, or taking a leisurely stroll, use walking as an opportunity to practice mindfulness. Pay attention to the sensation of your feet on the ground, the rhythm of your steps, and the movement of your body. Notice the sights and sounds around you without judgment or distraction.

4. Mindful Listening: In conversations, practice mindful listening by giving your full attention to the person speaking. Rather than thinking about what you're going to say next or being distracted by your phone, focus on

truly hearing and understanding what the other person is saying. Mindful listening deepens your connections with others and fosters empathy and understanding.

5. Mindful Work: Whether you're completing a project, attending a meeting, or answering emails, bring mindfulness to your work by focusing on one task at a time. Rather than multitasking or rushing through tasks, practice giving your full attention to the task at hand. This not only improves productivity but also reduces stress and increases satisfaction in your work.

The Profound Impact of Presence: How Mindfulness Transforms Life

The practice of mindfulness, as taught by Eckhart Tolle in The Power of Now, is not a temporary escape from the demands of life but a profound shift in how we relate to the world. By cultivating presence in each moment, we begin to experience life more fully, connecting with its richness and beauty rather than being consumed by the mental noise of past regrets or future anxieties.

Over time, mindfulness transforms not only how we experience daily life but also how we relate to ourselves and others. We become more compassionate, more grounded, and more resilient. We learn to navigate life's challenges with grace and clarity, finding peace even in the midst of chaos.

Ultimately, the practice of mindfulness reminds us that the present moment is all we truly have. When we learn to inhabit it fully, we discover that peace, joy, and fulfillment are not things we need to chase—they are available to us right here, right now.

CHAPTER 24: CREATING MENTAL SPACE

The Art Of Letting Go

In today's fast-paced world, our minds are often cluttered with endless tasks, obligations, and distractions. We juggle work, personal responsibilities, social obligations, and digital demands, often without pausing to question whether all these pursuits truly align with our core values and goals. The result is a sense of overwhelm, where we find ourselves stretched thin, constantly busy but rarely feeling truly productive or fulfilled.

Inspired by Essentialism: The Disciplined Pursuit of Less by Greg McKeown, this chapter explores the profound impact of letting go—the art of releasing unnecessary burdens and focusing only on what truly matters. McKeown's philosophy of essentialism is rooted in the idea that less is better. By stripping away the non-essential, we free up mental space, reclaim our energy, and gain clarity about our purpose in life.

Letting go is not just about decluttering our physical space but also about decluttering our minds, priorities, and commitments, allowing us to live with greater intentionality and focus.

In a world where we are constantly encouraged to do more, have more, and be more, the art of letting go can feel radical. Yet, it is only by learning to release the trivial distractions and burdens that we can fully embrace what is most essential. This chapter will explore how to identify and release the non-essentials in life, how to create mental space for what truly matters, and how letting go can transform your mental and emotional well-being.

The Problem of Overcommitment: The Tyranny of "More"

One of the greatest challenges in modern life is the pressure to say yes to everything. We live in a culture that celebrates productivity, achievement, and accumulation. Success is often measured by how much we can do, how much we can own, and how much we can accomplish. As a result, many of us fall into the trap of overcommitment, saying yes to every opportunity, task, or invitation, even when it drains our energy or distracts us from our most important goals.

This tyranny of more leads to a cycle of busyness that can be exhausting and unfulfilling. We take on more projects at work, commit to more social events, acquire more possessions, and try to maintain more relationships, all while feeling a growing sense of dissatisfaction. The more we try to do, the less effective we become, as our time and energy are spread too thin to make meaningful progress in any one area.

In Essentialism, Greg McKeown argues that the key to breaking free from this cycle is to prioritize what matters most and to let go of everything else. Essentialism is about discerning what is truly important and eliminating everything that distracts us from that focus. By doing less, we can accomplish more of what truly matters, and by letting go of the non-essentials, we create the mental space and energy to pursue our highest priorities with clarity and intention.

The Power of Saying No: Reclaiming Your Time and Energy

At the heart of essentialism is the ability to say no. This can be one of the most difficult but liberating skills to develop. Many of us feel compelled to say yes to every opportunity, whether it's a work project, a social invitation, or a favor for a friend. We fear disappointing others or missing out on potential opportunities, and as a result, we end up overloading our schedules and depleting our energy.

However, learning to say no is essential for creating mental space. Every time we say yes to something that doesn't align with our priorities, we are saying no to something else—often something more important. By learning to say no to non-essential commitments, we create room for the things that truly matter.

Here are a few principles to help you master the art of saying no:

1. Clarify Your Priorities: Before you can say no effectively, you need to have a clear sense of what

your priorities are. What are your most important goals, values, and responsibilities? What do you want to focus your time and energy on? By having a clear understanding of what matters most to you, it becomes easier to recognise when something is a distraction or a non-essential commitment.

For example, if your top priority is to advance in your career, you might decide to say no to social invitations that don't align with that goal. Similarly, if spending quality time with your family is a priority, you might choose to say no to work obligations that encroach on that time.

2. Be Polite but Firm: Saying no doesn't have to be confrontational or rude. You can decline an invitation or request politely, but be firm in your decision. A simple statement like, "Thank you for thinking of me, but I'm unable to commit to that right now," or "I'm focusing on other priorities at the moment, so I won't be able to take this on," can help you set boundaries without feeling guilty.

3. Recognise the Trade-Offs: Every decision involves a trade-off. When you say yes to one thing, you are saying no to something else. By recognizing the trade-offs involved, you can make more intentional choices about where to direct your time and energy. For example, if you say yes to a last-minute work project, you might be saying no to spending time with loved ones or taking care of your own well-being. Understanding these trade-offs helps you make decisions that are aligned with your priorities.

4. Trust Your Instincts: Often, we know when

something isn't right for us, but we ignore that instinct in favor of pleasing others or avoiding conflict. Trusting your instincts means listening to that inner voice that tells you when a commitment doesn't align with your values or when taking on something new will overextend you. By honouring your instincts, you are more likely to make decisions that support your well-being and long-term success.

Letting Go of Perfectionism: Embracing Imperfection as Essential

Another key aspect of letting go is learning to release the need for perfection. Many of us are perfectionists, constantly striving for flawless results in everything we do—whether it's our work, our appearance, or our relationships. While aiming for high standards can be valuable, the pursuit of perfection often leads to unnecessary stress, anxiety, and disappointment.

Perfectionism is a form of mental clutter. It consumes our thoughts with worries about how others perceive us, how we measure up to our own standards, and how we can avoid making mistakes. In reality, perfection is an illusion—it's an unattainable goal that keeps us in a state of constant dissatisfaction. Letting go of perfectionism means accepting that we are human, that mistakes and imperfections are a natural part of life, and that we can still achieve greatness without being flawless.

Here are a few ways to let go of perfectionism:

1. Set Realistic Expectations: Instead of holding yourself to an impossible standard, set realistic

expectations for what you can accomplish. Recognise that it's okay to do things well without doing them perfectly. By focusing on progress rather than perfection, you free yourself from the burden of trying to achieve the unattainable.

If you're working on a project at work, set a realistic timeline and goal for what you want to achieve. Rather than trying to produce a perfect outcome, focus on delivering something that meets the key objectives and allows for learning and improvement along the way.

2. Practice Self-Compassion: Letting go of perfectionism requires self-compassion—the ability to be kind and understanding toward yourself when things don't go as planned. Instead of criticizing yourself for mistakes or imperfections, practice acknowledging them without judgment. Remind yourself that everyone makes mistakes and that failure is often a stepping stone to growth and success.

3. Embrace "Good Enough": Sometimes, done is better than perfect. When you're caught in the cycle of perfectionism, you may spend excessive time refining, tweaking, and polishing something that is already good enough. Learn to recognise when something meets the necessary standards and let it go. By embracing "good enough," you free yourself to move on to more important tasks and avoid wasting time on unnecessary revisions.

4. Celebrate Imperfections: Instead of seeing imperfections as failures, celebrate them as part of the creative process. Mistakes and imperfections often lead to unexpected insights, innovations, and opportunities

for growth. By embracing imperfection, you allow yourself to take risks, experiment, and learn from your experiences.

Decluttering the Mind: Releasing Mental and Emotional Baggage

In addition to letting go of external commitments and perfectionism, creating mental space requires releasing mental and emotional baggage. Many of us carry around unresolved emotions, negative thought patterns, and limiting beliefs that clutter our minds and prevent us from living fully in the present. Letting go of this baggage is essential for achieving mental clarity and emotional freedom.

Here are some ways to declutter the mind and release what no longer serves you:

1. Let Go of Resentment and Grudges: Holding onto resentment or grudges is one of the most significant sources of emotional clutter. When we hold onto past hurts, we keep ourselves trapped in a cycle of anger and bitterness, which drains our energy and prevents us from moving forward. Letting go of resentment doesn't mean condoning the actions of others; it means freeing yourself from the emotional burden of carrying that anger.

Forgiveness is a powerful tool for letting go. By choosing to forgive, you release the hold that past wrongs have over your emotions and create space for healing and peace.

2. Release Negative Thought Patterns: Many of us have internal narratives that are filled with self-doubt, fear,

and negativity. These thought patterns clutter our minds and prevent us from seeing opportunities, taking risks, and believing in our own potential. Letting go of negative thought patterns involves recognizing when they arise and challenging their validity.

If you find yourself thinking, "I'm not good enough," or "I always fail," ask yourself whether these thoughts are based in reality. Often, negative thoughts are distortions of the truth, rooted in fear or past experiences. By challenging these thoughts and replacing them with more empowering beliefs, you create mental space for confidence and self-growth.

3. Unburden Yourself from Others' Expectations: Another source of mental clutter is the pressure to meet the expectations of others. Whether it's societal norms, family expectations, or workplace pressures, many of us carry the weight of trying to live up to what others want or expect from us. This can lead to feelings of inadequacy, stress, and dissatisfaction.

Letting go of others' expectations means embracing your own path and values. It requires you to get clear on what you truly want and to have the courage to pursue it, even if it goes against the grain. By releasing the need to please everyone else, you free yourself to live authentically and with purpose.

4. Practice Mindfulness and Presence: One of the most effective ways to declutter the mind is through mindfulness—the practice of being fully present in the moment. When we are caught up in worries about the future or regrets about the past, our minds become cluttered with thoughts that distract us from

the present. Mindfulness helps us let go of these distractions and focus on what is happening right now.

By practicing mindfulness, whether through meditation, breathing exercises, or simply paying attention to the present moment, you create mental space for clarity, peace, and intentionality.

Essentialism: The Disciplined Pursuit of Less

At its core, essentialism is about the disciplined pursuit of less—focusing on the few things that matter most and letting go of the rest. It's a mindset that challenges the modern assumption that more is better and invites us to question what truly adds value to our lives.

Essentialism is not about doing less for the sake of doing less. It's about doing less, but better. It's about making deliberate, thoughtful choices about where to direct your time and energy, so that you can achieve greater impact and fulfillment.

When we embrace essentialism, we give ourselves permission to let go of the non-essential—whether it's unnecessary tasks, toxic relationships, outdated beliefs, or material possessions that no longer serve us. By focusing on what is truly essential, we create space for creativity, growth, and meaningful progress.

The Freedom of Letting Go

The art of letting go is not about giving up or shrinking your ambitions. It's about creating the mental space and clarity you need to focus on what truly matters. Inspired by Essentialism by Greg McKeown, this chapter has explored the power of prioritizing what is most important, saying no to distractions, and releasing the mental and emotional clutter that weighs us down.

When we let go of the non-essential, we free ourselves to live more fully, more intentionally, and more joyfully. By practicing the art of letting go, we create the mental space needed to pursue our highest priorities with clarity and purpose, and we unlock the path to a life of greater meaning, fulfillment, and success.

CHAPTER 25: DEALING WITH LIFE'S UNCERTAINTIES

In life, we often find ourselves at the mercy of events beyond our control, swept up by circumstances we could never have predicted or planned for. From sudden personal crises to global catastrophes, uncertainty is an inescapable part of the human experience. Yet, despite its omnipresence, we spend much of our lives trying to minimize, control, or deny the existence of uncertainty. We create elaborate plans, build stable careers, and seek financial security in the hope that these measures will shield us from the unknown. But as the world constantly reminds us, no amount of planning or precaution can fully protect us from the unpredictable nature of life.

Inspired by The Black Swan by Nassim Nicholas Taleb, this chapter delves into the concept of uncertainty—not as something to be feared or avoided but as a force to be understood, embraced, and even used to our advantage. Taleb introduces the idea of "black swan" events: rare, unpredictable occurrences that have an outsized impact on our lives. These events—such as financial market crashes, political upheavals, natural disasters, or personal crises—often seem impossible to foresee, yet they reshape the course of history and individual lives alike.

Rather than trying to predict or control these black swan events, Taleb advocates for a mindset shift. Instead of fearing the unknown, we should focus on building resilience and adaptability so that when the unpredictable occurs, we are not only prepared to survive but capable of thriving. This chapter explores how to navigate life's uncertainties, how to build a mindset that embraces the unpredictable, and how to use uncertainty as a catalyst for growth and success.

The Myth of Predictability: Why We Overestimate Our Control

Human beings have a natural tendency to seek patterns, predict outcomes, and assume a degree of control over their environment. This is an evolutionary trait that has served us well throughout history. By identifying predictable patterns—whether in nature, social dynamics, or personal behaviour—we have been able to mitigate risks, plan for the future, and make informed decisions. However, this desire for predictability often leads us to overestimate our ability to foresee and control events.

In The Black Swan, Taleb argues that much of what we consider predictable is, in fact, illusory. We like to believe that the world is orderly and that we can anticipate the future based on past trends. However, the most significant and transformative events—the ones that truly shape history and our lives—are often those we never see coming. These black swan events are outliers, falling outside the realm of normal expectations, and their impact is both profound and unexpected.

Consider the financial crises that have rocked global economies—few predicted the exact timing of the 2008 financial collapse or the economic upheaval caused by the COVID-19 pandemic. Yet these events fundamentally altered the course of the world economy, reshaping industries, policies, and livelihoods in ways that no one could have foreseen. Similarly, in our personal lives, unexpected tragedies, health crises, or sudden career opportunities can dramatically change the trajectory of our futures.

One of the key lessons from Taleb's work is that uncertainty is not a problem to be solved but a reality to be embraced. The more we accept that we cannot predict or control everything, the more we can focus on what we can control: our responses, our resilience, and our ability to adapt to change.

Black Swan Events: Recognizing the Power of the Unforeseen

A black swan event, as defined by Taleb, has three key characteristics:

1. Rarity: Black swan events are rare and fall outside the realm of normal expectations. They are not the kinds of occurrences we can easily anticipate based on previous experience or patterns. For example, the

invention of the internet, the fall of the Berlin Wall, and the 9/11 terrorist attacks were all black swan events—completely unforeseen, yet they had a profound impact on the world.

2. Extreme Impact: These events have a disproportionate effect on our lives, industries, and societies. Black swan events are not minor disruptions but seismic shifts that fundamentally change the status quo. Whether it's a global pandemic, a technological breakthrough, or a personal loss, these events reshape the world in ways that are often irreversible.

3. Retrospective Predictability: After a black swan event occurs, we often rationalize it in hindsight, convincing ourselves that we "should have seen it coming." This phenomenon, known as hindsight bias, makes us believe that the event was more predictable than it actually was. In reality, black swan events are inherently unpredictable, and their occurrence defies logical explanation until after the fact.

After the 2008 financial crisis, many analysts and economists pointed to warning signs that had been present for years, suggesting that the crash could have been predicted. However, at the time, very few people actually foresaw the extent of the crisis or its global ramifications.

Black swan events remind us of the limits of our knowledge and the fallibility of our predictions. Instead of trying to forecast the next black swan, Taleb advocates for building robustness and antifragility—the ability to not only withstand shocks but to grow stronger as a result of them.

Antifragility: Thriving in the Face of Uncertainty

While traditional wisdom emphasizes building systems and strategies that are resilient—capable of withstanding shocks—Taleb introduces the concept of antifragility. Antifragile systems don't just survive uncertainty; they thrive on it. They are designed to gain strength, adaptability, and innovation from disorder and volatility. In many ways, the ability to embrace uncertainty and use it to our advantage is the ultimate form of resilience.

Think of a bodybuilder who grows stronger by subjecting their muscles to stress and strain. Each workout creates tiny tears in the muscle fibres, which then repair themselves and grow stronger. This is the essence of antifragility: stress, challenge, and uncertainty lead to growth.

How can we apply this concept to our own lives?

1. Diversify Your Investments and Skills: One of the most practical ways to build antifragility is by diversifying—whether in financial investments or personal skills. Instead of putting all your resources into one area, spread your risk across multiple domains. In financial terms, this means investing in a range of asset classes (stocks, bonds, real estate, etc.) so that if one market crashes, your entire portfolio isn't wiped out.

In your personal life, diversifying might mean developing a variety of skills that can be applied in different contexts. For example, learning new technologies, languages, or business strategies can make you more adaptable in an unpredictable job market. The more diverse your skill set, the better equipped you are to pivot when unexpected opportunities or challenges arise.

2. Embrace Trial and Error: Uncertainty often paralyzes people because they fear making mistakes or taking risks. However, one of the keys to antifragility is embracing trial and error as a necessary part of growth. Rather than trying to avoid failure or uncertainty, actively seek out opportunities to experiment, learn, and adapt. Every failure is an opportunity for feedback, and each attempt brings you closer to success.

In business, this mindset is often referred to as "failing forward"—the idea that each failure provides valuable lessons that can be used to improve future attempts. By experimenting with new ideas, strategies, or projects, you expose yourself to potential black swan opportunities—unexpected breakthroughs or successes that can propel you forward.

3. Stay Open to Serendipity: Life's most significant opportunities often come from unexpected places. By staying open to serendipity and chance encounters, you increase the likelihood of discovering new possibilities. This might mean being willing to take on new projects, meet new people, or explore interests outside your comfort zone.

Many successful entrepreneurs didn't set out to create the businesses they now run. Instead, they stumbled upon an idea or opportunity that they hadn't initially planned for. By remaining open to the unknown, they were able to seize opportunities that others may have overlooked.

4. Build Emotional Resilience: Antifragility isn't just about external strategies; it's also about developing the inner resilience needed to navigate uncertainty. This means cultivating the mental and emotional strength to handle setbacks, challenges, and unforeseen events with grace and adaptability. Practices like mindfulness, meditation, and self-compassion can help you stay grounded in the face of uncertainty, allowing you to approach challenges with a clear and balanced mind.

Emotional resilience also involves learning to detach from rigid expectations or specific outcomes. When you are flexible and open to different possibilities, you are better able to adjust to unexpected changes and find new paths forward.

The Opportunities Hidden in Uncertainty

One of the most powerful lessons from The Black Swan is that uncertainty is not something to be feared but something to be harnessed. While black swan events can bring chaos and disruption, they also create opportunities for innovation, growth, and transformation.

Consider the technological breakthroughs and innovations that have emerged in the wake of crises. The internet, once an obscure technology, became one of the most transformative forces in history after a series of unexpected developments. Similarly, many of today's most successful companies—such as Amazon, Apple, and Netflix—grew rapidly during times of economic uncertainty or technological disruption.

In our personal lives, too, uncertainty can be a source of unexpected opportunity. A career setback might lead to a new and more fulfilling path. A personal loss might inspire us to reevaluate our priorities and find deeper meaning in life. When we embrace uncertainty as a natural part of life, we open ourselves to possibilities we might never have considered.

Practical Strategies for Navigating Uncertainty

While we cannot predict or control black swan events, we can develop strategies to navigate uncertainty with greater confidence and adaptability. Here are a few practical approaches:

1. Focus on What You Can Control: In the face of uncertainty, it's easy to feel overwhelmed by factors beyond your control. However, focusing on what you can control—such as your mindset, actions, and responses—helps you regain a sense of agency. Identify the areas where you can take decisive action, whether it's improving your skills, strengthening your relationships, or building a financial safety net.

2. Prepare for Multiple Scenarios: Rather than trying to predict the future, prepare for a range of possible outcomes. This might involve creating contingency plans or building flexibility into your personal and professional life. For example, if you're starting a new business, consider how you would adapt if market conditions change or if key partnerships fall through. By planning for multiple scenarios, you increase your ability to pivot when the unexpected occurs.

3. Cultivate a Growth Mindset: A growth mindset—the

belief that challenges and setbacks are opportunities for learning—helps you navigate uncertainty with resilience and optimism. Instead of seeing uncertainty as a threat, view it as a chance to grow, adapt, and evolve. This mindset shift allows you to approach the unknown with curiosity and creativity, rather than fear.

4. Strengthen Your Support Network: Having a strong support network of friends, family, and mentors can make all the difference when navigating uncertain times. Surround yourself with people who can provide guidance, encouragement, and perspective. Building relationships based on trust and mutual support helps you weather life's challenges and embrace opportunities for collaboration.

Embracing the Unknown

Life's uncertainties, while daunting, offer profound opportunities for growth, transformation, and success. Inspired by The Black Swan by Nassim Nicholas Taleb, this chapter has explored how to navigate unpredictable events and use uncertainty as an advantage. Rather than fearing the unknown, we can learn to embrace it—building resilience, adaptability, and antifragility in the process.

By focusing on what we can control, preparing for multiple scenarios, and cultivating a mindset that thrives on challenges, we unlock the potential to turn life's most unpredictable moments into stepping stones toward success. In a world filled with uncertainty, the key to thriving lies not in avoiding black swan events but in learning to dance with them, using their unpredictability to propel us forward into new and uncharted territories.

CHAPTER 26: DISCOVERING YOUR PERSONAL VALUES

In a world filled with distractions, material pursuits, and societal pressures, the search for meaning is one of the most profound quests of human life. Beneath the surface of daily routines, achievements, and desires lies a deeper yearning—the need to live with purpose, to find significance in our actions, and to understand why we are here. At the heart of this search for meaning lies the discovery of our personal values—the guiding principles that shape our decisions, inform our behaviour, and give our lives a sense of direction.

Inspired by Viktor Frankl's seminal work, Man's Search for Meaning, this chapter delves into the importance of understanding your core values and how they serve as a foundation for living a purposeful life. Frankl, a Holocaust survivor and psychiatrist, famously argued that the pursuit of meaning is one of the most fundamental human drives. In the face of suffering, hardship, or uncertainty, it is the search for purpose and meaning that allows individuals to transcend their circumstances and find fulfillment, even in the most challenging conditions.

This chapter will explore how discovering your personal values is key to living a life that is aligned with your deepest sense of purpose. By understanding what truly matters to you—beyond external success, societal expectations, or fleeting desires—you can begin to make decisions that reflect your authentic self. In doing so, you unlock the potential to live with greater clarity, fulfillment, and resilience, no matter the challenges you face.

The Search for Meaning: Why Values Matter

At the core of Viktor Frankl's philosophy is the idea that life's meaning is not something we discover externally, but something we create internally. This meaning is deeply personal, unique to each individual, and often rooted in our values. But what are values, and why are they so essential to living a purposeful life?

Values are the fundamental beliefs that guide our choices and behaviour. They represent what is most important to us and serve as an internal compass that helps us navigate life's challenges, opportunities, and moral dilemmas. Values are not the same as goals or desires; rather, they are the underlying motivations that inform how we pursue those goals and desires. While goals may change over time, our values tend to remain relatively stable, providing a sense of continuity and meaning throughout our lives.

Someone who values compassion may choose a career

in healthcare, driven by a desire to help others. Another person who values adventure may prioritize travel and exploration, seeking experiences that challenge them and push their boundaries. In both cases, it is the core value—whether compassion or adventure—that provides meaning and direction, guiding the individual's choices and shaping their sense of purpose.

Understanding our personal values is essential because they serve as a lens through which we interpret the world and make decisions. When we live in alignment with our values, we experience a sense of authenticity and fulfillment. Conversely, when we live in conflict with our values—perhaps by pursuing a career or lifestyle that doesn't resonate with what we truly care about—we may feel disconnected, unfulfilled, or even lost.

In Man's Search for Meaning, Frankl observed that even in the most dire circumstances, such as the horrors of concentration camps, individuals who held onto a sense of purpose—whether through love, faith, or a commitment to a greater cause—were more likely to survive and find meaning in their suffering. Their values provided them with a reason to endure and a sense of hope, even when faced with unimaginable hardship.

Discovering Your Core Values: A Path to Self-Understanding

The journey to discovering your core values begins with self-reflection. While many of us are aware of certain values we hold dear, we may not always be fully conscious of the deeper values that shape our actions and decisions. To truly live a purposeful life, it's essential to explore and clarify what matters most to us at the deepest level.

Here are a few steps to help you discover your core values:

1. Reflect on Meaningful Experiences: One of the best ways to uncover your values is by reflecting on experiences that have been deeply meaningful to you. These are moments when you felt a strong sense of fulfillment, joy, or connection—times when you felt truly alive. Think about what these experiences had in common. What values were being expressed or honoured in those moments?

You might recall a time when you volunteered at a community event and felt a profound sense of purpose. The value at play here could be service or community. Or perhaps you remember a time when you took a solo trip and felt empowered by the freedom and independence it gave you, reflecting a core value of autonomy or exploration.

2. Examine What Triggers You: Another way to identify your values is by paying attention to situations that trigger strong emotional reactions—whether positive or negative. When we feel deeply upset, angry, or frustrated, it's often because one of our core values is being violated. Similarly, when we feel inspired or uplifted, it's often because our values are being affirmed.

For instance, if you feel angry when you see injustice or inequality, it may point to a core value of fairness or justice. If you feel joyful and energized in nature, it could reflect a value of connection to the environment or peace.

3. Identify Role Models: Think about people you admire —whether they are public figures, historical icons, or individuals in your personal life. What qualities or actions do you admire in them? Often, the traits we admire in others reflect the values we hold most dear. For example, if you admire someone's dedication to speaking out against oppression, it may indicate that courage or activism is an important value for you.

Similarly, if you admire someone for their creativity and ability to think outside the box, it may point to a value of innovation or individuality.

4. Consider Your Ideal Life: Imagine your ideal life —the life that would bring you the most fulfillment and happiness. What would it look like? What would you be doing? Who would you be surrounded by? By envisioning your ideal life, you can gain insight into the values that are most important to you. For example, if your ideal life involves spending time with loved ones, it may reflect a value of family or relationships. If it involves pursuing creative projects or intellectual challenges, it may reflect a value of creativity or knowledge.

5. Prioritize Your Values: Once you've identified a list of values that resonate with you, it's important to prioritize them. Not all values carry the same weight, and some may be more central to your identity and purpose than others. By prioritizing your values, you can gain clarity on which ones should guide your most

important decisions.

If you value both adventure and security, but adventure ranks higher, you may prioritize experiences that challenge you and push you out of your comfort zone, even if they involve some risk. On the other hand, if security ranks higher, you may make choices that prioritize stability and predictability.

Living in Alignment with Your Values

Once you've identified your core values, the next step is to align your actions, decisions, and goals with those values. Living in alignment with your values is essential for creating a sense of purpose and fulfillment in your life. When your actions reflect your deepest values, you experience a sense of coherence between who you are and how you live.

Here are a few ways to live in alignment with your values:

1. Make Value-Based Decisions: When faced with important decisions, ask yourself how each option aligns with your core values. Instead of making decisions based solely on external factors—such as money, status, or convenience—consider how the decision aligns with what truly matters to you. By making value-based decisions, you ensure that your choices are in harmony with your authentic self.

Don't just focus on the salary or benefits if you're considering a new job opportunity. Ask yourself how the job aligns with your core values. Does it provide opportunities for growth, creativity, or service? Does it allow you to work in an environment that reflects your values of integrity or collaboration? By making decisions that honour your values, you create a life that is more meaningful and fulfilling.

2. Set Value-Driven Goals: When setting goals, it's important to ensure that they are aligned with your core values. Goals that are disconnected from your values may lead to temporary success but are unlikely to bring lasting fulfillment. By setting value-driven goals, you create a sense of purpose and motivation that goes beyond external achievements.

If one of your core values is health, you might set a goal to improve your physical fitness, not just to lose weight or look a certain way, but because it reflects your commitment to taking care of your body and well-being. Similarly, if you value personal growth, you might set a goal to learn a new skill or pursue further education, not just for career advancement but because it aligns with your desire for continuous learning and development.

3. Assess Your Relationships: Our relationships play a significant role in shaping our sense of purpose and fulfillment. Take time to assess whether your relationships—whether personal, professional, or social—are aligned with your values. Are you surrounded by people who support and reflect your values, or are there relationships that conflict with what matters most to you?

Living in alignment with your values may mean making changes in your relationships—whether that involves setting boundaries with people who undermine your values or seeking out new relationships that affirm and support your growth.

4. Practice Integrity: Integrity is the practice of living in alignment with your values, even when it's difficult. This means being true to yourself and your principles, regardless of external pressures or temptations. Practicing integrity requires courage, as it often involves making choices that are not popular or easy, but that reflect your core beliefs.

For example, if honesty is one of your core values, practising integrity might mean speaking up about something that feels wrong, even when it's uncomfortable. If environmental responsibility is a core value, it might mean making choices that reduce your environmental impact, even if they require extra effort or sacrifice.

5. Reflect Regularly: Living in alignment with your values is an ongoing process that requires self-awareness and reflection. Take time regularly to reflect on whether your actions, decisions, and goals are in harmony with your values. Are there areas of your life where you've strayed from your values? Are there opportunities to bring more alignment into your daily routines or long-term plans?

By reflecting regularly, you can stay grounded in your values and adjust as needed to ensure that you are living a life that is true to yourself.

The Power of Purpose: How Values Create Meaning

At the heart of Viktor Frankl's philosophy is the idea that purpose is essential for enduring life's challenges and finding meaning, even in the most difficult circumstances. Our values provide the foundation for this sense of purpose, guiding us through adversity and helping us navigate life's complexities with resilience and strength.

When we live in alignment with our values, we experience a sense of purpose that transcends external achievements or circumstances. This purpose gives our lives direction and helps us find meaning in both the joys and sorrows of life. It provides us with a sense of agency—the belief that we can shape our lives and make choices that reflect our deepest sense of self.

For example, someone who values love and connection may find purpose in nurturing their relationships with family and friends, even during difficult times. Another person who values creativity and innovation may find purpose in expressing themselves through art, writing, or entrepreneurship, regardless of external recognition or success.

Ultimately, living in alignment with your values is the key to living with purpose and meaning. When your actions reflect your values, you experience a deep sense of fulfillment that comes from knowing you are living authentically and making choices that are true to who you are.

The Path to a Meaningful Life

Discovering your personal values is one of the most important steps in the search for meaning and purpose. Inspired by Man's Search for Meaning by Viktor Frankl, this chapter has explored how understanding your core values can guide your decisions, shape your goals, and create a life that is deeply fulfilling.

When you live in alignment with your values, you create a sense of coherence and integrity that transcends external circumstances. Your values provide a foundation for resilience, helping you navigate life's challenges with strength and clarity. By embracing your values and living with purpose, you unlock the potential to lead a life that is not only successful but also profoundly meaningful.

CHAPTER 27: PASSION VS. PERSISTENCE

The True Key To Fulfillment

In our culture, we are often told to "follow our passion." Whether in personal pursuits, relationships, or careers, passion is frequently positioned as the golden key to success and fulfillment. It is the spark that ignites excitement and enthusiasm, the force that propels us toward our dreams. However, what happens when passion wanes? What happens when the initial excitement fades, obstacles appear, and progress seems painstakingly slow? Does passion alone sustain us through these inevitable hardships?

Inspired by Grit by Angela Duckworth, this chapter delves into the fundamental difference between passion and persistence, exploring how true success and fulfillment are not born solely from the fire of passion, but from the steady and enduring force of grit—the relentless pursuit of long-term goals, sustained by perseverance and a deep commitment to seeing things through, even when the road gets tough.

Duckworth's groundbreaking research reveals that while passion is an essential starting point, it is persistence that ultimately determines whether or not we succeed. Grit, defined as "passion and perseverance for long-term goals," is the quality that allows people to continue working toward their ambitions despite challenges, setbacks, or the passage of time. It is the ability to stick with something even when it's no longer exciting or fun, when the novelty has worn off and the effort required feels overwhelming.

This chapter will explore the balance between passion and persistence, offering insights into how to cultivate grit and why it is the true key to fulfillment in any meaningful endeavor. By understanding the limits of passion and embracing the power of perseverance, we unlock the potential for long-term success, personal growth, and a deeper sense of purpose.

The Allure of Passion: A Powerful but Fleeting Force

There is no denying the power of passion. It is often the initial spark that ignites our interest in a particular field, project, or relationship. Passion can be exhilarating, filling us with energy, enthusiasm, and motivation. It inspires creativity, innovation, and bold action. When we are passionate about something, we are often willing to pour our time, effort, and resources into it, driven by a sense of excitement and possibility.

Passion is also deeply tied to our sense of identity. It helps us define who we are and what we care about. For many, discovering a passion feels like discovering a core aspect of themselves—whether it's a love for music, an interest in social justice, or a commitment to a particular career path. Passion gives us direction and purpose, making life feel more meaningful and engaging.

However, as powerful as passion can be, it is inherently fleeting. Passion, by its nature, ebbs and flows. It is subject to external conditions, emotional states, and changing circumstances. What excites us today may not excite us tomorrow. Passion is a force that, while initially strong, often diminishes over time as we encounter the inevitable difficulties and obstacles of any pursuit. The reality is that every meaningful endeavor—whether it's building a career, developing a skill, or maintaining a relationship—will eventually hit moments of frustration, boredom, or disappointment.

Consider the example of an aspiring writer who is deeply passionate about storytelling. In the beginning, they may be filled with creative ideas, eager to put words on the page, and excited about the possibility of publishing a book. However, as they progress, they encounter the difficulties of writing—writer's block, rejection from publishers, and the painstaking process of revising drafts. The initial passion that drove them to start the project begins to fade, and without the presence of persistence, they may give up before they achieve their goal.

This is where the limits of passion become clear. Passion alone is not enough to sustain long-term success or fulfillment. It is a powerful motivator at the start of a journey, but it cannot carry us through the inevitable hardships that arise along the way. Passion must be accompanied by another, more enduring quality: persistence.

Persistence: The Power of Grit

While passion may initiate a journey, persistence is what ensures we complete it. Persistence is the quality that allows us to keep going even when the excitement fades, when progress is slow, and when challenges seem insurmountable. It is the ability to stay committed to our long-term goals, even when the road is hard and the outcome uncertain.

In Grit, Angela Duckworth's research shows that persistence—often referred to as "grit"—is a far better predictor of success than talent, intelligence, or even passion alone. Those who possess grit are able to push through the inevitable obstacles and setbacks that arise on the path to achieving something meaningful. They are not deterred by failure or frustration; instead, they see these challenges as part of the process and remain focused on their ultimate goal.

Duckworth defines grit as a combination of passion and perseverance for long-term goals. While passion provides the initial motivation, it is perseverance that sustains us over time. Gritty individuals are not necessarily those who are the most talented or naturally gifted; rather, they are those who are willing to work hard, put in the time, and persist through difficulty.

One of the most famous examples of grit is Thomas Edison, the inventor of the electric light bulb. Edison famously failed thousands of times before finally inventing a working light bulb. When asked about his failures, he reportedly said, "I have not failed. I've just found 10,000 ways that won't work." Edison's success was not due to a singular moment of inspiration or passion; it was the result of relentless persistence and a refusal to give up, even in the face of repeated failure.

Similarly, J.K. Rowling, the author of the Harry Potter series, faced numerous rejections from publishers before her manuscript was finally accepted. Had she given up after the first or second rejection, the world would never have known the magic of Harry Potter. Her persistence, even in the face of adversity, is a testament to the power of grit.

The Myth of Effortless Success

One of the reasons persistence is often undervalued in our culture is because of the myth of effortless success. We are often drawn to stories of people who seem to achieve greatness with ease—whether it's a brilliant musician who seems to play effortlessly, a charismatic entrepreneur who appears to strike gold with their first business venture, or an artist whose talent seems to emerge naturally.

These narratives, however, are misleading. Behind every story of "overnight success" is a long and often grueling process of hard work, failure, and persistence. The world may only see the final result, but the reality is that most successful people spend years honing their craft, making mistakes, and learning from failure. Success, especially in meaningful endeavors, is rarely a straight path; it is a journey filled with detours, setbacks, and moments of doubt.

For example, Michael Jordan, widely regarded as one of the greatest basketball players of all time, was cut from his high school basketball team. Instead of giving up, he used that setback as fuel for his relentless work ethic, pushing himself to practice harder and improve his skills. Jordan's success was not the result of innate talent alone; it was the product of years of dedication, discipline, and persistence.

The myth of effortless success can be damaging because it creates unrealistic expectations. When people encounter obstacles or setbacks, they may mistakenly believe that they are not "good enough" or that they lack the necessary talent. In reality, what they may lack is not talent or passion, but the persistence to keep going in the face of difficulty. Understanding that success requires persistence helps us reframe setbacks as part of the journey, rather than signs of failure.

The Role of Passion in Grit

While persistence is the driving force behind long-term success, passion still plays an important role in the equation. Passion is what gives our efforts direction and meaning. It helps us identify what we care about and what we want to achieve. Without passion, persistence can become aimless or misdirected.

In Grit, Duckworth emphasizes that the most successful individuals are those who have both passion and perseverance for their long-term goals. Passion provides the "why"—the deep sense of purpose and commitment that keeps us motivated even when the work is hard. However, passion must be sustained by persistence, or else it risks fading over time.

The key to maintaining passion over the long haul is to cultivate a deep and enduring commitment to a goal or purpose, rather than relying on the fleeting excitement of new interests. Duckworth distinguishes between two types of passion: surface-level passion and deep passion. Surface-level passion is the kind of excitement we feel when we first discover something new and exciting. It's the thrill of starting a new project, learning a new skill, or pursuing a new opportunity. However, this type of passion is often short-lived and fades when challenges arise.

Deep passion, on the other hand, is rooted in a sense of purpose and meaning. It is not dependent on external excitement or novelty; instead, it comes from a deeper commitment to a long-term goal or value. People with deep passion are able to sustain their interest and effort over time, even when the initial excitement fades, because they are driven by something greater than momentary enthusiasm.

For example, a musician with deep passion may continue practicing their instrument even when they encounter difficult pieces or face criticism because they are deeply committed to their craft and their love of music. Their passion is not just about the thrill of playing; it's about the joy of mastering their art and expressing themselves through music.

Cultivating Grit: How to Build Persistence

While some people may naturally possess a high level of grit, Duckworth's research suggests that grit can be cultivated and developed over

time. Persistence is not a fixed trait; it is a skill that can be strengthened through deliberate practice and mindset shifts.

Here are a few ways to cultivate grit in your own life:

1. Develop a Growth Mindset: A growth mindset, as defined by psychologist Carol Dweck, is the belief that abilities and intelligence can be developed through effort and learning. People with a growth mindset view challenges and failures as opportunities for growth, rather than as reflections of their limitations. By adopting a growth mindset, you can build resilience and persistence in the face of difficulty.

For example, instead of thinking, "I'm just not good at this," you can reframe your thinking to, "I'm not good at this yet, but with practice, I can improve." This mindset shift helps you stay motivated and persistent, even when progress is slow.

2. Break Goals into Smaller Steps: One of the reasons people give up on long-term goals is that they can feel overwhelming or unattainable. To build persistence, break your larger goals into smaller, manageable steps. Each small victory reinforces your commitment and builds momentum, making it easier to stay persistent over the long term.

For example, if your goal is to write a novel, focus on writing a small number of words each day. Over time, these small efforts will accumulate into a finished book. By breaking the larger goal into smaller tasks, you reduce the sense of overwhelm and increase your ability to persist.

3. Embrace Challenges: Persistence is built by embracing challenges, not avoiding them. When you encounter a difficult task or a setback, approach it as an opportunity to learn and grow. Each time you push through a challenge, you strengthen your ability to persist in the face of adversity.

For example, if you're learning a new skill and find it difficult at first, resist the temptation to give up. Instead, keep practicing and seek out feedback. Over time, the challenge will become more manageable, and your persistence will pay off.

4. Stay Connected to Your Purpose: To maintain persistence over the long term, it's important to stay connected to your deeper sense of purpose. Remind yourself why you started your journey in the first place and what you hope to achieve. By keeping your ultimate goal in mind, you can stay motivated even when the work becomes difficult or monotonous.

For example, if you're training for a marathon and feel discouraged during long runs, remind yourself of why you decided to run in the first place—whether it's for personal achievement, health, or a cause you care about. Staying connected to your "why" helps you push through the tough moments.

The True Key to Fulfillment

The path to success and fulfillment is not paved with passion alone. While passion provides the initial spark, it is persistence—the ability to stay committed to long-term goals in the face of adversity—that truly leads to meaningful achievement. Inspired by Grit by Angela Duckworth, this chapter has explored the balance between passion and persistence, highlighting the importance of grit in navigating life's challenges and pursuing our deepest ambitions.

By cultivating persistence, developing a growth mindset, and staying connected to our sense of purpose, we unlock the power to achieve long-term success and fulfillment. Passion may light the way, but it is persistence that carries us to the finish line.

CHAPTER 28: ALIGNING YOUR LIFE WITH PURPOSE

In a world driven by goals, achievements, and constant progress, it is easy to get caught up in the whirlwind of doing without truly understanding the reason behind it all. We often focus on what we do and how we do it, while neglecting the most important question: why do we do it? What drives our actions, decisions, and the trajectory of our lives? For many, the lack of a clearly defined purpose—the absence of a strong "why"—leads to burnout, disconnection, and a sense of aimlessness.

Inspired by Simon Sinek's groundbreaking work Start with Why, this chapter explores the transformative power of defining your "why" and aligning your life with that deeper sense of purpose. According to Sinek, people and organizations that achieve the most profound levels of fulfillment and success are those who start with why—they understand the core reason behind their actions, decisions, and pursuits. The "why" is the driving force that gives meaning to everything else, providing clarity and direction.

This chapter will explore the importance of discovering your "why," how it shapes your sense of purpose, and how aligning your life with that purpose leads to greater fulfillment and satisfaction. By understanding the power of purpose and how to integrate it into every facet of your life, you can transform not only what you do but how you experience life itself.

The Importance of Why: More Than a Mission Statement

In Start with Why, Simon Sinek emphasizes that understanding your "why" is not just about crafting a mission statement or setting lofty goals. Rather, your "why" is the deep-seated belief, value, or purpose that fuels your actions. It is the reason you get up in the morning, the motivation that sustains you during difficult times, and the guiding principle that helps you make decisions.

Sinek's framework for understanding "why" is often applied to organizations, helping them clarify their core purpose to inspire employees, attract loyal customers, and build lasting success. However, this concept is equally applicable to individuals. Just as businesses thrive when they have a clear sense of purpose, so too do people when they understand why they are pursuing certain goals or living a certain way.

Your "why" provides a foundation for everything you do. It gives your life meaning beyond external achievements and provides a compass for navigating challenges and uncertainties. Without a clearly defined "why," even success can feel hollow, as it becomes disconnected from any deeper sense of purpose or fulfillment.

Defining Your Why: Discovering the Core of Your Purpose

Discovering your "why" requires deep reflection and self-awareness. It is not always immediately obvious and may take time to uncover, but once you articulate your "why," it becomes a powerful tool for guiding your decisions and aligning your life with a sense of purpose.

Here are a few steps to help you define your "why":

1. Reflect on Your Deepest Motivations: To uncover your "why," start by asking yourself what truly motivates you. What gets you out of bed in the morning? What brings you joy, satisfaction, and a sense of fulfillment? When do you feel most engaged or energized in your work, relationships, or personal pursuits?

Reflect on moments in your life when you felt a strong sense of purpose—times when you were fully aligned with what you were doing. What values or beliefs were driving you in those moments? Your "why" is often found in the intersection of what you love to do and what you believe is important or meaningful.

For example, someone who feels most fulfilled when helping others might discover that their "why" is rooted in service or compassion. Another person who finds joy in solving complex problems might identify innovation or curiosity as core elements of their "why."

2. Examine What Gives You Meaning: Meaning is a

crucial component of defining your "why." Think about the aspects of your life that give you the most meaning. What activities, causes, or relationships do you find deeply meaningful? What contributions do you want to make to the world or to the people around you?

Sometimes, discovering your "why" involves looking beyond your immediate circumstances to the larger impact you want to have. For example, a teacher might find meaning not just in the act of teaching but in the growth and empowerment of their students. A business owner might be driven by a desire to create opportunities for others or to build something that will last beyond their lifetime.

Your "why" is often connected to a sense of contribution or legacy—what you want to leave behind and how you want to influence the world in a positive way.

3. Identify Your Core Values: Your "why" is deeply connected to your values—the principles that guide your behaviour and decisions. Take time to identify your core values, which can serve as a foundation for understanding your "why." Values such as integrity, creativity, freedom, justice, or love often point toward a deeper sense of purpose.

For example, if freedom is one of your core values, your "why" may involve creating a life or business that allows you and others to experience more freedom—whether financial, creative, or personal. If justice is a central value, your "why" might involve working toward equality or advocating for those who are marginalized.

By identifying your core values, you can begin to see patterns in your motivations and choices, helping you articulate the driving force behind your life's purpose.

4. Look for Patterns in Your Life Story: Often, your "why" can be found by looking back at the experiences and challenges that have shaped you. Think about your life story and the moments that have had the greatest impact on you—both positive and negative. What lessons have you learned? What themes or patterns emerge when you reflect on your journey?

For example, someone who has overcome significant adversity might discover that their "why" is connected to resilience or empowerment—helping others find strength and overcome challenges. Another person who has experienced a deep sense of connection through art or music might identify expression or creativity as core elements of their "why."

By reflecting on your personal story, you can often uncover the deeper motivations that have guided you, even if you were not fully aware of them at the time.

Living in Alignment with Your Why

Once you've defined your "why," the next step is to align your life with that purpose. Living in alignment with your "why" means making decisions, setting goals, and taking actions that reflect your deeper sense of purpose. It involves prioritizing what truly matters to you and letting go of distractions or obligations that are not aligned with your core values.

Here are a few ways to live in alignment with your

"why":

1. Make Purposeful Decisions: When faced with decisions—whether big or small—ask yourself how each option aligns with your "why." Does this decision bring you closer to fulfilling your purpose, or does it pull you away from what truly matters? By using your "why" as a guide, you can make decisions that reflect your values and priorities.

For example, if your "why" is rooted in creativity, you might prioritize opportunities that allow you to express yourself artistically, even if they don't offer immediate financial rewards. If your "why" is connected to community, you might choose to invest more time in building relationships and supporting others, rather than focusing solely on individual achievements.

Making purposeful decisions helps you stay true to your core values and ensures that your actions are aligned with your deeper sense of purpose.

2. Set Meaningful Goals: When setting goals, it's important to ensure that they are aligned with your "why." Goals that are disconnected from your purpose may lead to temporary success but are unlikely to bring lasting fulfillment. By setting goals that reflect your deeper motivations, you create a sense of alignment between what you're working toward and the purpose that drives you.

For example, if your "why" is about empowering others, you might set a goal to mentor younger professionals or to create a platform that amplifies marginalized voices. If your "why" is about adventure and exploration, your goals might involve traveling to new places, learning new skills, or pushing the boundaries of your comfort zone.

Setting meaningful goals helps you stay focused on what truly matters and ensures that your efforts are directed toward achieving a life that reflects your purpose.

3. Let Go of What Doesn't Serve Your Purpose: Living in alignment with your "why" often involves letting go of activities, obligations, or commitments that are not aligned with your purpose. This can be difficult, especially if those activities once seemed important or brought you success. However, by focusing on your "why," you can make room for what truly matters and avoid spreading yourself too thin.

For example, if your "why" is connected to personal growth, you might need to let go of social obligations that feel draining or unfulfilling. If your "why" is about making a positive impact on the world, you might choose to step away from a career that no longer aligns with your values and pursue something more meaningful.

Letting go of what doesn't serve your purpose allows you to focus your energy and attention on the things that truly matter, leading to greater clarity and fulfillment.

4. Stay Grounded in Your Purpose During Challenges: Life is full of challenges, setbacks, and moments of uncertainty. During difficult times, staying connected to your "why" can provide a sense of stability and

direction. When you face obstacles, remind yourself of the deeper purpose that drives you and use it as a source of motivation to keep going.

For example, if you're pursuing a career in a challenging industry, staying grounded in your "why" can help you push through setbacks and disappointments.

If your purpose is about creating something meaningful, you'll be more likely to persist through difficult moments because you're connected to something greater than immediate success or external validation.

Staying grounded in your "why" helps you maintain resilience and perseverance, even when the path ahead is uncertain or difficult.

5. Cultivate Purpose in Everyday Life: While your "why" may be connected to long-term goals or significant life achievements, it's also important to cultivate purpose in your everyday life. Purpose is not just found in grand accomplishments; it is also present in the small, meaningful moments of daily living. By bringing awareness to your "why" in everyday activities —whether it's how you interact with others, how you approach your work, or how you spend your free time— you can live with greater intention and fulfillment.

For example, if your "why" is connected to compassion, you can practice it in small ways every day—whether by offering a kind word to a colleague, helping a neighbor, or simply being present with a loved one. If your "why" is about creativity, you can bring creativity into your daily routines—whether through cooking, journaling, or taking time to explore new ideas.

By cultivating purpose in the present moment, you create a life that is rich with meaning, even in the ordinary.

The Fulfillment of Living with Purpose

Living in alignment with your "why" brings a deep sense of fulfillment and satisfaction. When your actions, decisions, and goals are connected to your purpose, you experience a sense of coherence between who you are and how you live. This alignment provides a foundation for resilience, helping you navigate challenges with a sense of clarity and determination.

When you live with purpose, you are less likely to be swayed by external pressures or the pursuit of fleeting success. Instead, you are guided by a deeper sense of meaning, which allows you to stay focused on what truly matters, even when the path is difficult. Purpose provides a sense of direction that goes beyond immediate achievements, offering a lasting sense of fulfillment that can sustain you through the ups and downs of life.

Ultimately, defining your "why" and aligning your life with purpose is the key to living a life that is not only successful but deeply meaningful. When you start with why, you unlock the potential to live with greater intention, clarity, and joy—knowing that your actions reflect your deepest values and beliefs.

The Power of Purpose

The journey to discovering and living in alignment with your "why" is one of the most transformative paths you can take. Inspired by Start with Why by Simon Sinek, this chapter has explored the importance of defining your "why" and how living with purpose leads to greater fulfillment in all areas of life.

By understanding your core motivations, making purposeful decisions, and aligning your actions with your values, you create a life that is rich with meaning and deeply satisfying. Purpose is not just a destination but a way of living—one that brings clarity, direction, and a profound sense of fulfillment to everything you do.

CHAPTER 29: THE POWER OF GIVING

Why Helping Others Is The Key To Happiness

In a world often driven by the pursuit of personal success and achievement, the idea that true happiness comes from giving rather than getting seems almost counterintuitive. We are frequently taught to measure our lives by what we accumulate—whether it be wealth, status, or accomplishments. Yet, beneath this cultural fixation on self-interest lies a deeper truth: the greatest fulfillment in life comes not from what we gain but from what we give.

Inspired by Adam Grant's Give and Take, this chapter explores the profound impact that helping others can have on our happiness, success, and sense of purpose. Grant's research introduces a powerful distinction between givers, takers, and matchers—three types of people who approach social interactions and relationships in fundamentally different ways. Takers aim to get as much as possible from others without giving much in return; matchers seek balance, giving only when they receive something of equal value; and givers, by contrast, are those who focus on helping others, often without expecting anything in return.

Contrary to conventional wisdom, Grant argues that givers—those who prioritize helping others—are not only the most fulfilled but often the most successful in the long run. While it may seem like a selfless approach, giving unlocks a powerful cycle of reciprocity, trust, and collaboration, which leads to deeper connections, greater satisfaction, and, ultimately, lasting happiness. This chapter will delve into why giving is so powerful, how it transforms our lives, and why helping others is not just a moral imperative but the key to a more meaningful and joyful existence.

The Science of Giving: How Helping Others Boosts Happiness

Psychological research consistently shows that helping others increases happiness. Studies have found that individuals who engage in acts of kindness, generosity, and altruism experience greater levels of life satisfaction, mental well-being, and even physical health. The act of giving triggers the release of oxytocin, sometimes referred to as the "love hormone," which promotes feelings of warmth, connection, and joy. Furthermore, helping others activates the brain's reward system, giving us a natural "helper's high" that boosts our mood and sense of fulfillment.

But why is giving such a powerful driver of happiness? The answer lies in our evolutionary wiring. Humans are inherently social creatures, and our survival has long depended on our ability to form cooperative relationships with others. When we give, we strengthen social bonds, foster trust, and build a sense of community—all of which contribute to our overall well-being.

Helping others also shifts our focus away from our own problems and challenges. When we give, we move beyond the narrow confines of self-interest and connect with something larger than ourselves. This sense of connection is deeply fulfilling because it reminds us that we are part of an interconnected web of human life, and that our actions have the power to positively impact others.

For example, research has shown that individuals who volunteer their time regularly report higher levels of life satisfaction and lower levels of depression. This is not just because they are helping others, but because volunteering fosters a sense of meaning, purpose, and social connection—key ingredients for happiness.

The Three Types of People: Givers, Takers, and Matchers

In Give and Take, Adam Grant describes three types of people based on how they interact with others in social and professional settings:

1. **Takers**: Takers focus on maximizing their own gains and often see relationships as competitive. They are more concerned with what they can get from others rather than what they can give. Takers tend to view success as a zero-sum game—if someone else wins, they lose—so they focus on getting ahead at the expense of others. While takers may experience short-term success, their relationships often become strained, and

their approach can backfire in the long term.

2. Matchers: Matchers believe in fairness and reciprocity. They operate on a quid pro quo basis, giving only when they expect something in return. Matchers strive for balance in their relationships, ensuring that the scales are even. While this approach can lead to fair and equitable exchanges, it often lacks the deeper connection and trust that comes from selfless giving.

3. Givers: Givers focus on contributing to the well-being of others without expecting anything in return. They prioritize helping, supporting, and empowering those around them, often going out of their way to aid, advice, or encouragement. Givers operate from a mindset of abundance, believing that success is not a zero-sum game but something that grows when shared. While givers may sometimes be taken advantage of by others, Grant's research shows that, in the long run, givers often rise to the top in both personal fulfillment and professional success.

Givers, according to Grant, experience a unique form of success because they foster strong relationships built on trust, reciprocity, and collaboration. By focusing on helping others, they create networks of support and goodwill, which often lead to unexpected opportunities, shared successes, and deep satisfaction.

The Benefits of Giving: Why Givers Thrive

Contrary to the assumption that givers are taken advantage of or that their generosity makes them vulnerable, Grant's research demonstrates that givers often thrive—both personally and professionally. Here's why:

1. Giving Builds Trust and Reciprocity: When people see that you are genuinely interested in their well-being and success, they are more likely to trust you and offer help in return. This creates a cycle of reciprocity that benefits everyone involved. Trust is a crucial ingredient in any successful relationship, whether personal or professional. By giving first, givers earn the trust of others, which opens doors to collaboration, mentorship, and mutual support.

For example, in the workplace, employees who adopt a giving mindset by sharing their knowledge, offering help to colleagues, and mentoring others often build strong networks of trust. These networks, in turn, lead to greater opportunities for career advancement, as well as personal satisfaction in knowing they've contributed to the success of others.

2. Giving Strengthens Social Connections: One of the most powerful benefits of giving is the way it strengthens social connections. When we help others, we form deeper, more meaningful relationships. These connections are a source of emotional support, collaboration, and community—key factors in both happiness and success.

For example, someone who is known for their generosity—whether through time, advice, or resources—builds a reputation as someone others can rely on. This creates strong social bonds that are not only rewarding on a personal level but also lead to greater opportunities for teamwork, partnerships, and long-term success.

3. Giving Increases Meaning and Purpose: Givers often find that their lives are filled with a greater sense of meaning and purpose. When we help others, we connect to something larger than ourselves and contribute to the well-being of our communities, workplaces, or families. This sense of contribution is deeply fulfilling because it gives our actions significance beyond our individual desires.

For instance, a business leader who mentors young entrepreneurs, offering guidance and resources to help them succeed, may find profound satisfaction in seeing others flourish. The act of giving creates a legacy of impact, reminding us that our lives have value not only in what we achieve but in how we help others achieve their goals as well.

4. Giving Fosters Resilience: Helping others can also boost our own resilience. When we focus on the needs of others, we often gain perspective on our own challenges. Giving reminds us that we are not alone in our struggles and that we have the capacity to make a positive difference in the lives of others, even during difficult times. This perspective can help us navigate our own hardships with greater grace and resilience.

For example, individuals who volunteer in their communities during personal crises often report that helping others gives them strength and purpose, even in the face of their own struggles. The act of giving helps them feel connected and empowered, reducing feelings of helplessness or isolation.

The Myth of Self-Interest: Why Taking Doesn't Lead to

Lasting Happiness

While many people believe that accumulating wealth, power, or personal success will lead to happiness, research shows that the opposite is often true. Focusing solely on self-interest—what we can get from others or from life—rarely leads to long-term fulfillment. In fact, takers often experience higher levels of stress and lower levels of life satisfaction because their relationships lack depth and trust.

The pursuit of personal gain, without consideration for others, often leads to feelings of isolation and disconnection. When success is measured solely by individual achievements, the joy of those accomplishments is often fleeting. This is because human beings are wired for connection, not competition. When we prioritize our own needs above those of others, we cut ourselves off from the deep social bonds that are essential for lasting happiness.

Moreover, taking often leads to burned bridges and damaged relationships. Takers may rise quickly in their careers or social circles, but without the foundation of trust and reciprocity, their success is often short-lived. People may begin to distance themselves from takers, recognizing that their relationships are transactional rather than genuine. As a result, takers may find themselves isolated, lacking the support and goodwill that givers naturally cultivate.

The Joy of Giving: Why Helping Others Feels Good

There is a deep, intrinsic joy in giving that goes beyond external rewards or recognition. When we help others, we experience a sense of fulfillment that is rooted in our shared humanity. Giving taps into our natural capacity for empathy, kindness, and compassion, allowing us to connect with others on a fundamental level.

Here are a few reasons why giving feels so good:

1. Giving Makes Us Feel Connected: At its core, giving is an act of connection. Whether it's offering a listening ear, providing a resource,

or lending a hand, giving helps us form bonds with others. These connections are a source of joy because they remind us that we are part of a larger community, where our actions have meaning and impact.

2. Giving Boosts Our Self-Esteem: Helping others often enhances our self-esteem because it allows us to see ourselves as capable, generous, and kind. When we give, we reinforce our sense of self-worth, knowing that we have made a positive difference in someone's life.

3. Giving Creates a Sense of Accomplishment: There is a unique satisfaction in knowing that our actions have contributed to the well-being or success of others. This sense of accomplishment is not tied to external validation or rewards; it comes from the internal knowledge that we have used our skills, time, or resources to benefit someone else.

4. Giving Fosters Gratitude: When we help others, we often become more aware of the blessings in our own lives. This sense of gratitude enhances our overall happiness by shifting our focus away from what we lack and toward what we already have. Gratitude is a powerful emotion that amplifies our sense of joy and

contentment.

Becoming a Giver: How to Cultivate the Power of Giving

While some people may naturally adopt a giving mindset, giving is a practice that can be cultivated and developed over time. Here are a few ways to become more of a giver in your daily life:

1. Start Small: You don't have to make grand gestures to become a giver. Start by offering small acts of kindness, such as offering a helping hand to a colleague, sharing a resource with a friend, or simply listening when someone needs support. These small actions can have a ripple effect, creating deeper connections and opportunities for reciprocity.

2. Make Giving a Habit: Incorporate giving into your daily or weekly routines. Whether it's volunteering, mentoring, or donating to a cause you care about, making giving a regular part of your life ensures that it becomes a priority rather than an afterthought.

3. Focus on Relationships, Not Transactions: Shift your mindset from viewing relationships as transactional (i.e., what can I get?) to relational (i.e., how can I help?). By focusing on building genuine connections, you foster trust and goodwill, which naturally leads to a cycle of giving and receiving.

4. Give Without Expecting Anything in Return: True giving is selfless. Practice giving without expecting immediate rewards or recognition. The joy of giving comes from knowing that you've made a positive impact, not from receiving something in return.

5. Seek Out Opportunities to Help: Be proactive in finding ways to help others. Whether it's offering your skills, knowledge, or time, look for opportunities to contribute to the success and well-being of those around you.

The True Key to Happiness

The power of giving lies not only in the positive impact it has on others but in the profound sense of fulfillment and happiness it brings to the giver. Inspired by Give and Take by Adam Grant, this chapter has explored why helping others is the key to lasting happiness and how adopting a giving mindset can lead to deeper connections, greater success, and a more meaningful life.

By shifting our focus from what we can get to what we can give, we unlock the potential for true joy, purpose, and fulfillment. In the end, the greatest rewards come not from accumulating wealth, power, or recognition, but from making a positive difference in the lives of others. When we give, we not only enrich the world around us but also discover the true meaning of happiness.

CHAPTER 30: LEGACY

The Impact You Leave Behind

In the quiet moments of life, when we are still, when the world's noise fades and we are left with our thoughts, a question often echoes in the chambers of our hearts: What will I be remembered for? This question, more than any other, invites us to reflect on the true meaning of our lives, not in terms of wealth, power, or personal achievement, but in the impact we have on others. Our legacy is not the sum of our possessions, accolades, or accomplishments—it is the lasting imprint we leave on the lives we touch, the memories we create, and the values we pass on to future generations.

Inspired by The Last Lecture by Randy Pausch, this chapter explores the profound and often overlooked question of legacy. Pausch, a professor who was diagnosed with terminal cancer, delivered a moving and life-affirming "last lecture" about achieving your childhood dreams, but more importantly, about how to live a life that leaves a positive and enduring impact. As Pausch faced the end of his life, his focus was not on material success or recognition, but on the relationships he had built, the wisdom he could share, and the example he could set for his children and students.

At its core, legacy is not about what we leave behind, but who we leave behind. It's about the ripple effect of our actions, the influence we have on others, and the way we contribute to the lives of those around us. A meaningful legacy is not created by chance or through momentary success; it is built through intentional living, deep relationships, and a commitment to making the world better for those who come after us. This chapter will explore what it means to live a life of legacy, how to cultivate it, and why focusing on your impact on others is the key to true fulfillment and purpose.

The True Meaning of Legacy: Beyond Material Success

When many people think of legacy, their thoughts turn to material wealth or accomplishments. They imagine buildings with their names on them, family fortunes passed down through generations, or public accolades that cement their place in history. But while these symbols of legacy may endure, they are not the essence of what it means to leave a lasting impact.

Legacy is not about how the world sees us when we are gone; it is about how the world feels us when we are no longer present. It is not about fame or fortune but about the values, wisdom, and love that we instill in the people whose lives we touch. Our true legacy is found in the stories people tell about us, the lessons they learned from us, and the way our presence shaped their lives.

Randy Pausch understood this deeply. In his Last Lecture, he didn't focus on the accolades he had earned as a professor or the professional milestones he had achieved. Instead, he spoke about the importance of relationships, dreams, and living with integrity. His legacy wasn't about the things he had built or the recognition he had received; it was about the people he had mentored, the students he had inspired, and the love he had shared with his family.

Legacy, at its core, is about relationships. It is about the impact we have on others, the love we give, and the values we uphold. It is the way we live our lives day to day—how we treat others, how we handle adversity, and how we make choices that reflect our values. Material wealth may fade, but the impact of a kind word, a selfless act, or a life lived with purpose endures in the hearts and minds of those we leave behind.

Building a Legacy: How Actions Shape Your Impact

Legacy is not something that we create at the end of our lives. It is something we build, moment by moment, through the choices we make and the actions we take. Every interaction, every decision, every relationship is a thread in the tapestry of our legacy. Whether we are aware of it or not, we are always in the process of shaping the legacy we will leave behind.

Here are a few ways to consciously build a legacy that reflects your values and impacts others in a meaningful way:

1. Live with Integrity: At the heart of every meaningful legacy is integrity—the commitment to live

in alignment with your values, even when it's difficult. Integrity is the foundation upon which trust, respect, and influence are built. When people remember you, they will not remember the mistakes you made or the challenges you faced; they will remember whether you stayed true to your principles, whether you were honest, kind, and fair.

Living with integrity means making choices that reflect your deepest values, even when those choices are not easy. It means being consistent in your actions, treating others with respect, and holding yourself accountable for your behaviour. A legacy of integrity is one that inspires others to live with honour and to uphold the values that matter most.

Consider the legacy of figures like Nelson Mandela or Mahatma Gandhi. Their legacies are not defined by wealth or material success, but by their unwavering commitment to justice, equality, and peace. They lived with integrity in the face of incredible challenges, and their actions inspired generations to continue their fight for a better world.

2. Invest in Relationships: The most enduring legacies are built through the relationships we nurture and the love we share with others. No one's legacy is defined by the size of their bank account or the number of trophies on their shelf; it is defined by the people whose lives they touched. To build a legacy that lasts, focus on the relationships in your life. Invest time and energy into the people who matter most to you—your family, friends, colleagues, and community.

Building a legacy through relationships means being

fully present for the people you love. It means offering support when they need it, celebrating their successes, and walking with them through difficult times. It means showing kindness, empathy, and understanding. The love and support you give to others will become part of the legacy they carry forward in their lives.

Think about someone who has had a profound impact on your life. It may have been a teacher who believed in you, a mentor who guided you, or a friend who stood by you when times were tough. Their legacy lives on in you, in the lessons you learned from them, and in the way their presence shaped who you are today.

3. Teach and Share Wisdom: One of the most powerful ways to leave a lasting legacy is through teaching and mentoring. Every one of us has experiences, insights, and wisdom that can help others grow. By sharing what we've learned, we pass on our knowledge to the next generation, helping them navigate life's challenges with greater clarity and confidence.

Teaching doesn't have to be formal—it can happen in everyday conversations, in the way we lead by example, or in the advice we offer when someone seeks guidance. The impact of sharing wisdom often extends far beyond the moment, as the lessons we impart continue to influence others long after we are gone.

Consider the legacy of a great teacher or mentor in your life. Their guidance may have shaped your career, your character, or your approach to life. The wisdom they shared with you became part of your journey, and in turn, you may pass it on to others. This is the essence of legacy—the way our influence ripples out into the world through the people we teach and inspire.

4. Contribute to Something Greater Than Yourself: A meaningful legacy often involves contributing to something larger than your personal success or comfort. This could be through service to your community, advocacy for a cause you believe in, or the creation of something that benefits others—whether it's a business, a charitable organization, or a piece of art.

By dedicating yourself to a cause or purpose that transcends your individual needs, you create a legacy that impacts not just those close to you, but potentially thousands, even millions, of people. It could be the legacy of a scientist who develops life-saving medicine, an activist who fights for social justice, or a philanthropist who builds schools in underprivileged areas. These legacies create ripples of change that affect countless lives, often in ways the person may never fully realize.

Randy Pausch's legacy, for instance, was not just the work he did as a professor but the profound impact he had on his students and on millions of people who were inspired by his Last Lecture. His willingness to share his wisdom, even as he faced the end of his life, contributed to something far greater than himself—a legacy of inspiration, courage, and hope.

5. Lead by Example: Ultimately, the most powerful legacy you can leave is the example of how you lived your life. People may forget what you said, but they will never forget how you made them feel or how you

conducted yourself in the world. Leading by example means living in a way that reflects your values, treating others with kindness, pursuing your passions with courage, and facing challenges with resilience.

Your actions speak louder than your words, and the example you set—whether in your family, your workplace, or your community—will inspire others to follow in your footsteps. A legacy built on example is one that endures, as the people you influence carry forward the lessons they learned from watching how you lived.

Think of figures like Mother Teresa or Martin Luther King Jr., whose legacies are defined not just by their words but by the lives they led. Their courage, compassion, and dedication to service set a powerful example for others to follow, creating legacies that continue to inspire and uplift long after their passing.

The Ripple Effect: How Your Legacy Touches Lives

One of the most beautiful aspects of legacy is its ripple effect. When you impact one person's life, that impact doesn't stop with them—it ripples out to others, often in ways you may never see or know. A single act of kindness, a moment of encouragement, or a shared piece of wisdom can inspire someone to go on and impact the lives of many others.

Consider the story of a teacher who encourages a young student to pursue their dreams. That student, inspired by the teacher's belief in them, goes on to achieve great things and, in turn, becomes a mentor to others. The teacher's legacy lives on not just in the student's life but in the lives of everyone that student touches. This is the power of legacy—it multiplies, extending far beyond our immediate reach.

In The Last Lecture, Randy Pausch spoke about the importance of enabling the dreams of others. He understood that his legacy would not be defined solely by his personal accomplishments but by how he had helped others achieve their dreams. The ripple effect of his influence continues to touch lives around the world, as people who watched his lecture were inspired to live more fully, to pursue their passions, and to leave a positive impact on others.

Living with Legacy in Mind: Intentional Choices for Impact

While legacy is often thought of as something we reflect on at the end of our lives, the truth is that we are building our legacy every day. The choices we make—how we treat others, how we handle adversity, how we contribute to our communities—are all part of the legacy we will leave behind.

Living with legacy in mind means making intentional choices that reflect the impact we want to have on others. It means thinking beyond immediate gratification or short-term success and focusing on how our actions will resonate in the lives of others. It means asking ourselves: What kind of example do I want to set? How do I want to be remembered? What values do I want to pass on to the next generation?

When we live with legacy in mind, we approach life with greater purpose, clarity, and intention. We recognise that our time on this earth is limited, and that the true measure of our lives is not what we accumulate but what we give. By focusing on how our actions impact others, we create a life of meaning, connection, and lasting significance.

The Legacy You Leave Behind

In the final analysis, your legacy is not about the accolades you receive or the possessions you accumulate. It is about the people you touch, the values you uphold, and the impact you have on the world. Inspired by The Last Lecture by Randy Pausch, this chapter has explored the profound importance of living a life that leaves a lasting and positive legacy.

Your legacy is built not through grand gestures but through the everyday choices you make—the kindness you show, the wisdom you share, and the love you give. It is the ripple effect of your influence on others, the example you set, and the contribution you make to something greater than yourself. By living with integrity, investing in relationships, sharing your wisdom, and leading by example, you can create a legacy that endures long after you are gone—a legacy that inspires, uplifts, and transforms the lives of others.

As you move forward in life, remember that every action you take is part of the legacy you are building. Focus on how your actions impact others, and strive to live in a way that leaves the world better than you found it. In doing so, you will create a legacy that is not just remembered, but felt in the hearts of those you leave behind.

CHAPTER 31: THE FINAL LESSON

A Symphony Of Unwritten Wisdom

And so, we arrive at the threshold of culmination, where the threads of knowledge that have been carefully spun throughout this tome now intertwine to form a grand symphony—a resounding crescendo of unwritten rules, hitherto scattered like stars, now unified into a constellation. The final lesson is not a mere summary, but a call to arms, a clarion cry that implores you to rise above the mundane, the ordinary, and grasp the reins of your destiny. This is where reflection and action collide, where knowing transforms into becoming, and where the ethereal truths we have explored must manifest in the tangible essence of your existence.

In this climactic chapter, we shall not merely recall the wisdom gleaned but forge it into the bedrock of your life. Here lies the alchemy of self-awareness, the subtle art of relationships, the mastery of careers, the elusive dance with financial freedom, the sinews of emotional resilience, and, above all, the sacred flame of purpose.

These are not disparate lessons, but facets of a single, multifaceted gem that you now hold in your hand, shining with the potential of the life you are meant to live.

But before we immerse ourselves fully in this final revelation, remember that each rule, each insight, is not an abstract principle, but a living force, waiting to be wielded by those bold enough to embrace it. You stand on the edge of transformation, and the final lesson is not to turn back—but to step forward into the unknown with audacious intent.

The First Principle: Self-Awareness as the Root of All Power

We began this journey by peeling back the layers of illusion that so often cloud the human experience. The power of self-awareness—the profound knowledge of oneself, one's emotions, one's strengths and failings —was unveiled as the foundation upon which all greatness is built. For how can one master the external world if they have not first mastered the inner kingdom?

In the dance of life, where chaos often masquerades as progress, it is self-awareness that acts as the anchor, the unmoving centre in a maelstrom of distractions. Yet self-awareness is not static; it is a dynamic force, one that grows, evolves, and sharpens with each moment of introspection, with every experience that deepens our understanding of who we truly are beneath the masks we wear.

To be self-aware is to know the contours of your soul

as intimately as an artist knows the canvas they paint upon. It is to recognise your triggers, your aspirations, your shadow, and your light. It is the compass that guides you through the forests of confusion, that points unfalteringly toward the true north of your authentic self. Without it, one is adrift, tossed by the winds of circumstance, subject to the whims of fate. With it, one becomes the master of their fate, the architect of their destiny.

In this final moment, let the lesson be clear: Know yourself, for in knowing yourself, you will know the world. The universe within mirrors the universe without. Self-awareness is not a solitary act, but the gateway to wisdom, to understanding the very fabric of existence.

The Second Principle: The Art of Relationships

As the soul is revealed through self-awareness, so too is it reflected and tested in the crucible of relationships. It is here, in the interplay of human connection, that the truest measure of your growth, your wisdom, and your love is revealed. Relationships, whether they be fleeting or eternal, are not mere accidents of proximity; they are the mirrors that reflect our deepest truths, our hidden vulnerabilities, and our boundless capacity for empathy and compassion.

The unwritten rule here is simple but profound: To give of yourself without expectation is to receive the world. In the art of relationships, we learned that active listening, the ability to truly hear another, is more powerful than any act of persuasion or eloquence. In the quiet space between words, in the soft gaze that acknowledges another's existence, lies the key to forging bonds that transcend the superficial and touch the eternal.

But relationships are not only the domain of love and friendship; they extend into the realm of the professional, the communal, and the global. In the art of networking, we discovered that true opportunity comes not from talent alone, but from the bridges we build with others. To succeed is to serve, to uplift those around you, for no one rises alone. The legacy of your life will be written in the hearts of those you touch, not in the pages of a résumé.

In this, the final crescendo of understanding, embrace this truth: You are not an island, but part of an intricate web of connections. Cherish those bonds, nurture them, for they are the vessels through which your impact on this world will be felt long after you have departed. Let your relationships be the foundation upon which you build not just success, but significance.

The Third Principle: Career as the Mastery of Time

We then turned our gaze to the realm of the professional—the domain where time becomes currency and purpose is often clouded by the pursuit of status and wealth. In our exploration of career management, we discovered that success in one's career is not merely a matter of talent, nor is it dictated by the whims of luck. It is, instead, the deliberate alignment of your skills, values, and time with a mission that transcends mere occupation.

The unwritten rule here is that your career should be

an extension of your purpose, not a deviation from it. Too often, we are led astray by the glittering allure of prestige or the seductive promises of financial gain, only to find ourselves lost in a labyrinth of discontent, where time is traded for dollars and meaning is sacrificed on the altar of convenience. But the true masters of career are those who understand that their work is not a separate entity from their life but a vital expression of their essence.

The mastery of career is not just about achieving success in the eyes of others; it is about crafting a life where your work becomes a reflection of your innermost passions and values. It is about managing time as the most precious resource you possess —knowing when to say "yes" and, perhaps more importantly, when to say "no."

As we reach the apex of this lesson, let the truth resound in your mind: Do not merely pursue a career; cultivate a vocation, a calling that resonates with the deepest parts of your soul. Let your work be a song that you sing, a craft that you hone, not for the sake of accolades, but for the fulfillment of purpose. And in doing so, time itself will become your ally, not your adversary.

The Fourth Principle: Financial Independence as Freedom's True Name

From career, we wove the thread into the realm of financial wisdom—that elusive domain where freedom is measured not by the number of zeroes in your bank account, but by the liberty to live life on your terms. In a world that so often equates financial success with happiness, we uncovered the truth that money is not the goal, but the means to the goal.

The unwritten rule of financial independence is simple: True wealth is the ability to say "no." It is the freedom to walk away from what does not serve you, to chart your course not based on necessity but on desire and principle. Money, when wielded wisely, becomes a tool for creating opportunity, for investing in your future, for empowering others. But when pursued blindly, it becomes a cage, trapping you in a cycle of accumulation with no end in sight.

We explored the concept of multiple income streams, the idea that security comes not from a single source, but from diversification—of investments, skills, and opportunities. But the most powerful lesson is that financial independence is not about wealth alone; it is about the freedom to live in alignment with your values, your passions, your purpose. It is about being free from the fear that comes with financial instability, and free to pursue the life that truly fulfills you.

As we close this chapter, let the final note of this principle ring clear: Seek financial independence not for its own sake, but for the freedom it grants you to live a life of meaning, integrity, and joy. Let money be your servant, never your master.

The Fifth Principle: Emotional Resilience as the Forge of Strength

No life, no matter how purpose-driven, is without hardship. And so we turned our attention to the hidden fortress within each of us: the power of emotional resilience. In this journey, we learned that the path to greatness is not paved in gold, but in trials, tribulations, and setbacks that forge the strength of character needed to rise again and again.

The unwritten rule of emotional resilience is that failure is not the enemy; it is the teacher. Every fall is an opportunity to rise with greater wisdom, every heartache an invitation to deepen your capacity for empathy, every disappointment a chance to strengthen your resolve. Emotional resilience is not about avoiding pain or struggle; it is about transforming those experiences into fuel for growth, for wisdom, for compassion.

In the crucible of emotional resilience, you learn to embrace the full spectrum of the human experience—the highs and the lows, the joy and the sorrow. You understand that life's greatest gifts often come wrapped in adversity, and that true strength is found not in avoiding hardship, but in facing it with courage and grace.

As the final embers of this lesson glow, remember this: The storms of life will come, but they need not destroy you. Instead, let them carve you into the person you were always meant to be. Emotional resilience is the forge in which your soul is tempered, and through it, you will discover a strength you never knew you possessed.

The Sixth Principle: Purpose as the Flame That Illuminates All

And now, we arrive at the heart of the matter—the flame that has burned at the centre of this entire journey. Purpose. It is the final, most essential lesson, the one that ties all others together. Without purpose, self-awareness, relationships, career, financial independence, and resilience are hollow pursuits. It is purpose that gives them meaning, that transforms them from individual goals into a cohesive whole.

Purpose is not a destination; it is a journey. It is the guiding light that illuminates every step you take, the deeper "why" that drives you forward even when the path is unclear. To live without purpose is to wander aimlessly through life, but to live with purpose is to stride confidently toward the horizon, knowing that every step is part of a grand design.

In this final lesson, understand that purpose is not something you find—it is something you create. It is born from your values, your passions, your relationships, and your experiences. It is the reason you rise in the morning, the motivation that carries you through the darkest nights. Purpose is not static; it evolves as you grow, as you learn, as you change. But it is always there, a steady flame that flickers in the wind but never extinguishes.

As we close this final chapter, let the last note ring out like a clarion call: Do not wait for purpose to find you. Seek it, shape it, live it. Let purpose be the flame that lights your path, the wind that carries your sails, the foundation upon which you build your life. And know this—when you live with purpose, you leave a legacy that endures far beyond your time on this earth.

The Symphony of Unwritten Rules

And now, the symphony is complete. The unwritten rules, those invisible threads that guide the dance of life, have been revealed in their full glory. These are not mere lessons, but principles, pillars upon which you can build a life of meaning, joy, and impact. But knowing them is not enough. You must live them.

Self-awareness will root you. Relationships will sustain you. Career will sharpen you. Financial independence will free you. Emotional resilience will strengthen you. And purpose will elevate you. Together, they form the foundation of a life well-lived, a life that leaves behind not only accomplishments but a legacy.

The final lesson, dear reader, is this: You are the author of your life. You hold the pen, and the unwritten rules are yours to command. Go forth with intention, with courage, with love, and with purpose. Write your story, and let it be one that inspires others long after you have turned the final page.

EPILOGUE: THE QUIET ECHO OF UNWRITTEN TRUTHS

And now, as the final words settle softly on the page, as the symphony of thoughts fades into a quiet hum, you find yourself standing on the precipice of a new beginning. The journey through the unwritten rules has led you here—not to an ending, but to an unfolding. For while the chapters may have drawn to a close, life itself continues its inexorable march forward, ever offering fresh horizons, ever asking you to apply the lessons gleaned.

In the stillness that follows this book's last breath, something profound lingers—an echo of all that has been learned, a whisper of all that is yet to be. These unwritten rules, now inscribed upon your heart, are not static laws bound by time or circumstance. They are living truths, fluid and adaptable, bending to the rhythm of your life as it unfolds in ways both expected and unforeseen. They are less a map than a compass, not dictating the exact steps you must take, but gently guiding you toward the true north of your existence.

The beauty of these rules lies in their simplicity, in their quiet insistence that you are the architect of your life. No external force holds the power to define your journey, no circumstance can strip you of your agency, no challenge can eclipse your potential. You are the still point in the turning world, the sovereign over the choices you make, the artist of the narrative you weave. These rules are the brushstrokes, the colors you have been given, but the painting—oh, the painting—is yours to create.

The Weight of the Moment

What remains now is the weight of the moment you inhabit—the infinite potential of the present. You are here, in this moment, with all that you have learned, all that you are, and all that you aspire to be. Before you lies the vast expanse of possibility, stretching like an endless ocean, its waves beckoning you to dive deeper into your purpose, your truth, your destiny.

The question that hums in the air is no longer, What will you learn? but, What will you do with what you have learned? How will you live now, knowing that the unwritten rules of life are within your grasp? How will you transform this wisdom into action, into change, into a life that is not only lived, but truly lived well?

The choice is yours, always yours, to take these lessons, to make them your own, to breathe life into them with each step you take from here onward. You have seen that self-awareness is the foundation of all mastery, that relationships are the sacred bonds that anchor us to the world, that careers are not just pathways to success but expressions of your innermost calling. You know now that financial freedom is not about wealth but about autonomy, that emotional resilience is the forge where strength is born, and that purpose is the flame that lights your way.

The Eternal Dance of Becoming

In truth, life is not about achieving a final state of being. It is an eternal dance of becoming, a constant evolution in which we shed the skin of the past to step into the luminous unknown of the future. The unwritten rules are not destinations—they are the steps in this dance, guiding you with grace and subtlety, asking you to embrace the ebb and flow of life's tides with open arms.

You will falter. There will be moments of doubt, of fear, of seeming failure. But now, with the wisdom of these rules as your guide, you will understand that each stumble is not an ending but a part of the process. Each challenge is a crucible, refining you, honing your spirit, preparing you for the next chapter of your journey.

And as you move forward, remember this: The rules are not written in stone, but in the softness of your heart. They bend to your will, shaped by your choices, illuminated by your growth. They are the invisible threads that bind together the fabric of your life, not constricting you but empowering you to live fully, freely, authentically.

A Quiet Promise

Let this epilogue be a quiet promise—a reminder that life, in all its complexity and beauty, is yours to shape.

There are no guarantees, no certainties, no roadmaps that lead unerringly to happiness. But within you lies the power to navigate this world with wisdom, with courage, with grace. The unwritten rules are now written within you, etched into the core of your being, waiting for you to give them form through the actions you take, the love you share, the dreams you pursue.

As the final echoes of this book fade, know this: You are enough. You have always been enough. The journey you are on is not about becoming someone else or achieving some distant perfection. It is about embracing who you are—here, now, in this moment—and allowing that truth to shine through everything you do.

The final lesson is not found in the pages of this book, but in the life you will live from this day forward. It is found in the quiet choices, the moments of courage, the acts of kindness that will ripple outward into the world, leaving behind a legacy of love, purpose, and meaning.

The Journey Continues

And so, dear reader, as you close this book, the journey continues. The unwritten rules are no longer unwritten, but living within you, ready to be acted upon. Your life awaits—vibrant, full of potential, rich with possibility. The path ahead is yours to walk, and though it may be uncertain, it is yours to define.

Go now, with the lessons of this journey etched into your heart. Go with the knowledge that you are the author of your destiny, the creator of your legacy. Live boldly, love deeply, and pursue your purpose with unwavering passion. For that is the final lesson, the one that cannot be spoken but must be lived: Life is yours, and it has always been yours to shape.

GLOSSARY OF TERMS

This glossary provides definitions and explanations of key concepts, terms, and ideas that have been explored throughout the book. These terms, while appearing familiar, hold profound meanings within the context of the unwritten rules of life. Each concept is central to understanding how we navigate our personal growth, relationships, careers, finances, and the pursuit of a purpose-driven existence.

Active Listening
The act of fully focusing, understanding, and responding to someone in a conversation, beyond just hearing their words. It involves being present, empathetic, and engaged, which fosters deeper connections and trust in relationships.

Antifragility
A concept that describes systems or individuals that grow stronger through challenges and stress. Unlike resilience, which is about withstanding pressure, antifragility implies thriving and improving in the face of adversity.

Career Management
The conscious and deliberate planning, pursuit, and development of one's professional life. It involves aligning your career choices with your values, skills, and long-term goals to create a meaningful and fulfilling professional path.

Emotional Resilience
The ability to recover from or adapt to life's adversities and challenges. Emotional resilience involves developing strength through adversity and using setbacks as opportunities for growth, rather than letting them cause defeat.

Financial Independence
A state where an individual has enough financial resources to support their lifestyle without needing to rely on external income sources, such as employment. Financial independence allows one to live with autonomy and freedom, focusing on pursuits that align with personal values rather than financial necessity.

Grit
A combination of passion and perseverance for long-term goals. Grit involves maintaining effort and interest over years despite obstacles, adversity, and plateaus in progress. It is the engine behind sustained achievement and success.

Growth Mindset
A belief that intelligence, talents, and abilities can be developed through effort, learning, and perseverance. Those with a growth mindset view challenges as opportunities to improve rather than as threats to their self-esteem or status.

Legacy
The impact and influence one leaves behind after they are gone. Legacy is not only about wealth or achievements but the lasting effects of one's actions, values, and relationships on others and the world. It reflects how one is remembered and the ripple effect of their contributions.

Networking
The process of building and nurturing relationships with others for mutual benefit. In the professional context, networking is often used to create opportunities, exchange knowledge, and collaborate, but true networking involves offering value to others without the expectation of immediate return.

Passion vs. Persistence
A concept that highlights the distinction between passion (the initial excitement and emotional drive for a pursuit) and persistence (the long-term commitment to continue despite challenges and setbacks). Success often relies not just on being passionate, but having the

perseverance to see efforts through to completion.

Personal Values
The deeply held beliefs and principles that guide an individual's decisions, actions, and behaviours. Personal values shape how one defines purpose, interacts with others, and prioritizes life goals. They are often the foundation of a purpose-driven life.

Purpose
The driving force or reason behind one's actions, goals, and life decisions. Purpose provides a sense of meaning and direction, acting as a compass that aligns actions with long-term aspirations and values. Living with purpose ensures that life's pursuits contribute to something greater than oneself.

Relationships as Currency
A metaphor for the idea that relationships are valuable assets in life, capable of opening doors to opportunities, collaboration, and support. Building strong, trusting relationships is often more powerful than individual talent or wealth when it comes to long-term success and fulfillment.

Self-Awareness
The conscious knowledge of one's character, emotions, desires, strengths, and weaknesses. Self-awareness allows individuals to understand their inner worlds and how they are perceived by others, which in turn enables

more authentic and effective decision-making.

The Power of No

The ability to set boundaries and protect one's time, energy, and well-being by declining requests or commitments that do not align with personal priorities. Saying "no" is an essential skill in maintaining focus on one's goals and living a purpose-driven life without being overwhelmed by unnecessary obligations.

Time Management

The process of organizing and planning how to divide time between specific activities. Effective time management allows individuals to maximize productivity, achieve goals, and ensure that time is spent on meaningful pursuits that align with their values.

Unwritten Rules

The implicit, often unspoken guidelines that govern life, relationships, and success. Unlike formal education or societal rules, unwritten rules are learned through experience and self-awareness. These rules shape how individuals navigate personal growth, career development, and interpersonal relationships.

Vulnerability

The willingness to open up emotionally and show one's authentic self, including weaknesses and fears.

Vulnerability is often seen as a strength because it allows for deeper connections, greater empathy, and the ability to embrace imperfection in oneself and others.

Work-Life Integration
The concept of creating harmony between professional and personal life, where each complements the other, rather than compartmentalizing the two. It suggests that success in both realms is interconnected, and true fulfillment comes from balancing career aspirations with personal well-being and relationships.

Why
A central concept derived from Simon Sinek's work, the "why" refers to the core reason behind actions, decisions, and life pursuits. Understanding one's "why" leads to greater clarity, focus, and purpose, ensuring that all efforts are aligned with personal values and goals.

REFERENCES

The following is a compilation of influential books, authors, and thought leaders whose work has inspired the ideas, lessons, and principles explored throughout this book. These references provide a rich foundation of knowledge across personal growth, emotional intelligence, relationships, career management, financial independence, and purposeful living. Each work contributes to the broader understanding of the unwritten rules of life and offers deeper insights into the themes discussed in this book.

Brown, Brené.
Daring Greatly: How the Courage to Be Vulnerable Transforms the Way We Live, Love, Parent, and Lead.
New York: Gotham Books, 2012.
In Daring Greatly, Brené Brown explores the power of vulnerability and the importance of embracing imperfection. Her work emphasizes the courage required to open up emotionally, fostering deeper connections in both personal and professional relationships.

Carnegie, Dale.
How to Win Friends and Influence People.

New York: Simon & Schuster, 1936.

This classic book provides timeless advice on the art of building meaningful relationships through effective communication, active listening, and empathy. Carnegie's principles continue to be valuable in fostering personal and professional success.

Covey, Stephen R.
The 7 Habits of Highly Effective People: Powerful Lessons in Personal Change.
New York: Free Press, 1989.
Covey's work is foundational in the realms of time management, personal growth, and leadership. His seven habits offer a framework for living a purposeful and productive life, emphasizing principles of integrity, proactivity, and balanced success.

Duckworth, Angela.
Grit: The Power of Passion and Perseverance.
New York: Scribner, 2016.
Angela Duckworth's groundbreaking research on grit reveals that long-term success is not just a matter of talent or intelligence, but of passion combined with perseverance. Her work underscores the importance of resilience in achieving personal and professional goals.

Ferrazzi, Keith, and Tahl Raz.
Never Eat Alone: And Other Secrets to Success, One Relationship at a Time.
New York: Crown Business, 2005.
Ferrazzi's book on networking and relationship-

building stresses the value of generosity in creating meaningful professional connections. He emphasizes that the best opportunities arise from genuine relationships, not just talent or qualifications.

Frankl, Viktor E.
Man's Search for Meaning.
Boston: Beacon Press, 1959.
This profound work, based on Frankl's experiences in Nazi concentration camps, explores the human search for meaning. Frankl's existential philosophy, known as logotherapy, teaches that the pursuit of purpose is the key to enduring life's inevitable suffering.

Goleman, Daniel.
Emotional Intelligence: Why It Can Matter More Than IQ.
New York: Bantam Books, 1995.
Goleman's pioneering work on emotional intelligence explores how self-awareness, empathy, and emotional regulation play a critical role in success, both personally and professionally. His ideas are central to understanding interpersonal dynamics and leadership.

Grant, Adam.
Give and Take: Why Helping Others Drives Our Success.
New York: Viking, 2013.
Adam Grant's work challenges conventional notions of success by emphasizing the power of giving. Through research and real-life examples, he demonstrates how generosity and helping others can lead to personal and

professional fulfillment.

Johnson, Spencer.
Who Moved My Cheese?: An Amazing Way to Deal with Change in Your Work and in Your Life.
New York: G. P. Putnam's Sons, 1998.
This allegorical book teaches lessons about change, adaptability, and the importance of flexibility in an ever-evolving world. It emphasizes the value of being proactive and embracing uncertainty as a key to thriving.

Kiyosaki, Robert T., and Sharon Lechter.
Rich Dad Poor Dad: What the Rich Teach Their Kids About Money That the Poor and Middle Class Do Not!
Scottsdale, AZ: Plata Publishing, 1997.
Kiyosaki's personal finance classic contrasts the mindsets and strategies of his "rich dad" and "poor dad," revealing essential lessons about financial independence, investing, and wealth-building that are often overlooked in traditional education.

McKeown, Greg.
Essentialism: The Disciplined Pursuit of Less.
New York: Crown Business, 2014.
In Essentialism, Greg McKeown advocates for the disciplined pursuit of fewer, more important things. His philosophy emphasizes the importance of focus, clarity, and the intentional elimination of distractions to achieve a life of purpose and productivity.

Pausch, Randy.
The Last Lecture.
New York: Hyperion, 2008.
Randy Pausch's inspiring final lecture, delivered after his terminal cancer diagnosis, centres on the importance of living fully, realizing childhood dreams, and leaving behind a meaningful legacy. His reflections on life and purpose resonate deeply with readers.

Ramsey, Dave.
The Total Money Makeover: A Proven Plan for Financial Fitness.
Nashville, TN: Thomas Nelson, 2003.
Dave Ramsey's financial planning guide offers practical advice on managing debt, building savings, and achieving financial freedom. His step-by-step approach focuses on financial discipline and long-term planning for personal security.

Robin, Vicki, and Joe Dominguez.
Your Money or Your Life: 9 Steps to Transforming Your Relationship with Money and Achieving Financial Independence.
New York: Penguin Books, 1992.
This book provides a holistic approach to financial independence, emphasizing mindfulness, intentionality, and aligning financial goals with personal values. It teaches readers how to rethink their relationship with money and achieve a more fulfilling life.

Sinek, Simon.
Start with Why: How Great Leaders Inspire Everyone to Act.
New York: Portfolio, 2009.
Sinek's Start with Why introduces the concept that successful individuals and organizations begin with a clear sense of purpose—their "why"—which drives their actions and decisions. His work emphasizes that knowing your "why" leads to greater focus and fulfillment.

Taleb, Nassim Nicholas.
The Black Swan: The Impact of the Highly Improbable.
New York: Random House, 2007.
In The Black Swan, Taleb explores the profound effects that rare, unpredictable events—"black swans"—have on history, society, and individual lives. His work teaches the importance of adaptability, resilience, and the acceptance of uncertainty.

Ury, William.
The Power of a Positive No: Save the Deal, Save the Relationship, and Still Say No.
New York: Bantam Books, 2007.
William Ury's book offers practical techniques for saying no with confidence and integrity, without damaging relationships or losing sight of one's goals. His work is essential for learning to set boundaries and protect personal priorities.

Additional Acknowledgments

Throughout this book, the insights and research of countless thinkers, writers, and professionals have shaped the ideas and lessons presented. Although not directly cited, the fields of psychology, philosophy, business, and personal development have significantly influenced the content. Special acknowledgment goes to the ongoing work in emotional intelligence, leadership, and resilience, which forms the backbone of this exploration into the unwritten rules of life.

ACKNOWLEDGEMENTS

This book is the culmination of many years of reflection, learning, and collaboration, and I am deeply grateful to everyone who has contributed to its creation.

First and foremost, I extend my deepest thanks to my readers, whose curiosity and commitment to personal growth inspire me to continue exploring the unwritten rules of life. Without your dedication, this book would not have been possible.

I would like to express my profound gratitude to my family, especially my parents, whose unwavering support and encouragement have been my bedrock throughout this journey. Their belief in me has been a constant source of strength and inspiration.

To my colleagues, mentors, and friends, your insights, challenges, and thought-provoking conversations have enriched my understanding of the themes in this book. You have helped shape its structure, content, and depth, and for that, I am immensely thankful.

I also wish to acknowledge the invaluable contributions of the thinkers, authors, and researchers whose work has informed and inspired the concepts presented here. Their writings have provided a solid foundation on which I have built, and I am honoured to add my voice to the ongoing conversation around personal growth, emotional resilience, and purposeful living.

Finally, my heartfelt thanks to the team at Irene Minds, whose belief in this project brought it to life. Your editorial expertise, creative input, and tireless efforts have ensured that this book reaches its highest potential. It has been a privilege to collaborate with you.

Thank you all for being a part of this journey.

– Dr. Bhaskar Bora

COPYRIGHT INFORMATION

© 2024 Dr. Bhaskar Bora. All rights reserved.

This book, including its content and layout, is protected under copyright law. No part of this publication may be reproduced, distributed, or transmitted in any form or by any means, including photocopying, recording, or other electronic or mechanical methods, without the prior written permission of the author, except in the case of brief quotations embodied in critical reviews and certain other non-commercial uses permitted by copyright law.

For permission requests, please contact:

Dr. Bhaskar Bora
Email: bora.dr@gmail.com

Published by Irene Minds, 2024.

DISCLAIMER

The material in this book is provided for educational, informational, and self-improvement purposes only. While every effort has been made to ensure the accuracy of the information contained herein, neither the author, Dr. Bhaskar Bora, nor the publisher, Irene Minds, assumes any responsibility for errors, omissions, or contrary interpretations of the subject matter.

This book is not intended as a substitute for professional advice in the areas of finance, career management, mental health, or relationships. Readers are encouraged to seek professional guidance tailored to their individual needs.

The examples provided in this book are illustrative and are not intended to represent specific individuals or situations. Any resemblance to actual persons, living or dead, or to specific events or circumstances, is purely coincidental.

By reading this book, you agree that neither the author nor the publisher will be held responsible for any direct or indirect consequences resulting from the use of this information. Readers are encouraged to use their own discretion and judgment in applying any of the ideas or principles discussed in this book.

For any inquiries or feedback, please contact:
Dr. Bhaskar Bora
Email: bora.dr@gmail.com

www.ingramcontent.com/pod-product-compliance
Lightning Source LLC
Chambersburg PA
CBHW052237220526
45471CB00001B/84